The
Nomadic
Handbook

Other Books by the Author

Nomadic Furniture 1 (with Victor Papanek)
Nomadic Furniture 2 (with Victor Papanek)
How Things Don't Work (with Victor Papanek)

THE NOMADIC HANDBOOK

A Guide to Moving and to Finding and Adapting Your Next Home

James Hennessey

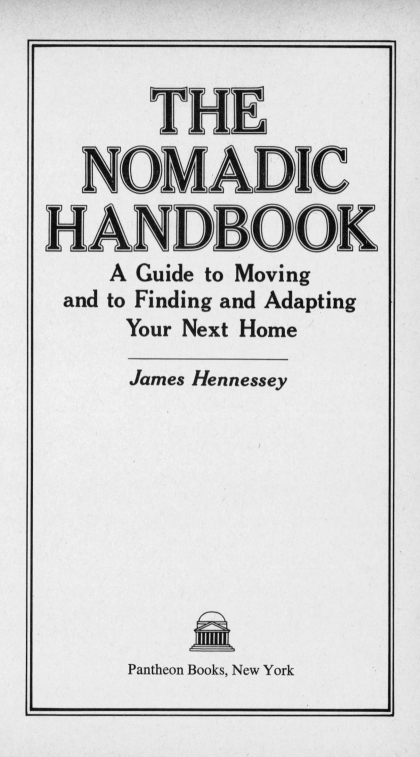

Pantheon Books, New York

Library of Congress Cataloging in Publication Data

Hennessey, James.
  The nomadic handbook.

  Bibliography: p.
  Includes index.
  1. Moving, Household. 2. House buying.
I. Title.
TX307.H46   643   78–73962
ISBN 0–394–73782–2

Manufactured in the United States of America

First Edition

This book is dedicated to those people who influenced my life and guided my direction: my parents, for their support and love; my wife, Sara, for her warmth and understanding; Jay Doblin, for teaching me the meaning of Innovation; Vic Papanek, for helping me to realize my own potential; and all my students, present and past, who honestly teach me more than I teach them.

CONTENTS

LIST OF ILLUSTRATIONS

LIST OF CHARTS

Introduction

WHETHER YOU REALIZE IT OR NOT, YOU ARE READING THIS book because you are going to be moving in the very near future. Statistics show that one-fifth of America's population moves every year and that it is unlikely you will stay in one location for longer than five years.

This book is for all of you who have moved before and suffered through countless miseries, as well as for all of you who anticipate moving for the first time and want to avoid any mistakes. It is hoped that this book will provide many insights into the entire spectrum of moving and that you will use it as a guidebook. It can help you through all of the stages of moving and getting situated, finding a place to "call your own," and adapting that place to the particular needs of you and your family.

These tasks are not easy ones. Moving is not a subject to be taken lightly. Quite a few people get into trouble for lack of sufficient education and preparation. It seems that each of us who moves approaches the act of moving as if no one else had ever done it before. Few of us really talk with others who have moved or share our own moving hints. We tend to rely mostly on information supplied by the professional moving companies or on an occasional news article or television program. Most of this information is so negative that it is downright depressing! We seem to hear only from people who complain that their move was a disaster and who regret ever making it in the first place. However, people usually make a move in order to improve their conditions, better their lives, and seek new horizons. To present yourself with an entirely new range of possibilities is an exciting challenge and adventure. You should look forward to moving with great anticipation because of the opportunities it offers you and your family.

It is indeed possible to have an extremely pleasant and trouble-free move. The keys to the entire process are organization and control. This book will assist you in decision making and strategy in order to help you make your move simple, enjoyable, and successful. The book is divided into three major sections: *The Move, The Acquisition*, and *The Adaptation*. Each of these is a major portion of a move and can be considered a separate and complete step.

The Move deals primarily with getting your belongings from one place to another. Chapter 1 contains basic information on professional movers: the kinds of services they provide and what you can expect from them. The chapter discusses both the positive and negative aspects of a professional move and how you might anticipate and avoid problems associated with it. Professionals send out stacks of booklets, pamphlets, and other information, most of which is designed to convince you to use their services. This chapter does not contain any of it. Instead, it presents straightforward and understandable information that clarifies the role of the professional mover.

Chapter 2 is for the do-it-yourself mover. It introduces the different types of rental agencies and equipment presently available. It also helps you determine what to move, estimate the size of your belongings, and suggests methods for saving money.

Chapter 3 deals with alternatives moves. Here, there are a number of possibilities that are variations of the "normal" moving methods. If you cannot afford a professional mover and lack the mental or physical motivation to move yourself, this chapter is for you. It talks about the possibilities that can be found between these two extremes, as well as the kinds of savings in time, energy, and finances you can anticipate.

The fourth chapter contains information and guidance, comparisons and shortcuts, charts and checklists, that other people have shared with me over the years, as well as my own experiences, so that you can prepare your house for moving. Hints on how to pack, methods for crating and boxing, and ideas on putting it all into a truck efficiently are included. There are suggestions on lightening your load and deciding what to take and what to leave. There is information on auctions, garage sales, flea markets, and other methods for disposing of unwanted belongings. Lastly, advice on all matters that you must attend to when you change your address is presented in simple and easily understood checklists, which will help you keep track of things during your move.

The Acquisition covers finding a place to live in your new location. There are a number of conventional methods of looking for places to buy, rent, or lease, which are briefly discussed, such as the information on existing housing in Chapter 5. This chapter also talks about locating housing, what to expect from real-estate agents, and how to locate alternative types of housing.

Chapter 6 discusses these alternatives to conventional housing: portable housing, factory-built homes, mobile and modular homes. Concepts for housing such as geodesics, inflatables, and tensile structures are other options you might consider investigating instead of a conventional house. Also presented are some of the more exciting kit homes.

The chapter on The American Dream covers buying land and building your own house; related legalities and restrictions; mortgage and loan problems; well, water, and waste disposal issues; and the possibilities of alternative power and energy sources.

Chapter 8 deals with adaptive-use structures, the renovation and use of buildings that were not originally intended to be living environments. Here, information is offered on how to find and where to look for structures that are adaptable and how to adapt them. These alternatives present tremendous possibilities for people who want to live somewhere really unique.

The third section, *The Adaptation*, concentrates on the architectural interior space of your living environment and making changes to it that relate to the needs of you and your family. These changes are done without altering the exterior architecture or changing the structure of the building.

People who are confronted with living in a single room will want to focus on Chapter 9. The chapter is geared for those who live in one-room efficiency apartments, in dorm rooms at college, or even cabins, cottages, and trailers. The subject is the simplification of space: how to take one room and put a lot of things into it and still end up with a simplified appearance. Advice is given on storage and how to utilize space best in situations where space is at a premium.

Chapter 10 deals with apartments and how you can bring your personality into one without making great changes to the apartment itself, changes which you would have to leave behind when you moved out. It talks about change without permanence and adaptation without investment.

Chapter 11 is about home improvements. It is primarily intended for people who own their homes and are thinking of making various improvements. It discusses what types of improvements really pay off in the long run, the logic of fixing up a house you are going to sell, and the kinds of repairs that will return your investment. It also suggests the kinds of interior changes, such as levels, lofts, and built-ins, that can really alter the look and appearance of a home.

I think you will find this book to be extremely comprehensive. Above all else, it should provide the inspiration that will help you approach your move with a different outlook. Hopefully, it will give you the chance to enhance the changes that your move will bring about by enriching your environment and your living conditions as well.

Part I

THE
MOVE

Chapter 1
_____

The Professional Mover

THE PROFESSIONAL MOVER IS OFTEN DESCRIBED AS AN experienced, knowledgeable, courteous, and efficient person who will take care of both you and your belongings and, were we to believe current television advertising, will take even better care of Greatgrandma's rocker than you yourself. Indeed, if this were the case, there wouldn't be any questions about how to move your belongings from one place to another. Everyone would choose the professional regardless of price because his service is unbeatable.

The professional can and does provide a lot of different services; and for people who have the funds, this is generally the simplest and easiest way of moving their belongings. If someone else is paying your moving bill, it is almost automatic that you will choose a reliable professional and chalk up whatever happens to experience. It is when you are paying the bill yourself that you begin to look into the business of professional moving with much more caution. There is no question that moving with a professional is an expensive venture, and each year the cost increases tremendously in order to keep pace with inflation and the cost of living. You will probably find it to be the most expensive method of moving outlined in this book.

There is a general assumption that all professional movers are basically the same and provide comparable services. Naturally, the laws of human nature dictate that this is somewhat of an impossibility. Moving companies do indeed differ; and when the time comes for you to decide which one will do your move, you will want to know as much as you can about all of them in order to make an educated decision.

The first step is to poll your friends and associates who

have moved to find out who they recommend. If the results of your poll are anything like the one I did before our last move, you will be surprised to learn that few people will recommend the mover they had and will, instead, have all kinds of complaints to lodge against the company. At least you may find out who *not* to use.

If your company is moving you, ask them for a recommendation. A mover who has a vested interest in your firm and who wants to maintain good relations with them will probably take better care of you and your household of things.

The best way to begin is with the assumption that most of the companies are equal. Then, as you learn more about them, you will eliminate those you have mixed feelings about. First contact those professional interstate movers listed in the Yellow Pages. Telephone each one and ask them to send you information about their services. Tell them that you want to look at their material before you see one of their

Carrier performance reports: reading up on the track record of professional movers

salespeople and that you do not want an estimate at this time. Make sure they understand that you are interested just in reading about the company. You will find that moving companies have a wealth of pamphlets, booklets, and brochures; and it will be apparent through these that some companies have a greater interest in communicating their services than others. The way to tell is to look carefully at the literature that has been sent to you. A well-designed graphic package and related brochures suggest that the company is concerned about its image and impact on the consumer. A plain envelope containing a hodgepodge of papers, mimeos, and cheaply printed pamphlets usually indicates that the company is disorganized and doesn't consider client communications to be very important.

Once you have done this homework, you can combine the results of your friends' recommendations with your firm's recommendation and the information in the brochures, along with each company's performance record (which tells you how many moves the company made during the previous year and how many complaints were lodged against them), to help you reach a decision about the mover you want. At this point you can telephone the moving company and request that a representative come to your home for an estimate of your moving expenses. Many publications suggest that you contact at least three movers for estimates, but unless you are evenly divided among two or three companies, I wouldn't recommend it. Since all interstate movers have rates regulated by the Interstate Commerce Commission, it is unlikely that the estimates would be that different. If they did differ greatly, you should have great concern that one of the company representatives is "lowballing" you (giving you an especially low estimate) just to get you to sign up with his company. It is much better for you to make your decision in your own time. Once you have selected a company, focus only on their representative and estimate.

When the representative calls, it is best to be friendly and courteous and at the same time very cautious. Remember that the representative is a salesperson who makes a commission on your move if he can persuade you to sign on the dotted line. Too often, overly zealous salespeople will promise just about anything to get you to sign. Only afterwards do you realize that, except for that one evening, you will never see that salesperson again and that he has no personal liability for the things he promised you. Be nice but totally untrusting. Get any promises down on paper along with the salesperson's signature. Only then can the company be held responsible for "special favors" or "free, thrown-in items."

In order to obtain a relatively accurate estimate, you must show the salesperson everything you intend to move. It won't help you to hide a refrigerator with the intention of "sneaking it on the truck." Because you will ultimately be paying for the *total weight* of your items and the distance to be traveled, the *number* of items is inconsequential.

You may also be interested in additional services that the company can provide, such as transporting your family car. Again, be cautious about exactly what you are to receive for these services. In the case of my automobile, for example, the salesperson showed me several nice photographs of a car being placed into a crate within the moving van to avoid damage to it from other things packed into the truck. I remember paying extra just for the crate. When the van arrived, however, it was obvious that my car had traveled over 3,000 miles with no crate at all and with boxes packed all around the car. These boxes rubbed right through the paint and down to the metal of the car during the long journey. Nothing in my moving contract said anything about my having paid for a crate for the car, and I made the gross mistake of assuming that my car would be treated like the automobile presented in their brochures. If in the same situation today, I would insist that a carefully worded sentence describing the crate and method for transporting the car be added to my contract.

Probably the most widely used additional service is that of

professional packing and unpacking of your belongings. Because of the time it takes and the cost of labor these days, not to mention the cost of cartons and rolls of tape, this can be an incredible expense. Again, this is an option for people who have their moving expenses paid by someone else. It is understandable that most consumers elect to pack their own belongings, which might explain why many items don't arrive in the new location in one piece. (Chapter 4 explains the how-to's of packing.)

Another service often mentioned by professional movers is storage. This should be avoided at all costs. One tends to forget about things placed in storage; and at a rate accumulated daily, it doesn't take long for the storage charges to exceed the value of the items stored. A much better price can be found at storage centers located in larger cities and operated by U-Haul and store-it-yourself companies. If none of these places is available, try renting a garage for a period of time. You would be best advised to install a loud alarm on the garage door if you do this. One of the best ideas involves talking a friend into renting his garage to you, especially during the summer months when he wouldn't mind leaving his car(s) outside. However, don't accept a friend's gracious offer to store your things free for a while. Offer your friend a set amount of money and mutually sign an agreement. Should something come up, you will find that without the commitment of money or contract, even your friend can move your things outside without mercy. The signed agreement ensures that for an agreed sum of money, you can safely store your things—and at a fraction of the cost that a professional storage outfit would charge. The agreement also states exactly when you have to remove all your things so that your friend knows well in advance the extent of his commitment. If well planned, this suggestion can save you a bundle in storage fees, give you time to find a permanent place, and allow you to rest easy with the knowledge that your possessions are secure.

The time of year when you move can be crucially important to you and can make quite a difference in the quality of treatment you receive from a professional mover. If possible, you should avoid the three summer months, during which over 75 percent of all moves are made. Obviously, the summer has its advantages: nice weather and the kids are not in school. But consider that the professional moving companies, faced with this unusual increase in business, must hire a large number of independent truckers and inexperienced helpers. If you are moved by this kind of crew, you can expect some damage to your belongings. The best time to move is in the early spring, just prior to summer. You can make your professional move before the summer rush; it generally won't hurt the kids to pull them from school a bit early; and your family will have more time to adjust to the new area, develop some friendships, and prepare for a new school year. Autumn moves are the second-best choice, since the weather is still dependable. But your children will have to start school late and may have to overcome being called "the new kids" in school. You might also consider a move during the winter months if you are going east-to-west, as weather conditions should improve as you go; but for the most part, the unpredictability of the weather can lead to more problems than you'd like to face. It is often during the cold months that professionals find themselves snowed in somewhere and you find yourself in an empty house waiting for your five-day-late shipment to arrive. It happens to approximately 8 percent of the moves a company makes each year.

Be sure to get a sufficient amount of insurance for your household goods. All movers have a maximum liability of 60¢ per pound unless you increase that figure by paying an additional amount. The cost for this insurance is a pittance compared to the total moving expenses, so it is more than a worthwhile investment. Consider what would happen if the company lost your entire shipment and all you got back was 60¢ on the pound! It has happened. The company representative can outline the different insurance options when he comes to your home in order to make the estimate.

Before the moving van comes to your home to pick up your belongings, it goes to a weighing station where its weight is recorded on your bill of lading. This is called the tare weight. Call the company and find out when and where this weighing is to be held and ask to be there. There are two things for you to look out for: 1. only the truck driver should be in the truck; 2. the gas tank should be full. It doesn't matter if there are other shipments on the truck (as is often the case), because you are interested only in the difference between the weight of the van before it goes to your house and the weight of it when your goods are packed into it. After your load is on the truck, follow it back to the weighing station. Check that only the same driver as before is in the cab and that no extra weight has been added. (There have been instances where four guys have hung on the truck or a horse has been put on the scale to up the weight.) Your presence will keep any funny business from occurring. They are allowed to top off the gas tanks before the weighing, so, again, be sure those tanks were at the top before your goods were loaded. Be a bit pushy if necessary and unscrew the gas caps on both side tanks and look in; you should see your reflection. Don't trust a gauge on the dashboard, as these can easily be rigged to register full. Those tanks constitute several hundred pounds of weight, which you might end up paying for. Also, be sure all equipment such as hand trucks, dollies, and pads are in the truck at both weighings. Your attendance to both matters will ensure an accurate weighing. Some professional moving companies won't allow you to attend that first (tare) weighing. This kind of action would make me very dubious about the accuracy of the weight, and I'd find another company that *would* allow me to be there.

When the movers arrive to pack the cartons and boxes into the van, they will tag each article with a self-stick identification number, which goes onto a tally sheet along with a description of the article. Keep track of the proceedings by making sure that everything gets a tag and that the descriptions are accurate to the article and correspond to the right number. When your goods are unloaded at the new location, the process is reversed; then you must check off each item and its number as the item is brought into the house. Beware of double-tagging. This is a practice that an unscrupulous mover might use to steal some of your belongings. As the movers unload boxes from the van and bring them into your house, they remove a number tag from a box they want to keep and put that tag on the opposite side of a box that already has a tag, which gives the box *two* number tags. When they bring the box into the house, they show you one of the numbers, which they remove and destroy once they put the box down in the corner of a room. Later, when you go through the inventory, you note that a box is missing, but a quick search around the house will, sure enough, locate the number on that box in the corner. Obviously, all of these boxes look the same to you, and you don't realize that the box is not correctly numbered. Meanwhile the movers have secreted the other box away in the van, and you are now less one box of your belongings. Movers tend to unpack things at a frenetic pace, and you find yourself in a flurry of activity, very often confused and barely able to keep up. A pair of disreputable movers will take advantage of your predicament and make off with as many as ten boxes of household goods by using this method. You must be certain that when the mover comes through the doorway with your boxes of goods, you check all sides of each box to ensure that it has not been double-tagged. Take your time and make them work at *your* pace!

The rest of the procedure for moving with a professional is pretty much taken care of for you. Most professional moves go smoothly with a minimal number of problems and complaints. Nonetheless, you should be as knowledgeable as possible about the events that are to take place and you should read everything you can find about moving. Most important is the Interstate Commerce Commission's red booklet, *Summary of Information for Shippers of Household Goods*, which your mover must supply you, by law, free of charge. In addition, there are some books listed in the bibliography which you should glance at.

Professional movers are not ogres waiting to pounce upon every unsuspecting consumer who comes along. Rather, they are representatives of an immense business that has all the good and bad points of a large organization, and they rely heavily on word-of-mouth recommendations and on private, individual moves. It is understandable that they want your move to be as uneventful as you do, and most of them will try their hardest to make it so. Couple this knowledge with the insights and cautions mentioned above, and you will be in an extremely good position to organize and control your move by a professional company so that the results are pleasant as well as effective.

Chapter 2

The Do-it-yourself Move

IF YOU WERE TO LOOK AT THE NATIONAL TREND, YOU would see that professional movers do not have a corner on the moving market. Quite surprisingly, they have only a 25 percent share of it. The remaining 75 percent consists of people who have decided to move themselves. And there seems to be a number of good reasons why people might reach this decision.

One of the primary concerns of the average consumer is expense. Without question, a professional move is the most costly method of transporting your goods. This partially stems from the fact that professional movers are regulated by the Interstate Commerce Commission, which establishes the rates that can be charged for interstate moves, thereby eliminating competitive pricing. People who move themselves, on the other hand, can expect to save somewhere between 50 and 75 percent (according to U-Haul and Ryder). Because companies that provide rental vehicles and equipment are not government-regulated, their rates are affected by "friendly competition." It is thus possible to find lower rates by shopping around. In addition, savings also result from the do-it-yourselfers supplying their own labor for packing, loading, unloading, and unpacking.

Most professional movers require cash or a certified check upon delivery of your items. Not too many consumers have access to large sums of money at that particular time, a time when they need their money for many other things related to the move. Rental agencies, however, very often accept major credit cards, which makes payment more convenient.

The professional does have experience in one area that the do-it-yourself mover just doesn't: the art of packing. Many years of testing and evaluation have given the professional a basis for his techniques, so it is unrealistic for the do-it-yourselfer to think he can do a better job at it. However, he will probably offset his lack of packing expertise with extra special care and handling, the kind of "babying" one really can't expect from a professional company, regardless of its advertising claims.

There is again the matter of convenience when comparing these two types of moves. The do-it-yourselfer can leave when he wants to and take almost as long as he cares to— perhaps even take a short side trip. When he arrives, his goods are there with him with no delays, no waiting. He always knows where his goods are, and it is unlikely they will be "lost en route." Late pickups and deliveries remain problems for professional movers.

Choosing a Rental Firm

Because 90 percent of the people who move themselves pay for the move out of their own pockets, it is the cost-conscious individual who ultimately chooses to do it himself. Consequently, he will want to find the best equipment at the best rate. Choosing the best rental firm for your move will probably be a relatively easy task, since there are only three major companies operating within the United States: U-Haul, Ryder, and E-Z Haul. These three should be dependable and reliable because of the volume of business they do and the quality of their equipment. If you find or hear of other rental agencies in your area, try to learn more about them. Are their rates really lower or are there hidden charges? Talk to anyone who has used them before and, perhaps, even call your local Better Business Bureau to see if there have been complaints lodged against them in the past. Smaller companies such as these could really save you money, especially if your move is a local one and you intend to return the van to the same location you rented it from. The primary rule of thumb here is to investigate them before renting.

To determine the best rental firm for your move, first get an estimate of the rates from each one. Telephone them (it's a lot quicker), tell them what equipment you need and when, tell them your destination, and ask them to mail you their information package, as well as an estimate of the charges. You should gather these estimates from all the major companies in your area, as well as from a few of the smaller ones.

Another factor to consider is the proximity of rental-firm outlets to both your present location and the location of your new home. For local moves this is not so important, since you will return the equipment to the same agency. But for interstate moves, it is extremely important that the agency have a convenient representative in both the city you're moving from and the city you're moving to.

In your choice of rental companies, also consider the size of the van you are going to require (this chapter later tells you how to determine that size), what it rents for, and the types of moving aids and equipment the company has to offer. You might discover that only one of these companies has available the size van you need.[1] If the number and size of your household belongings are particularly large and you find that a single van will still not have enough room, then talk to each of the rental companies about giving you a special price for the rental of a van and a trailer or, perhaps, two smaller vans for the price of the single large one. Again, these firms have negotiable rental rates, so you can bargain with them to some extent.

Another factor to consider is your destination. If you are moving to an area in which a large number of moves are made, you'll be taking the van to a location where the company has many other rentals, which may mean that the company will have to transport the truck to some other area where it is needed. You are often charged for this redistribution. So, while shopping around for a rental agency, you might want to locate one that will not charge you for this.

Once you have found the best price and best equipment

for your move, it is advisable to put down a deposit on the vehicle and equipment you are going to need at least one month before the move. This is especially important if you plan to move during the summer months. The deposit will "hold" the equipment and avoid a charge that companies often put on rentals during the peak season. Ultimately, the best idea would be to place your deposit around April for a move you plan to make in June or July, thus avoiding the surcharge.

Insurance

Naturally, we all want to have a safe move. But there are pitfalls you should be aware of and prepared to deal with. What if your van were stolen? Who would be responsible for it? What about your personal belongings? An accident or breakdown could present a financial tragedy in addition to physical or emotional hardship. It is wise to prepare your move by making sure you have adequate insurance coverage for the types of mishaps that could occur.

Both U-Haul and Ryder have optional insurance policies that offer comprehensive coverage for do-it-yourselfers. U-Haul's "Safemove" pays up to $5,000 for loss or damage to your possessions during a one-way move with one of their trucks. In addition, their policy provides personal injury protection for you as well as your passengers, and it frees you of any responsibility for the rental truck and equipment. Ryder's "Safeguard" policy offers similar protection for renters of their equipment. Considering the reasonable cost, I would suggest that you subscribe to one of these optional policies when you move.

You should note that neither of these insurance policies protects you from theft. Were your truck and belongings stolen en route, you would be liable for the rental equipment as well as for the loss of your household items. Check with your insurance agent to see if your goods are covered during a move by your homeowners' policy. If not, it may be possible to add a temporary clause to your policy that will provide such coverage. The rental truck and its equipment might be covered by your present automobile insurance. Since this policy may also provide some comprehensive and accident insurance, find out from your agent exactly what the limits of your policy are.

Another easily overlooked event requiring insurance protection is accident or injury to a third party, such as someone who helps you load or unload your truck. Because this operation takes place at the site of your home, your present homeowners' insurance policy may cover such misfortune. But, again, contact your insurance representative to be sure.

Many people naïvely move without adequate insurance coverage and find themselves in serious trouble when complications arise. The additional cost of comprehensive insurance coverage is easily overshadowed by the proportional cost of the move itself and the comfort of knowing that all possible events are taken care of. A synopsis of insurance coverages can be found in the following chart.

CHART 1.

INSURANCE COVERAGE

Fill in the personal-insurance column after consulting with your agent(s).

Personal Protection	Your Own Insurance	U-Haul "Safemove"	Ryder "Safeguard"
Loss of life		$10,000	$15,000
Medical expenses		$500	$500
Ambulance		——	$50
Passenger Protection			
Loss of life		$5,000	$5,000
Medical expenses		$500	$500
Ambulance		——	$50

Household Goods[1]

One-way rental, Truck	$5,000	$5,000
Trailer	$2,000	——
Local rental, Truck	$2,000	$2,500
Trailer	$1,000	——

Third-party Protection

Accidental injury while loading or unloading van	——	——

Damage

Rental truck and equipment	complete coverage[2]	complete coverage[3]
Third-party vehicles or property	——	——

---

[1] See the actual policies to determine exactly what types of accidents are covered. Ryder, for example, covers "accidental loss or damage from collision, overturn, upset, landslide, flood, explosion, hail, windstorm, lightning or fire." It does not cover theft or burglary!

[2] Without the optional "Safemove" policy, you are responsible "for all accidental damage to the rental vehicle."

[3] Your liability without the optional "Safeguard" coverage is "the first $500 or the entire amount if the accident is the result of insufficient clearance."

Breakdowns

You should also be ready for the possibility of truck or tire failure. While such occurrences are rare, it is important to know what to do were such a mishap to deter your trip.

Rental companies differ in the way they approach some of these breakdowns. Take tires, for example. Ryder suggests that you pay for the repair and promises that you will be reimbursed when you show the paid receipt to the Ryder dealer at the end of your trip. For tires damaged beyond repair, you must locate the nearest Ryder office (found in the consumer information section of the log book that comes with the truck), call them collect, and have them arrange for the correct tire replacement. There is no way of telling how long this could take. U-Haul has a similar policy regarding tire repair (at your expense, to be reimbursed later), but they have an arrangement with Goodyear Tire and Rubber to provide free replacement if a tire cannot be repaired. The ease and speed with which this can be accomplished depends on the location of the nearest Goodyear dealer. You may still have to pay out-of-pocket expenses such as towing, so be sure to obtain receipts and show them to the dealer when you return the equipment.

In terms of repairs or breakdown, most companies expect *you* to pay for anything less than $25.00 and to get a receipt. Ryder promises to reimburse these expenses at the end of the trip, while U-Haul expects you to mail the receipts to them for reimbursement. For major breakdowns involving expenses over $25.00, both companies have a nationwide emergency telephone number you can call to obtain help. Ryder indicates that it is prepared to "send a mechanic to repair your vehicle on the spot or to tow it to a shop for repairs or even to replace it if the repair would cause you undue delay." U-Haul says that "partial rental refunds will be made when U-Haul mechanical failure causes premature termination of your move." In any event, the cost of the delay and possible transfer of your goods from one truck to another will inconvenience you.

These are risks you take when deciding to move yourself, but they are not as bad or as frightening when you have made sufficient preparation for them. For this reason, I would suggest you take along at least $100 in cash to cover out-of-pocket expenses such as towing and repairs.

There are a number of factors that should be added together to determine the total cost of your do-it-yourself move. There is the initial cost of the van, and this expense is given to you in advance by the rental company when you call them for an estimate. You will also have to allow for the cost of gasoline along the way. To get a reasonable estimate, figure that the truck will average 6 MPG, which you might stretch to 7 MPG if you drive at a slow yet comfortable rate of speed. Multiply this by the number of miles you intend to travel and then by the cost, per gallon, of regular gasoline to get your estimate.

6(7) MPG × Total Miles × ¢/Gallon of Gas = Gasoline Estimate

For a cross-country move, it wouldn't be surprising to tally up gasoline costs of $300 or so.

In addition to gasoline, you will have to pay road and bridge tolls, depending upon the highway system and route you travel, as well as special taxes and surcharges each state requires of trucks weighing over a certain tonnage. You will have to pull into every open weigh station along your route, where your van will be weighed and taxed accordingly. Check with the rental company for details.

Figure in a buffer of $100 to account for oil and road maintenance, as well as possible towing fees. You may have minor repairs and vehicle expenses for which you will need cash.

Be sure to include in your estimate the distribution fee if you are being charged one and also the amount required (and returned) for your deposit. Include the rental rates for any additional moving aids, such as dollies and hand trucks.

Altogether, these costs constitute your estimate for each rental company. Combined with the convenience factors of close pickup and drop-off locations, you should be able to select the best rental company to handle your move.

CHART 2.

CALCULATING TOTAL MOVING EXPENSES

Van or trailer rental—$

Gasoline—$

Tolls—$

Towing/Maintenance—$

Distribution fee—$
Deposit—$
Meals and lodging—$
Additional moving equipment—$
_____

Total Expenses

Moving Needs

Before you begin collecting various estimates, you must know what to request in terms of truck size. Rental firms do not have estimators who come to your house; rather, you must do the job of categorizing your belongings and determining just what size van you are going to need. This is obviously one area where you don't want to fall short and have to leave something precious behind, but you also don't want to overestimate and pay for a larger van than you need. The following is an inventory checklist that will give you a very good idea of what you have and how much space each item will occupy. Simply mark off each item on the list that you have, and write its estimated cubic-foot size in the empty column. After inventorying the entire house, total the cubic feet to determine how much space your belongings will require.

CHART 3.

"ESTIMATED SIZE" CHECKLIST

Household Item	Cu. Ft.	No. of Pieces	Total Cu. Ft.
Barbecue	5		
Bathinette	4		
Beds			
King	67		
Queen	50		
Double	45		
Single	30		

Youth	20
Cot (folding)	2
Bicycle	6
Birdbath	3
Birdcage	2
Bookcase	12
Boxes	
Book	2
Dish-pak	5
Utility	3
Wardrobe	15
Breakfast table	10
Buffet	25
Buffet with hutch top	30
Bureau, dresser, chest	20
Card table	1
Cedar chest or trunk	10
Chairs	
Arm	10
Occasional	14
Overstuffed recliner	20
Rocker	12
Straight	4
Chaise longue	10
China cabinet	20
Clothes basket	1
Clothes hamper	3
Corner cabinet	14
Couch, sofa, davenport	35
Crib	8
Desk	20
Dishwasher	15
Double dresser	25
Drapes	3
Dresser chair or bench	4
Dryer, Clothes	20

Extension table	14
Fan	1
Filing cabinet	8
Fireplace tools	3
Floor lamp	3
Footlocker	5
Footstool	2
Freezer	45
Garden cart	3
Garden hose and tools	10
Golf bag and clubs	2
Heater	3
Hide-a-bed	35
Highchair	3
Ironer (mangle)	10
Ironing board	2
Lawn chair	3
Lawn mower, Hand	5
Lawn mower, Riding	20
Lawn swing	20
Magazine rack	2
Mirror	3
Night table	4
Oven, Portable microwave	4
Packing barrel	10
Phonograph, Portable	2
Picnic bench	5
Picnic table	20
Playpen	6
Range	25
Refrigerator	40
Roaster, rotisserie	3
Rugs or pads (each)	8
Sewing machine, Portable	3
Upright	8

Sled	2
Stepladder	5
Stereo components (each)	2
Swingset	20
Table chair	4
Table lamp	2
Tables, Coffee or end	4
Television, Combination	18
Portable	8
Console	12
Toolbox	3
Toy chest	4
Tricycle	4
Utility cart	3
Vacuum cleaner	3
Wagon	5
Wardrobe closet (armoire)	36
Washing machine	20
Wheelbarrow	6

Total Cubic Feet _____

As you travel through each room checking this list, estimate the number of boxes you will need for the smaller items that are tucked away in drawers and cabinets. Consider the special-purpose cartons you can buy from your rental company: small, strong boxes for books; medium-sized utility boxes; padded and divided cartons for dishes (Dish-paks); and large wardrobe cartons complete with hanging rods for clothes. (For more box information, see Chapter 4.)

Once you have completed your tally and have added up the cubic feet for every item in your household, as well as for the cartons and boxes you intend to pack, compare this number to the various sizes of trailers and vans available at the rental company. The following chart indicates the approximate cubic-foot capacities of the trucks and vans currently available.

CHART 4.

TYPICAL TRUCK AND TRAILER SIZES

Van Size	Cubic Feet	Rental Firm
24-foot truck	1,128	U-Haul
22-foot truck	1,091	Ryder
20-foot truck	1,054	U-Haul
18-foot truck	950	Ryder
16-foot truck	847	U-Haul, Budget
14-foot truck	600	U-Haul, Budget
12-foot truck	538	U-Haul, Ryder, Budget
Large trailer	378	U-Haul
Medium trailer	200	U-Haul
Small trailer	102	U-Haul
* "Combo" 24-foot van with large trailer	1,506	U-Haul

* NOTE: *This option, while it allows for the greatest amount of goods to be shipped, prevents you from towing the family car behind the van. Budget, as well as others not mentioned, has trucks only for local moves. Check your phone book.*

It is important to note that you will need a trailer or van that is slightly larger in its capacity than the cubic-foot estimate you made of your household belongings. It is unlikely that everything in your shipment can be packed snugly together with no air spaces in between. You must, therefore, include in your estimate enough additional space to accommodate bulky, misshapened items that just don't pack together well. (Bicycles and tricycles are notorious for this!)

In addition to the van, you will want to carry along some aids to assist you in moving large, obstinate articles out of the house and into the van with relative ease. Some of these aids can be rented from the same company that rents you the van.

One of the primary aids is furniture pads. These are heavy, durable cloth blankets that are used to prevent scratching or breaking of furniture and appliances. Usually rented by the dozen at a reasonable charge, they are a wise investment. Any item that is not boxed for packing into your van should be protected from gouges, scratches, and rubbing, so it is a good idea to wrap your fine wood furniture in pads and to cover visible surfaces like tabletops with them. This is not necessary for overstuffed sofas and already padded items. These upholstered furnishings just need some protective plastic sheeting to keep them from getting soiled.

It is also well worth your while to rent an appliance dolly, a tall two-wheeled truck designed for, and therefore extremely well suited to, moving heavy major appliances, such as washers, dryers, refrigerators, ovens and ranges, and other bulky items. The dolly has a relatively short step, and just above the small, heavy, ball-bearing wheels is a set of rubber belts that allow the dolly to roll smoothly up or down

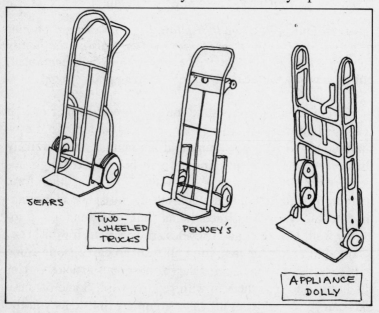

SEARS

TWO-WHEELED TRUCKS

PENNEY'S

APPLIANCE DOLLY

stairs. The dolly is wheeled up to an appliance, and the step is positioned underneath the edge of one side. There is a quick-release strap arrangement that can be brought around the appliance so the dolly can be strapped tightly to it. This provides great control and maneuverability for bringing your appliances out of tight situations, through doorways, and up or down stairs in your home.

The appliance dolly, however, is not well suited to moving cartons and boxes because its bottom step is too short. For this purpose, I would recommend the use of a regular two-wheeled hand truck. Because these are usually not found at the van rental firms, you should buy or, if you know someone

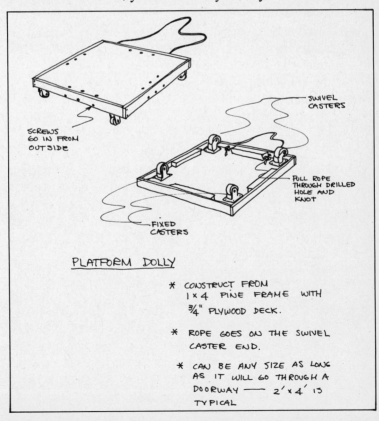

SWIVEL CASTERS

SCREWS GO IN FROM OUTSIDE

PULL ROPE THROUGH DRILLED HOLE AND KNOT

FIXED CASTERS

PLATFORM DOLLY

* CONSTRUCT FROM 1 x 4 PINE FRAME WITH 3/4" PLYWOOD DECK.

* ROPE GOES ON THE SWIVEL CASTER END.

* CAN BE ANY SIZE AS LONG AS IT WILL GO THROUGH A DOORWAY — 2' x 4' IS TYPICAL

who owns one, borrow. You could rent one from some other company, but this would be impractical if your move is across the country, since you have to return it to the same place from which you rented it. I have found enough uses for it around the house to warrant the purchase. The two-wheeled truck is much shorter than an appliance dolly, and its wheels are much larger, so they are not prone to getting stuck in sidewalk cracks. It has a much smoother and canti-levered handle arrangement, as well as a broader step that can easily accommodate the width of an entire book box, for example. With one of these hand trucks you can whisk four or five cartons of goods back and forth with great ease— certainly greater ease than you could with the heavier ap-pliance dolly. Additionally, it is a good practice to leave the appliance dolly strapped to the last heavy item you packed on the van. This way you won't inadvertently forget the dolly when you leave, and it will be in a convenient place when you unload. The two-wheeled truck then takes over in the carting of all the boxes and cartons and other smaller items that constitute the remainder of your household goods.

One piece of moving equipment that is really hard to find anywhere and that I would suggest you construct yourself is called a platform dolly. Basically, it is a reinforced ¾-inch plywood platform roughly 2 feet square onto which four heavy-duty swivel casters have been mounted. This kind of platform provides a smooth rolling surface for large, heavy items which would be difficult to manage otherwise, and es-pecially for items which do not have casters of their own and are not easy to balance on either of the other dollies. One such item that comes to mind is a dehumidifier, whose casters are not suitable for traveling over rough, coarse surfaces. Other items include large, portable color televisions; electric typewriters; ornate brass cash registers (some of us keep the strangest things around the house); and an assortment of machine-shop tools, such as table saws, band saws, scroll saws, and planer-jointer combinations. Since this dolly is so inexpensive and easy to make, it is well worth the time and effort to put one together solely for the purpose of transporting these hard-to-categorize unwieldy items. The following illustration gives you all the information necessary for putting one together at a minimal expense.

Another moving aid for which you will undoubtedly find a number of uses is a good-quality, durable rope. You should probably have two different weights of rope. One is a relatively lightweight rope that you can use to secure items within the van via the tie-downs positioned at various locations along the van's interior. The common securing method is to pack about a fourth of the van, from floor to ceiling, and tie it down. Then proceed to the next quarter. The other rope should be much heavier, as it is often used to pull or lift an object into position, especially large appliances. The ropes should be well made and reasonably priced, as well as smooth to the touch. Avoid using sisal rope, which is too coarse and of too sharp a texture to handle well.

You may consider adding to these aids a small block and tackle. I have successfully used such a device in pulling a washer and dryer from a basement location up a steep staircase where there was just enough room for the appliance. It was easy to make a ramp out of 2×6's and slide each appliance up the ramp by using the block and tackle as the pulling device.

This brings us to the use of a few 2×6's, which can serve as makeshift ramps, pry bars, and other related devices. They could make a big difference in the ease of moving some large pieces of furniture; and if you don't bring a pair of them, you'll wish you had. These boards are preferable to 2×4's because they are wider and provide a better track along which to guide a dolly. They are also easy to stash inside the van along one wall.

You should also have a good pair of leather or heavy fabric work gloves. Moving a houseful of belongings is a difficult task which takes its toll on your hands. Use gloves to prevent such injuries as blisters, pinching, scratches, and splinters, which can so easily occur.

To go along with the work gloves, you might consider a hat of some kind. A hat can provide a certain amount of shade, which you will welcome if you find yourself working in bright midday sunlight. One with a padded brim will help keep sweat out of your eyes, which can be really annoying when you are in the middle of "horsing" an upright piano down a flight of stairs. Here, even a nice clean terrycloth towel tucked into your belt will be handy for wiping perspiration off your forehead and arms. Besides adding to your comfort, the towel will help you maintain a decent grip and better control of the object you are moving.

This list of moving aids is certainly not essential for everyone's move. You will have to analyze what items you are moving and their location in your house in order to determine which of these aids you will really need. Some people use simply a few furniture pads and an appliance dolly, and are very successful. But if your household is anything like mine, you will probably find that every item mentioned will come in handy and will alleviate a lot of the problems, strain, and effort. The reasonably small investment in terms of purchasing a two-wheeled hand truck and some decent rope, as well as a small block and tackle, will certainly pay for itself in the end and save much physical labor and valuable time.

CHART 5.

MOVING-AIDS CHECKLIST

- ☐ Furniture pads ⸺ dozen
- ☐ Appliance dolly
- ☐ Two-wheel hand truck
- ☐ Platform dolly
- ☐ Tie-down rope (medium strength)

☐ Hauling rope (heavy strength)
☐ Block and tackle
☐ Two 2 × 6 boards
☐ Gloves (enough for all helpers)
☐ Hats
☐ Towels
☐ First-aid kit

Readying Your Major Appliances

There is one other area worth discussing for do-it-yourself movers, and that is the disconnection and preparation of major appliances for moving. Most professional movers suggest that you contact an electrician or gas company representative to disconnect your appliances; but if you follow these reasonable safeguards, there is no reason why you cannot make the disconnections yourself.

First you'll need an appliance tool kit. This is a very simple, no-frills kind of kit that contains just seven items:

a roll of wide masking tape
a Vise-Grips or large slip-joint pliers
a standard slotted screwdriver
a Phillips screwdriver
a simple electrical tester (neon type)
a small container of soap bubbles
a flashlight

Using these tools, you should be able to disconnect every appliance in your home, from the kitchen to the laundry. So let's go through a list of major appliances and discuss the disconnection and preparation of each one.

The Refrigerator

This is probably the largest bulky major appliance you own; but since it is basically an empty box, it tends to be lighter than most other items. The refrigerator does not require much preparation before moving. Roll it out from the wall and unplug the electric cord. Most units these days have built-in casters that allow them to roll in a straight (front-to-back) line. Now is a good time to clean the interior well and vacuum the dust from the evaporator coil in the rear on the outside. Everything not permanently attached to the interior must be emptied out; and things like butter bin doors and crisper lids should be taped down with masking tape. Also be sure to tape the doors shut to prevent them from swinging open during the move.

The dolly is always positioned on a side, never on the front or rear, since it may mar or dent the doors if put on the front or seriously damage the evaporator coil tubes if put on the back. (One small pinhole in the evaporator coil tubes and you can junk your refrigerator!) Place a pad between the dolly and the refrigerator, then secure the dolly strap around the refrigerator to hold the dolly in place. Be careful: too much tension here could crease the refrigerator doors or sides. Coil up the electrical cord and bind it with a "twist-tie" (they come with plastic trash bags, but you can buy them separately), then stash the cord into some available opening or behind the evaporator coil. If this is impractical, tape the cord to the refrigerator back.

The width of a refrigerator is normally designed to be just narrow enough to allow the appliance to fit through an average doorway, so plan the easiest route through your house to the van. Never try to move a refrigerator alone—it is definitely a two-person operation. One person controls the move by balancing the refrigerator on the dolly, while the other guides the refrigerator over steps and thresholds and through doorways. It is often better to position the refrigerator on the van with the doors facing the wall, as this tends to protect the front from scratches. Just be careful about what is packed next to the evaporator coil. Always hang a furniture pad over and around the refrigerator after it is in place.

Ovens and Ranges

Ovens and ranges are normally not very difficult to move.

Electric stoves are simply unplugged from the heavy socket on the wall behind them. It is a safe procedure to locate the appropriate circuit breaker or fuse and shut down power to the oven outlet before pulling the plug. Obviously, you don't need to be an electrician to perform this task. Store the heavy cable in some opening in the back or tape it securely. Remove anything that might fall off during the move, including oven racks, broiler pans, pots and pans stored in a separate compartment, burner elements and rims, griddle tops, and even control knobs. All of these can go into a carton marked OVEN. Tape the oven and storage doors closed; and if you have the type of electrical surface elements that do not unplug, tape them to the range with long strips of masking tape.

Everything mentioned above applies to preparing a gas range as well, except for the disconnection, which is a little more involved. After pulling the oven from the wall, locate the gas line and valve. The shut-off valve allows gas to flow through it when its handle is in line with the valve body. Give the handle a quarter turn in either direction to the off position. Using the slip-joint pliers, unscrew the flexible hose coupler where it connects to the valve. As soon as it is off, listen for the sound of escaping gas. The gas companies add a strong odor to their product which you should also notice, especially if it continues for longer than a few seconds after the connector has been taken off. If the valve continues to leak gas and no adjusting of the valve handle will stop it, then reconnect the oven and call the gas company for help. But if all seems in order and the sound as well as smell of gas has gone away, you can proceed with the leak test. Take the soap-bubble solution and slop some over the valve, valve handle, and pipe. Watch carefully to see if bubbles form around any of the joints or cracks. No bubbles? Then you are all set to move the oven away.

Ovens should also be dollied from the side. You will find that an oven is much more unwieldy than a refrigerator because so much of it hangs over the edge of the dolly. The wider the oven, the greater your predicament. You must really swing the dolly back to achieve the balance point, and with the oven up in the air, careen through your house to the van. Your assistant can be of extreme value here by helping you keep the oven in balance and by guiding and lifting when necessary. In fact, you may find the platform dolly more useful. As with the refrigerator, position the oven in the truck with the front toward the wall for protection, and hang a furniture pad over and around it.

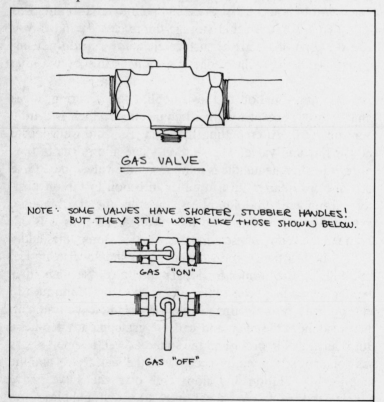

GAS VALVE

NOTE: SOME VALVES HAVE SHORTER, STUBBIER HANDLES!
BUT THEY STILL WORK LIKE THOSE SHOWN BELOW.

GAS "ON"

GAS "OFF"

(NOTE: When testing a gas valve, *never* use a match or open flame. Soap bubbles are nonflammable and provide something for your kids to play with when you get to the new house.)

Washing Machines

These appliances can sometimes cause the greatest consternation to the do-it-yourself mover, since they are large, awkward, and heavy. Additionally, they are often located in

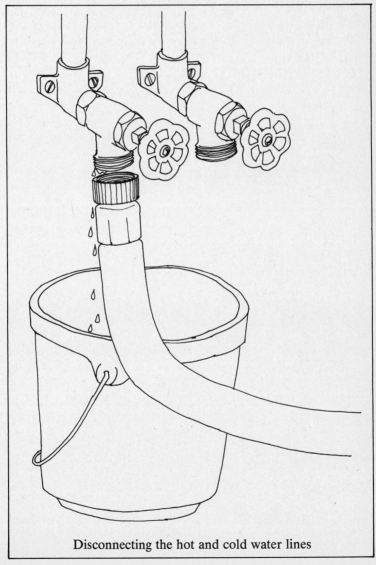

Disconnecting the hot and cold water lines

some dark corner of a basement, which can provide a real challenge to their removal. Washer disconnection is not much of a problem. It is a good idea to run the machine through a rinse-spin cycle to assure that the water is out. The weight of a water-filled machine would make it difficult for you and your assistant to tug it away from the wall and expose the hoses. *Step one:* Unplug the electrical cord, secure it with a twist-tie, and stash it into an opening or tape it to the back. *Step two:* Remove the hot and cold water hoses. First close down the two faucets (water valves). Then, before unscrewing the connector, place a bucket underneath,

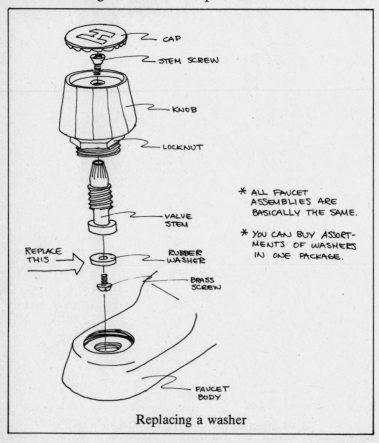

CAP

STEM SCREW

KNOB

LOCKNUT

VALVE STEM

REPLACE THIS →

RUBBER WASHER

BRASS SCREW

* ALL FAUCET ASSEMBLIES ARE BASICALLY THE SAME.

* YOU CAN BUY ASSORTMENTS OF WASHERS IN ONE PACKAGE.

FAUCET BODY

Replacing a washer

as there is still water under pressure in each hose. Unscrew each connector from each faucet, using the slip-joint pliers to loosen them, and allow the hose ends to drain into the bucket. These faucets are notorious for leaking, since they have been in an open position for many years and the rubber washers inside may have deteriorated and cracked. Another good reason for the bucket: if the faucets leak, you can replace the washers before continuing. The illustration shows a typical faucet and how to replace the washer. Once the area is dry, loosen and remove the hoses from the back of the washer. Now is the time to carefully inspect them and look

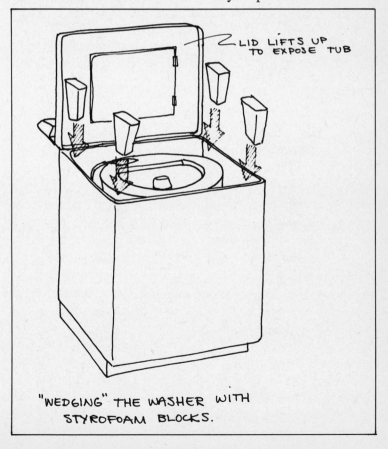

LID LIFTS UP TO EXPOSE TUB

"WEDGING" THE WASHER WITH STYROFOAM BLOCKS.

for cracks and signs of wear. You may want to replace them, but wait until you are in the new house, because you may need longer or shorter ones than what you have presently. *Step three:* Protect tub and motor. Vacuum the motor compartment well and wedge a few Styrofoam blocks between the motor and the frame. The tub can be reached by prying up the top and hinging it back while you wedge some Styrofoam between the tub and the interior walls in four places. Some rental firms (including U-Haul) sell these inserts, so you might ask about them when you pick up the truck. *Step four:* Put the hoses inside the tub and secure the lid with tape.

Like all appliances, you should dolly the washer from either side to prevent damage. Since washers tend to be even heavier than some refrigerators, this is definitely a two-person job. To load the washer onto the truck, it is easier to go up the ramp first while pulling the dolly behind you. The assistant can push on the appliance and help you guide the wheels. Once inside, you can quite easily turn the appliance around and position it in some secure spot.

Clothes Dryers

Dryers, like stoves, are either electric or gas, and can be disconnected in the same way. Be sure to clean and vacuum the appliance well before putting it on the truck. Also be sure to tape the door closed and pack away anything that is not already secured. Most dryers do not require drum protection; but if you want to be on the safe side, you can remove the back and secure the drum and motor with Styrofoam, as was done with the washing machine.

Portable Dishwashers

Although portable dishwashers have quick-disconnect features and are designed to be rolled around, you should still dolly them to the van. Since the light-duty self-contained casters are made only for smooth kitchen floors, they are too easily broken or bent on hard concrete. Again, be sure that all of the water is out of the unit and that anything not permanently secured has been removed and packed away.

These are the basics for preparing and disconnecting appliances for your move. Do not overlook the fact that most of these appliances have the capacity to store and protect a number of household items that might otherwise be difficult to box, such as large quilts, blankets, pillows, and other soft objects. A checklist for disconnecting any appliance follows.

CHART 6.

APPLIANCE DISCONNECTION

- ☐ 1. Disconnect the power source (gas or electric).
- ☐ 2. Disconnect the water source, if any.
- ☐ 3. Thoroughly clean the appliance.
- ☐ 4. Pack soft goods inside.
- ☐ 5. Secure all items and doors with wide masking tape.
- ☐ 6. Dolly from either side only.
- ☐ 7. Position in van with front toward wall.
- ☐ 8. Wrap with furniture pad to protect finish.

Now that you have seen what is involved in a do-it-yourself move, you should be better able to evaluate this alternative in relation to the professional move. In addition to the information provided above, another important factor is the kind of savings you can expect over a professional move. Ryder estimates that costs can be cut up to two-thirds by doing the work yourself, while U-Haul claims that, on the average, you can save 50 percent of the costs of moving and up to 75 percent if you rent a trailer instead of a van. The amount saved is also proportional to the distance traveled: the farther you go, the more you can expect to save. Compared to the very high cost of a professional move, these figures can be very alluring indeed and might easily persuade you to manage the move yourself. However, remember that a do-it-yourself move requires planning, organization, and a good deal of sweat and strain. If you are sufficiently prepared, you will find it a rewarding and money-saving effort.

Chapter 3

Alternative Moves

IN THE PREVIOUS TWO CHAPTERS, I FOCUSED ON THE more conventional methods of moving a household of belongings; discussed the pluses and minuses of each move, and compared the conveniences of a professional move with the savings of a do-it-yourself move. This chapter suggests a number of alternatives that run the gamut from the professional move to the do-it-yourself move. Some of these alternatives are a bit off-beat, but they are intentionally so. Yet all of them are intended to provide the eye-opening realization that other possibilities do exist. In order for some of these methods to work for you, you should look at them with an open mind; and if they're not directly appropriate, you can adapt them to your needs. Perhaps you will want to borrow part of one method and combine it with part of another, making the possibilities of combinations appear endless. In any event, what follows are other avenues of moving you should know about and consider, so that you can make a more knowledgeable choice when the time comes for you to make that big move.

The Crate Method

The crate method is designed for anyone who intends to move, but it is most beneficial to people who choose the professional move and want to eliminate the negatives associated with it, such as the mishandling of goods, breakage, delays in packing and unpacking, and the disorganization of your house when you arrive at your new location. This method involves building a relatively sophisticated crate for each room of your house. If you have, say, a seven-room house, it means consolidating everything you own into seven well-designed and fabricated crates. This will ultimately provide the professional mover with only seven items to put into the van; and because these items are rectilinear, they are easily "nested" and packed. In addition, since these crates have been packed by you, the movers will not be directly handling any of your goods. Another advantage of this method is that it allows for a very simple organization of your goods: the living-room crate goes into the living room, the master-bedroom crate goes into the master bedroom, and so on. Thus, loading and unloading procedures are simplified, and the ultimate savings is in the shorter time it takes to handle these crates.

Some moving companies are beginning to experiment with a system similar to this, in which you are provided with 10 foot by 8 foot by 8 foot containers into which you pack roughly 4,000 pounds of goods.[2] The actual moving is done on a flat-bed truck. Unfortunately, this method has not yet picked up sufficient popularity to be offered except in a few of the major cities. Besides, this service is more costly (about 5 to 10 percent higher) than a regular professional move, which might very well offset the savings one could expect.

The ultimate solution is to design and build the specialized crates yourself. There is a simplified method for building crates; and in addition to the illustrations shown here, you will want to see the construction diagrams in the packing section of Chapter 4.

Part of the design parameters of building such a crate is that, regardless of its length, its height and width must be able to pass through doorways, which limits these dimensions to around 30 inches in width and 76 inches or so in height. It also means that some of the furniture you are accustomed to having (particularly large, bulky, overstuffed items) may have to be eliminated in lieu of furniture that can fit within the crate. The illustrations indicate just a few possibilities. In addition, it is possible to locate furniture that can be easily dismantled for packing into such a crate, and you are advised

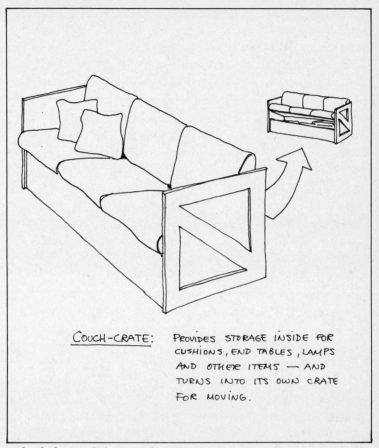

COUCH-CRATE: PROVIDES STORAGE INSIDE FOR
CUSHIONS, END TABLES, LAMPS
AND OTHER ITEMS — AND
TURNS INTO ITS OWN CRATE
FOR MOVING.

to look for such items whenever you replace one of the older pieces of furniture in your home.

This is a costly method initially. Good materials are not cheap, and the cost of wood has been rising steadily for the last decade. You might be dissuaded from using this method because of the expense; but if yours is a qualified move (based on the Internal Revenue definition), the cost of materials for these crates may be as valid a tax deduction as the move itself. You will also have the crates for every subsequent move you make, which, according to the national average, will occur once every five years. You can imagine the feeling of

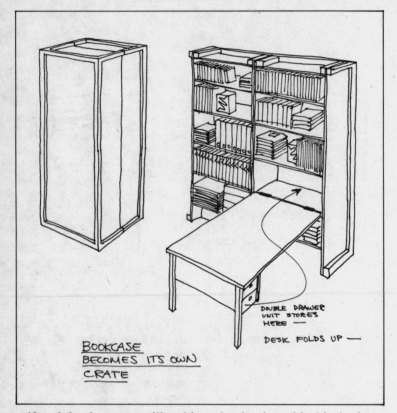

DOUBLE DRAWER
UNIT STORES
HERE —

DESK FOLDS UP —

BOOKCASE
BECOMES ITS OWN
CRATE

self-satisfaction you will achieve by having this kind of organization for your household move, not to mention the fun of seeing the expression on the face of the moving-company representative when he comes to give you an estimate. There is also the very pleasant fact that you can take as much time as you like to carefully pack your belongings before the move and unpack them after, with each item having a specific protected place in the crate.

There is the possibility that the crate itself could be a piece of furniture. By some simple adjustment of its panels or by folding a section out, it can easily become a bed platform for the bedroom, a contemporary couch for the living room, or even a bookcase for the den. The following illustrations show

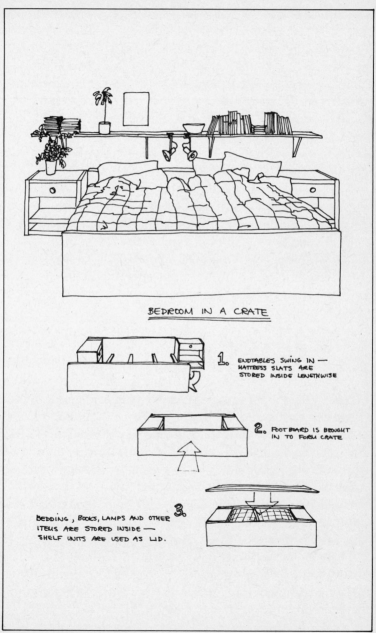

BEDROOM IN A CRATE

1. ENDTABLES SWING IN — MATTRESS SLATS ARE STORED INSIDE LENGTHWISE

2. FOOTBOARD IS BROUGHT IN TO FORM CRATE

3. BEDDING, BOOKS, LAMPS AND OTHER ITEMS ARE STORED INSIDE — SHELF UNITS ARE USED AS LID.

you some of the possibilities and should get you thinking about this exciting alternative. Such a method as crating would make your professional move a lot easier and less troublesome, as well as save you quite a bit of heartache brought about by numerous broken objects. Even if you intend to move yourself, a well-organized crating system will greatly accelerate your packing. For more ideas, see Chapter 9.

Put-it-all-in-boxes Method

The put-it-all-in-boxes method is one that subscribes to the same theory as the crate-for-each-room idea. This method will save a bit more time and energy, and will be considerably less expensive, resulting in significant savings, which make it preferable to a straightforward do-it-yourself move. The concept is a simple one: pack your entire household into cardboard boxes, using as many uniform-sized boxes as possible.

The best way to move is to have items that are easy to transport and that nest together in the van. Most do-it-yourself moving guides suggest that you begin packing a van by first loading all the boxes. They suggest this approach because boxes are the easiest items to pack and create a well-organized appearance in the van before the appliances and other bulky, heavy, and/or oddly shaped objects are loaded. Consider, then, that if your entire household were composed just of boxes, it would be an extremely easy task to move them into a van, stack them up, and drive away. Another advantage to boxing your belongings is that the boxes allow for no-tolerance close packing, and so would lower the cubic-foot van size you need (and lower the price, too).

It stands to reason that some articles around your home will not easily fit into a cardboard box. If the item is something that you just cannot part with, you will have to find or create a box big enough to contain it. It is even better to get rid of large, unwieldy items. Now is the time to sell your

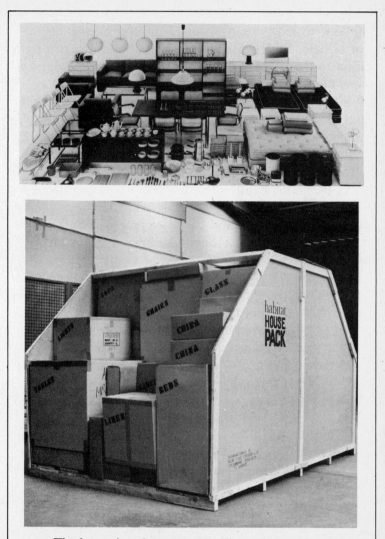

The house-in-a-box concept. The ultimate way to
move. Sell everything you have and order the
House Pack from Habitat. It can be flown to any
location in the world and will be waiting for you
when you arrive at your new home. (Habitat,
28 Neal St., London, England)

appliances; they weren't working quite right anyway. Now is the time to sell those overstuffed furniture items; they're so out of date. Now is the time to give away that extra refrigerator in the basement; it seems to have only ice cubes in it these days, anyhow. Consider the fun you can have buying all new things for your new home. Why not? Selling most of your obsolete appliances and furnishings will give you some money to play around with when you arrive in your new home.

If your move is with a professional mover, large, bulky, or heavy items will greatly affect the weight of your shipment. If you are moving yourself, not only will they be a handling problem, but their size will cut down on the amount of space in your truck. By eliminating these items you will be able to reduce the weight of the shipment or rent a trailer your car can tow instead of a truck. In either case, you can expect considerable savings,[3] and boxing everything is the major step toward achieving them.

But let's be practical. It would be almost impossible to find one carton size that could accommodate everything you own. A box containing books should be small enough to be portable when full, but almost everything else in the house won't fit in so small a carton. And a box sufficiently large to hold those other items would be impossible to lift with books in it. So it looks like at least two box sizes will be necessary.

Although you can buy boxes from most rental companies, you'll find they're not a bargain. The standard book carton is about 12 inches by 12 inches by 18 inches; the standard utility carton is 18 inches by 18 inches by 16 inches. If you were to buy them from a rental agency, you would have to pay a dear price for each one. Since this method of moving requires a great number of boxes, you should be able to find a much better bulk or wholesale price.[4] Go through the Yellow Pages and look at the advertisers under CARTONS, CORRUGATED. Try to locate a dealer who specializes in used or surplus cartons. He can give you the best price on cartons, as long as you are willing to transport your goods in boxes printed with some company's old graphics.

To realize your goal, try to pack every item in your house into a carton of some kind. You may locate some larger cartons, into which you can put furniture pieces, at a nearby appliance store. But in the future, it would be far easier to shop for furniture that is not only comfortable but knocks down for packing. Most knockdown furniture was shipped in a carton at some time; and if you have the opportunity, you should obtain and save the carton it comes in.

Hire Nonprofessionals

Hiring nonprofessionals is particularly suited to people who cannot afford a professional move and would like to do it themselves but are not interested in packing and loading a truck, as well as unloading it after driving some great distance. This alternative would be ideal for older couples or people with heart conditions. With this method, you must take over the responsibility of organization. This includes arranging for a van from the rental company, providing certain moving aids, and packing up the household. The actual move is accomplished by one or two nonprofessionals whom you have hired.

The best candidates would be a couple of college students, home for the summer and interested in some lucrative work. Very often they would welcome the chance to drive a truck to some other location where they could spend a vacation and receive a salary at the same time (which could subsidize all or part of that vacation). It would help, of course, if the students were people you knew—say, from your neighborhood or perhaps the children of your friends. But careful screening should easily provide a candidate or two who are trustworthy and mature.

Advertise for help in the student newspaper of the local college sometime toward the end of the school year. Invite those who seem promising to your home so they can see what you have to move and so you can meet them and get acquainted. Once you have chosen your "crew," clearly spell out the responsibilities of both parties. Avoid any scheme to pay by the hour, as it is impossible to determine how long any move will take, and arguments are sure to develop. Instead, offer to pay a set, fair amount for the work. As long as the amount is agreed to by all parties before the move, there should be no problems.

Your crew should be responsible for picking up the van at a specified time, carefully loading your household belongings onto it, and driving to the new location within a set number of days. They should also be responsible for unloading the van, arranging the items in your new house, and returning the van to the rental firm. If they want to tow their car behind the van, they should pay for the tow-bar rental.

Your responsibilities would include the preparation of your household goods for moving by a certain date and the prepayment of rental fees for the van and other moving aids. You should also provide a set amount of money for travel expenses to cover gasoline costs and food and lodging for the crew. Upon delivery of your belongings, you should pay them the agreed-upon salary in cash.

All these responsibilities should be clearly spelled out in a written agreement. This document should be reasonable, understandable, and familiar to both parties before the move begins. It is important to allow the students to see their responsibilities on paper and to know what they're getting into before they fully commit themselves. Once the agreement is written and found to be satisfactory to everyone, all parties should sign it. There is an air of legality to this procedure which emphasizes the important point that your move is not a "joy ride," and that when it comes to safely transporting your goods, business definitely comes before pleasure. Because students' compensation for this burden and responsibility is their salary, do not be a tightwad or bargain hunter.

CONTRACT FOR MOVING

THIS IS AN AGREEMENT BETWEEN _____(THE OWNER)
AND _____
AND _____   (THE MOVERS).

IT IS AGREED THAT ON_____THE MOVERS WILL PICK UP
A PRE-ARRANGED RENTAL TRUCK FROM_____AND WILL ARRIVE
READY TO WORK AT_____O'CLOCK AT THE RESIDENCE OF THE OWNER_____
_____.

THE MOVERS WILL LOAD THE TRUCK WITH CARE AND DRIVE TO_____
_____WHERE THEY WILL ARRIVE ON
_____AT_____O'CLOCK, NO LATER. THE MOVERS WILL
THEN UNLOAD THE TRUCK WITH CARE AND DISTRIBUTE THE ITEMS IN THE HOUSE AT THE
OWNERS DIRECTION.

ON THE SAME DAY, THE MOVERS ARE TO RETURN THE TRUCK TO_____.

DURING THE MOVE THE MOVERS ARE TO BE PROFESSIONAL, CAREFUL AND RESPONSIBLE.

IT IS AGREED THAT THE OWNER WILL PRE-ARRANGE FOR THE TRUCK RENTAL AND WILL
PREPAY ITS ENTIRE COSTS. THE OWNER WILL BE RESPONSIBLE FOR THE PACKING AND
BOXING OF HIS SHIPMENT AND ASSURES THAT THIS PACKING WILL BE COMPLETED BY THE
DATE OF THE MOVE. THE OWNER ALSO AGREES TO BE AT THE NEW LOCATION AT THE TIME
SO DESIGNATED SO THAT NO TIME IS WASTED BY THE MOVERS.

PAYMENT: THE OWNER WILL PREPAY THE RENTAL TRUCK AND THE NECESSARY MOVING
EQUIPMENT TO INCLUDE DOLLIES, PLATFORMS AND PADS.

THE OWNER WILL ALSO PROVIDE $_____ AS TOTAL PAYMENT FOR THE MOVE TO BE
PAID TO THE MOVERS FOR THEIR SERVICES IN THE FOLLOWING MANNER.

$_____ WILL BE PAID AT THE TIME OF PICKUP AND WILL BE USED BY THE MOVERS
FOR NECESSARY EXPENSES TO INCLUDE GASOLINE, MEALS AND LODGING.

THE REMAINING $_____WILL BE PAID AFTER THE MOVE IS COMPLETED AND THE TRUCK
RETURNED.

ALL PAYMENTS ARE TO BE IN CASH.

EACH OF US AGREES TO THESE CONDITIONS AND ACCEPTS THE RESPONSIBILITIES THAT
THEY IMPLY ON THIS DAY _____.

_____   _____

_____   _____

Even though you must cover the salary and travel costs of your hired crew, the total is still far less than what you would pay a professional.

You might be interested in how a reasonable agreement looks, so I've prepared a sample, which you can adapt to your own particular needs.

Although this method of moving certainly does involve some risk, the hazards can be avoided by good planning, organization, and forethought.

Bring-along-a-friend Method

For many of you, a professional move seems to be the only answer, but after reading about this method you may change your mind. Most people will find this method appealing, since it involves inviting a friend, and it is only marginally more expensive than a straightforward do-it-yourself move in which you do all the work yourself. The arrangements between you and your friend can be as simple as your friend volunteering his time and energy, to your providing him with some compensation for his help. This kind of scheme certainly removes any of the risks inherent in hiring people you don't know, but it does mean that your commitment is greater in terms of your own output of physical labor. If you are single, recently divorced, or a single parent, it is obvious that some help could make your move easier and more enjoyable. In return, you can offer your friend a free trip, an interesting experience, and a few more days of friendship and camaraderie.

Many psychologists tell us that it is important for children to be physically involved in a family move and to assist in some of the packing and moving chores. This certainly is true, but it is also a full-time job keeping them under control, which usually takes the parent away from his or her responsibilities. The additional help that a friend provides will be quite welcome; and since it is likely that the children know the friend too, roles can be easily exchanged from time to time to alleviate boredom or feelings of helplessness. Also, it might be necessary for you to be at the new location before the move, or perhaps you will have to fly to the new location (a parent with four children, for example, or someone with physical disabilities). In this case, you could rely on your friend to drive your things to the new house by himself. If your friend is required to make this long journey without your assistance and companionship, you must compensate him for this as well. Consider paying him a reasonable salary. Friends usually try to turn this down, but insist on paying anyway.

Unlike the hiring of nonprofessionals, this method doesn't require a written contract or agreement; but it is important, for the sake of preserving the friendship, to come through with all of your promises, especially monetary ones involving return airfare or a salary. You should take the responsibility for packing and crating your belongings, and bring your friend into the move on the day you intend to pick up the van and load the belongings into it. Your friend will provide comfort and solace through the bad times and enjoyable companionship during what could be a long and tedious drive. Also, he will be there when you arrive at the new location, providing a friendly face amidst a new and often alienating environment. So, even though this method may involve a bit more expense than hiring nonprofessionals, it certainly will be much more pleasant for you and, perhaps, enjoyable and fun for your friend as well.

You may be interested in the comparison I did recently for a move from New York City to Los Angeles. The chart shows the relationship of costs between a professional move and one in which a friend helps with the loading, unloading, and driving.

CHART 7.

MOVING COMPARISON

Professional Mover			*Move with Friend*	
Estimate of				
moving	$3,500		$1,500*	Ryder 22-foot van
Family airfare	400	Dad	500	Salary for friend
	300	Mom	400	Airfare for friend
	200	Kid 1		
	200	Kid 2	1,100	Airfare for family
	$4,600		$3,500	

* *The van rental figure includes $300 for gasoline and maintenance.*

As you can see, this alternative holds a number of advantages. The first is that you save $1,100 as compared to a professional move. And the friend makes out pretty well, too! For his efforts and willingness to help during your time of need, you could afford to pay a salary of $500, provide a vacation with free lodging at your new home, and offer airfare home.

This particular comparison is based on just one possible moving scheme, and some of the costs are purposefully overestimated. If this method intrigues you, collect the same kind of data for your particular situation. The amount of savings is increased as the distance increases; but even on a short haul, it would pay to look seriously into this alternative. It is also possible to save more money by accompanying your friend in the van and eliminating the cost of your airfare. But there is no question that the benefits in terms of savings, as well as sharing an enjoyable experience with a friend, make this method a strong alternative.

Share-a-move

You and a friend are moving to the same place and decide to share all expenses. As simple as this sounds, you can save quite a bit of time and money by going in with someone who is moving to the same location. Truck rental, gasoline, and labor can be shared. This method is worth pursuing early, since if you find someone, you will have to plan mutual strategies and schedules.

Buy a Truck

This option is one that is so simple it escapes the imagination of most people. It involves looking through the used-truck section of your newspaper and visiting used-truck lots in order to find a good truck to buy. It is very often possible to find a truck of sufficient capacity that is from five to ten years old, that still has a lot of "life" in it, and that can be purchased for a reasonable amount of money.[5] The best buy would probably be an American-made 14- or 16-foot truck. These are the standards of the truck industry, and great numbers of them have been produced, giving you a better selection to choose from. You should look for something that is clean, in the box as well as the cab, and has a good maintenance record. Company-owned vans tend to be abused, so look for something that was privately owned, and keep your eyes open for bankruptcies or business auctions. If you can, find a truck that has a ramp which slides out from the back. Hydraulic lift gates can be found on some trucks; but as they tend to be somewhat dangerous and not altogether suited to household moving, avoid a truck that has one, unless it is the best buy you can find.

Buying a used truck is much like buying a used car. Your first impression will tell you what kind of treatment it has had. Are there cigarette burns on the seats? Is the body full of dents and scratches? Are the steering wheel and gearshift knob so worn that the paint has been rubbed off? Since a truck chassis is more exposed than a car chassis, look at it from all angles: front, back, top, and underneath. Is the engine leaking oil all over the pavement? Is the frame bent or rusted? Check the condition of the tires. Will they get you to your destination? How many miles are on the speedometer? The truck should start well when it is cold. It should have a steady idle and should accelerate easily with no stalling or hesitation. Ask if it has a governor and, if so, what speed it is governed to. Most rental trucks have governors that prevent driving over 55 mph. Be sure the truck you are interested in is not governed to 35 mph as are some inter-city vans.

Take the truck for a drive around the block, and note its stability and handling, as well as the odd rattles and other noises it might make. Be sure to drive it over a bumpy road to test the condition of the shock absorbers, springs, stabilizers, and other suspension parts. How it handles here will determine the kind of ride your household belongings will have on the way to their new home. A six-cylinder truck will give you slightly better gas mileage, but an eight-cylinder tends to be more dependable. If you have done your shopping well, you will have found an inexpensive and durable truck that will transport your goods without major problems—which is the whole idea of this alternative.

The way to recover a portion of your investment is to sell the truck upon your arrival at your destination. Be prepared to suffer a slight loss in the resale of your truck, but the amount that represents won't be anywhere near the cost of a comparable truck rental. Moreover, it is possible, depending upon what part of the country you are driving to, to sell your truck at a profit. Some states and regions are truck-minded, and there is a great demand for good used trucks. California is one area where eastern trucks tend to be a treasured commodity because they are not burdened with the California-required emission control devices that hamper fuel economy.

When you are established in your new home, check the local newspapers for the kinds of prices vehicles similar to yours are getting. You may be surprised to see a figure well above the price you paid.

You should be aware that while this alternative sounds terrific, it does have a few possible pitfalls. For example, you may be unable to locate a truck to buy after months of searching, which could cause you to miss out on your best opportunity to move. You might then be too late to reserve a rental truck, which could seriously delay your move. There is also the possibility that your used "bargain" may collapse halfway between here and Albuquerque. It is even possible that you won't find a buyer for your truck after you arrive at your new destination; this would leave you with an 18-foot delivery truck as your second car.

But considering the amount of savings possible, and even the fact that you may make a profit on the venture, these risks are not too serious. This alternative could be just the right solution for someone who is sufficiently experienced with trucks to know a good buy when he sees one. If you fit this description, think about the possibilities of this alternative.

Borrow a Truck

Obviously, borrowing a truck is one of the cheapest ways to move if you have a friend, neighbor, or relative who owns a sufficiently large truck you can borrow. If you can latch on to one of these "bargains," your move could be accomplished for almost no cost at all. If you don't have any neighbors or friends who own a truck, perhaps you can arrange something with the company you work for. Or how about the company you *will* be working for? Sometimes a truck full of products is rushed to a client in your town, and after being unloaded, it is returned empty to its place of origin. If you knew when that would happen, that truck could have your household belongings on it, saving you a lot of money. You won't know unless you ask.

However, borrowing a truck does have some inconvenient aspects to it. The major one is that the truck must be returned to its owner, which means a round trip. If your move is across town, there is no real problem; but a move across the country would quickly put an end to this idea.

It may be possible to find someone who has a truck to sell. You could offer to take it on consignment, move your belongings in it, and sell it for him in your new location. He will probably want some formal written agreement signed by both of you which would assure that you take responsibility for his truck and that by a certain date, you send him a check for the agreed selling price regardless of whether or not you had sold the truck. Risky, perhaps, but in terms of moving costs it may be worth it.

You should also look into some of the auto and truck delivery companies that have offices in your area. These companies transport vehicles for private owners, and sometimes they are looking for people to drive them. Very often car manufacturers and dealers make swaps with each other and utilize these companies to transport the cars to other cities. These companies usually have periodic ads in the newspapers for qualified, safe drivers. They often pay a salary in addition to a gasoline allowance. There is no reason why these companies would be limited to passenger cars as their only source of business. It is also quite possible that a truck dealer would be interested in transporting a number of vehicles cross-country to a better market area. So it wouldn't hurt to look these companies up in the Yellow Pages and call them to see what they have available. The listing to look for is AUTOMOBILE TRANSPORTERS AND DRIVE-AWAY COMPANIES.[6] Be sure to check the same listing under TRUCKS.

If your household is small, you might be able to make the move with a trailer. Since many more people own trailers than trucks, trailers are a lot easier to find and, consequently, to borrow. Don't overlook the possibility of borrowing a large motorhome, vacation trailer, or schoolbus, which may have just enough interior space to accommodate your belongings.

With this method, the best way to find something is to ask

around. If you are lucky, the "grapevine" will steer you in the direction of a vehicle available to borrow.

Get-rid-of-everything Method

One of the best ways to avoid an expensive move is to liquidate everything you own. Certainly this means that you wouldn't have the problems of a professional move or the physical work of a do-it-yourself move or the hassles of renting, buying, or borrowing a truck. As unrealistic as this idea sounds, everyone is capable of doing it. What prevents us is our attachments to luxuries, the memories we associate with our heirlooms, and the attitudes we have of how others might perceive the selling of things we have received from them as gifts. It may be possible to save a few items to pack into the trunk of your car; but for this method to really work well, you should plan to sell, give away, or toss out everything in sight.

There are, of course, a number of ways in which you can sell your belongings. You can place ads in the newspaper or local swap sheet. The latter represents a number of publications—*Pennysaver* and *Buy-Wiser*, just to name a few—which comprise weekly listings of articles for sale by private owners. These publications are usually available in drugstores and grocery stores for free or at little cost.

You can have a garage sale or house sale. You can take everything to a flea market or swap meet. All of these are good ideas, but nothing will sell an entire household of things better than an auction. Auctioneers specialize in liquidating estates, and they have a knack for obtaining the best price for each item. Some auctioneers will handle the sale of your things for just a percentage of the profits; some ask for a straight fee; and others ask for both a fee and a percentage. So it pays to shop around for an auctioneer.

The auctioneer and his company are responsible for preparing and selling your goods. They will come to your home and appraise your belongings. Having been in business for some time, they will be able to tell you rather quickly what things are simply not worth putting on the auction block, and you should plan to discard or donate these. They may combine your things with someone else's to increase the number of items and thereby attract more buyers. Another advantage of auctions is that you can expect to sell everything that is up for bid. Auctions are infectious! People who come to them get caught up in the activity and tend to bid on everything. The auctioneer usually has a following of bargain hunters, antique buffs, and store owners who attend every session. You can usually get a fair price for your things, and sometimes you get much more than you would have at a garage sale or flea market, since people at auctions tend to overbid.

So, in terms of selling everything and in terms of one-step convenience, the auction is by far the best method for liquidating your possessions.

The proceeds from the auction will pay for airfare to your new location and will probably finance your setting up a new household there. This method will have greatest appeal to those of you who are single, students at college, and people with very few personal belongings. Even if you have a large family and large house, don't discount this way of selling a great volume of goods. During our lives we tend to accumulate as much as our living environments can hold. Each successive move usually brings us to a larger environment, and we accumulate more to fill in the empty spaces. It doesn't take long to acquire objects and devices for every nook and cranny in the house, and much of them go unused for years at a time. If you had to evaluate all the things you presently own, how many of them would be so important to you that you couldn't live without them? Compared to the number of your possessions, these treasured objects represent a small percentage.

So, if your move is going to bring about a new change in job and a new change in lifestyle and area, you might as well enhance the effect of these changes by making a totally new change in your living environment. When the professional mover's representative comes to your house and tells you that you have two and a half tons of household clutter, or when you go through the cubic-foot checklist in Chapter 2 and discover that you will need not one but two 20-foot trucks to carry your belongings, you can then imagine the immeasurable joy you could have by not having to move a thing.

Don't Own Anything

Certainly the easiest way to eliminate the need to get rid of a lot of belongings—or even have to move them—is to not own anything in the first place. It seems, however, that pride of ownership is much too ingrained in American life and culture for most people to be able to adhere to this suggestion. But young people starting out just after their schooling should try to keep the number of their possessions as small as possible. After all, it is during these early years that life is most unsettled and changeable, and moves are most frequent. Realize, then, that it is possible for a person to exist without any privately owned possessions and still be content and satisfied with life.

If you were such a person, you would presently be living in a totally furnished apartment near your place of work, enabling you to walk to and from each day and eliminating your need for a car (or even a bike). Your apartment is entirely furnished and includes silverware, plates, glasses, and even towels.[7] When the time comes for you to change jobs and move to the opposite end of the country (or even to Europe), you pull out a few suitcases, pack your clothes, and hop on the next flight to your destination. After a few days of looking around, you eventually find a suitable apartment which, like the one you left, includes everything you could possibly need. You move in, unpack your suitcases, and resume your life.

This kind of move sounds like a vacation, and in a sense it

is, because all of the worries of ownership have been carefully avoided and your treasured possessions are small enough to be transported easily. As we go through life, marry, and start families, this method becomes less viable, since the attitudes and habits of a group are now involved. This suggestion is for the person who is single and can keep his life simple and nomadic. Perhaps you will find that a possessionless life is a possible alternative for you.

Of course, there are a great many alternatives in addition to the ones mentioned here. You could buy a motorhome to live in; and should the time come for you to move, your entire home would go along with you. You could even buy a suitable truck to live in, with part of it a storage area and the rest a foldout, tentlike system that increases the floor space and lets in light and air. You will find a number of other living environment suggestions in chapters 6, 7, and 8.

I hope that by reading through these alternatives, it becomes apparent to you that the professional move and the do-it-yourself move are just two methods of moving and that a number of other creative possibilities do exist. Below is a chart that summarizes the methods I've discussed and that relates them to an "apparent-cost" scale. You are welcome to plug in any of your alternatives wherever they may fit.

Also, if you develop a really ingenious moving idea that has been proven to work, I would like to know about it. Write to: Jim Hennessey, c/o Pantheon Books, 201 East 50th Street, New York, New York 10022.

CHART 8.

ALTERNATIVE MOVES COMPARISON

$$$ _____ Costs _____ $

Professional
Move _____

Do-it-yourself
Move _____

Crate for each room

Put everything into boxes

Rent truck—Hire nonprofessionals

Rent truck—Use friend

Buy truck

Borrow truck or trailer

Get rid of everything—Auction

Don't own anything

Chapter 4

Moving Hints

IN THIS CHAPTER I HOPE TO GIVE YOU THE KIND OF IN-formation you need to organize your move and get it under way. There are specifics on packing, as well as on loading the truck and organizing the things in it. There is advice on how to lighten your shipment of goods—how to know what to take and what to leave behind. And there are suggestions that cover various ways of selling your belongings and the types of arrangements that you should make to effect a well-organized and efficient move.

If you are interested in knowing more about any particular topic, you can refer to the bibliography in the back of the book.

Packing

Probably the greatest amount of information I've collected over the years concerns packing. Having read through all of it, I am amazed at how complicated people can make so simple a task! There are no real tricks to packing; and with the sophistication of specialized packing cartons available these days, the only thing you need is common sense.

To do this job properly, you should develop the ability of "putting yourself in the box along with the object"—that is, imagining how it would feel to be bumped around in the back of a truck for 3,000 or so miles. Your response to that image will guide you in safely packing any object. As you fold over the flaps of each box you pack, also consider: What would happen to this box if someone dropped it? What would happen to this box if another, heavier box fell on top of it? What if this box were jabbed in the side with a broom handle or indiscriminately kicked by a heavy work shoe? All these mishaps can occur during a move. Common sense, coupled with the ability to "objectify" yourself, will tell you how to support and protect any item you pack into a box.

My advice on packing, then, will not belabor the importance of wrapping and padding every item. Rather, the discussion will focus on the types and sizes of boxes you will use in your move; then, using the checklist from Chapter 2, we will cover packing procedures for every item in your inventory.

What follows is an analysis of each inventory item, including special packing hints you may find important. First, let's talk about the standard boxes and their characteristics.

CHART 9.

STANDARD CARTONS

The A Carton   1 ½ cubic feet   13 by 13 by 16 inches
This is the book carton. It is perfect for small, heavy items because its size limits the total weight to something manageable. It holds about 2 lineal feet of books or about sixty record albums, as well as shoes, canned goods, tools, and small appliances.

The B Carton   3 cubic feet   18 by 18 by 16 inches
This carton is the workhorse of the moving trade. Almost everything else will go into this one except unusually large or fragile items.

The Dish-pak   5½ cubic feet   18 by 18 by 30 inches
This is a double-walled box specially adapted to carry dishes. It usually includes egg-crate dividers for individual cups and packing cardboard for each dinnerware item. It will hold service for eight.

The Wardrobe   14 cubic feet   21 by 24 by 48 inches
A large carton with a built-in hanger bar designed for clothes, this carton is extremely convenient, and it eliminates

the need to carefully fold and pack each clothing item. It keeps suits and dresses on their respective hangers both clean and unwrinkled.

Specialty Cartons

Rental companies normally don't have specialty cartons, but you can buy new or used ones from professional movers without obligation. They come in various sizes for transporting paintings or mirrors, and in all the standard mattress and box-spring sizes.

Now, let's go through that inventory list.

Barbecue—Unless this is an expensive propane model, it probably isn't worth taking along. By now it is dirty and rusty and more trouble than it's worth. Give it away or toss it out.

Bathinette—The first question is: Are you still using it? If it is in the attic waiting for the next baby, it isn't worth keeping. Consider holding onto it only if it is a family heirloom. Otherwise, sell it.

Beds—Beds can be pretty bulky, but at least most of them knock down. Bundle the rails together and pad the headboard. Get a specialty carton for the mattress. Before moving your waterbed, make sure your new house can support its weight.

Bicycle—Consider how often you use it. Generally, even though it is awkward to pack, it is worth keeping, since its value continues to rise and it provides good exercise and cheap transportation. Put it on the truck last.

Birdbath—This is heavy and of little utility. A good garage-sale item.

Birdcage—Kind of useless without a bird in it. If you have a bird, you will want to transport it in your car or by air. The best thing for the animal is to keep it in familiar surroundings, so the cage should go with you.

Bookcase—Large, one-piece units are a pain to move. Sell them with the house. Movable bookcases, on the other hand, are modular and can be disassembled into easily packed components. Next time buy units like these.

Boxes—Boxes usually go on the truck first because they are easy to handle and arrange. Build up a solid wall of them and secure it with rope.

Breakfast table—Not too tough to move. Does it fit into your new home? Is it pretty old and beat up? Do the legs come off for easy packing?

Buffet—Is this in keeping with your new lifestyle? Early American furniture tends to look strange in contemporary homes. This is a big, heavy item that could easily be sold. Do you really need it?

Bureau, dresser, chest—Take out the drawers before moving these things. Pack soft goods into the drawers, and replace them once the chest is positioned in the truck.

Card table—Since it folds, it's easy to take along. As a matter of fact, one of the best ideas involves making a beautiful walnut or oak surface that fits over the tabletop. This conversion ups the quality to that of a fine piece of furniture that looks terrific in the kitchen or, in multiples, in the dining room. Need more space? Add more tables. Think about replacing what you have now with these very contemporary solutions that transport easily.

Cedar chest or trunk—This is already a packing device. Fill it with soft goods and delicate things that need extra protection.

Chairs—These can be a problem. Kitchen chairs are gangly but lightweight. Overstuffed armchairs and recliners should

Telescope director's chair

be sold, not moved. The typical recliner these days is a good idea gone berserk. It is far too heavy and bulky besides being incredibly ugly. Sell and replace at your new location with a nice, simple relaxer and matching footstool. Rockers are usually heirlooms; and if your inventory includes one, save it for the end of the truck and pad it well. Put it on top of the load. Still one of the best nomadic chairs is the Telescope director's chair.[8]

Chaise longue—The chaise longue is a good sellable item, particularly the well-made, redwood variety. It does take up a lot of space and should be sold before moving. Your new home might require a different type of seating, so you are better off starting from scratch.

China cabinet—This is another big item that you might want to sell. Besides, putting your dishes on display is not a contemporary notion, since few people these days invest in fragile china. Practicality is the key word, and everyday dishes don't need to be behind a glass window. If you still want to display them, why not build in some shelf surfaces in your new kitchen?

Clothes basket—An inexpensive item, this can be sold or given away and replaced at your new location.

Clothes hamper—A hamper can be used as a packing device if you feel it is necessary to bring along and it fits into your new home.

Corner cabinet—Another decorative and barely functional piece of furniture, it could easily be replaced with a simple set of shelves mounted on standards. In this manner, the supporting surfaces won't dominate, and the articles exhibited would take on more importance, which is the way it should be.

Couch, sofa, davenport—Big, overstuffed items should be sold. Buy a well-made and well-designed sofa at your new location, one that can be knocked down for shipping. Many Scandinavian and contemporary pieces do this beautifully.

Crib—Question again: Is it being used? Items in storage in the attic should be sold; heirlooms can be passed on to some other member of the family, especially if you are no longer in the "baby business." Port-a-cribs are still the easiest to transport.

Desk—Small, standard desks should be sold, as they are easy to come by. Antiques, especially roll-tops, are quite heavy, but at least they break down into components that can be moved. You will probably want to keep an antique, since it represents an investment that is continually going up in value.

Port-a-crib: Port-a-crib, Inc., Ballwin, Mississippi

Dishwasher—Unless this item is brand-new, you should sell it. Most newer models have innovations like forced-air drying and energy conservation features. Your new place may have a built-in model already installed. If it doesn't, then after the move is a good time to buy one.

Double dresser—This is an animal to move. Although it can be used to contain some things during the move, the drawers have to be taken out while you lug it to the truck. You might consider selling it.

Drapes—Don't move these. It is extremely unlikely you will require the same size, color, or texture in your new place. Offer them along with your old house.

Dresser chair or bench—These went out in the fifties along with the dressing table. Sell them (if you can). The new idea is to make better use of your bathroom for makeup and primping. Install a good mirror and lighting in your new home. They will be worthwhile investments.

Dryer, Clothes—You really don't want to move this if you can help it. Make it part of your house deal when you sell. You can include all of your appliances and tack a reasonable amount for them onto the selling price of your home. The extra money can go a long way in buying you a new one, and you will be spared moving the old one as well.

Extension table—Not too bad if the legs can be removed. The Swedes have some nicely designed gateleg tables that seem to extend forever and don't have the separate sections that get dusty and banged-up in the hall closet.

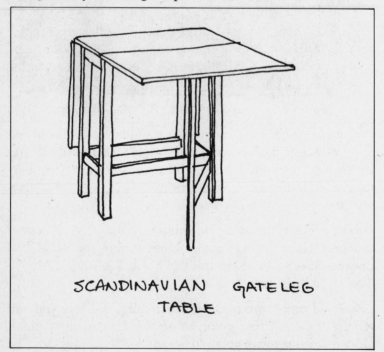

SCANDINAVIAN GATELEG TABLE

Fans—Box fans are handy everywhere, so hold onto them. Save the box they come in for storage and packing. Small oscillating fans are dangerous and not too effective, so get rid of these.

Filing cabinet—Big and heavy but worthwhile. Truck it out to the van with the platform dolly, and keep all the papers in it. Just don't turn it on its side (as my professional movers once did).

Fireplace tools—Indispensable, but only if your new place has a fireplace.

Floor lamp—These are usually tall and skinny enough to slide in almost anywhere in the truck. Remove the shade and bulb, and pack them separately in a box. Coil the cord, secure it with a twist-tie, and tape it to the lamp column. Wrap the lamp in a plastic leaf bag.

Footlocker—Like the cedar chest or trunk, this is already a packing device. Metal footlockers are nice for shop tools and heavy, awkward objects because they are reinforced and sturdy.

Footstool—If this is a mate to a chair you intend to keep, then pack it along. Otherwise, sell it.

Freezer—Long, chest-type freezers are almost impossible to handle. Sell yours and plan to replace it at your new location.

Garden cart—Depends on the condition, but for the most part, sell and replace later.

Garden hose and tools—These fit nicely in a B carton. By all means bring them.

Golf bag and clubs—People into the sport must take them. People not into the sport don't own them. Self-resolved.

Heater—A portable heater can be essential in climates that are cold, but it can also take the chill out of a brisk evening in places like Florida and California. I would bring it along.

Hide-a-bed—Like the overstuffed recliner, this has become over-designed. It is just too heavy to move. If you have one down in the basement rec room, leave it there. I have seen some elegantly simple ones in Scandinavian import places.[9]

Highchair—The same question about the bathinette and the crib applies. Many highchairs have the nice concept of being convertible into a work stool for Mom or Dad later, when the baby outgrows it.

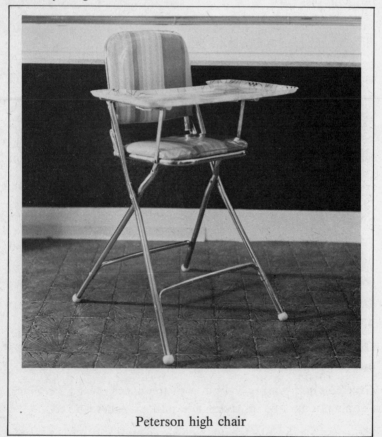

Peterson high chair

Iron (mangle)—You don't see many of these any more. They are still popular in Europe and rural America; but with the advent of permanent-press sheets and pillowcases, they aren't really needed. Sell it to a European or rural American.

Ironing board—I'm still looking for one that does not (1) rock when open and (2) pinch your fingers when being closed. Old-time wooden ones are still the best, if you can find one. Heavy and sturdy, they will not conduct electricity from a frayed cord as an aluminum or metal ironing board could.

Lawn chairs—Go the route of the chaise longue. Most people bring their aluminum folding chairs because no one else wants them and they haven't the heart to pitch them. At least they are light.

Lawn mower, Hand—Manual ones are a nice, simple product that, with minimal care, will last forever. Certainly you should keep it if your lawn is small enough to be mowed by hand. A gasoline mower should be drained both of gas and oil, and the handle demounted to make it more compact. You might also wrap it in a perforated plastic bag to keep it from staining adjacent articles in the truck.

Lawn mower, Riding—You may not need it where you are going, so check first. Really large lawns require it. Is your mower an old one? Maybe now is the time to step up to one with more capabilities, such as a snowblower option. After draining the gas and oil, put it on the end of the truck.

Lawn swing—This should probably be sold. It is too big to move unless it can be unbolted and broken down into manageable parts.

Magazine racks—Magazines are better out of sight. Most magazine racks are clutter producers. Sell yours.

Mirrors—Measure and buy a specialty carton of sufficient

size. If you measure your paintings as well, you may find the ideal carton size in which to pack them all together.

Night table—Sell this if it doesn't knock down. The simplest ones are inexpensive plastic Parson's tables, which have removable legs that store underneath and are really easy to move.

Oven, Portable microwave—Certainly small enough to move easily, and it is energy-efficient as well. The food still tastes funny, though.

Phonograph, Portable—This may fit into a B carton along with the records. Otherwise, it should travel in its own case.

Inexpensive plastic Parson's tables

Tape down the tone arm to keep it from flying around during handling.

Picnic table and bench—Like other large pieces of lawn furniture, it may be easier to sell these before moving. You can consider moving them if they can be disassembled.

Playpen—If you still have a toddler around the house, you should plan to bring this. Your new house may have stairs and other hazards that your toddler is not used to, and the playpen will keep baby out of trouble.

Range—This is pretty well covered in the appliance section of Chapter 2. Sell it if you are moving into a home that already has one, especially a built-in. Sell it even if you are just looking for a home with a built-in. If you don't find one, you can always buy another range.

Refrigerator—This is also covered in Chapter 2.

Roaster, rotisserie—Another out-of-date item. It may come in handy at the new place as a cooking substitute while you look for a new stove; but if someone at the garage sale offered a few bucks, I wouldn't turn it down.

Rugs or pads—Here again it is extremely unlikely that you will have the same requirements and taste in your new home. Most rugs that are laboriously moved end up in the attic or at someone else's house. The exceptions are small neutral or valuable rugs. They should be rolled up and wrapped in brown paper for protection.

Sewing machine, Portable—This may fit into a B carton; otherwise, it will hold up well in its own case.

Sewing machine, Upright—This should be carefully wrapped in pads.

Sled—Snow? Go! No snow? No go!

Stepladder—Sell the aluminum one; keep the wooden one. Wood is better because it lacks the electrical shock hazards the metal ones are noted for. Keep the large extension ladder, too, unless your new house is a one-story ranch.

Stereo components—These will usually fit into A or B cartons. Turntables should be packed in their original cartons because of the special protective Styrofoam inserts. If you no longer have the original cartons, secure the tone arm with tape, and tape down anything else that can move. Pack the components into a box, and wedge with foam or rolled-up towels.

Swingset—I've always been disappointed in these. They rust away in the first year and present all kinds of hazards for the kids. Leave it in the backyard. There are companies that make wooden sets which, besides being weather-resistant and durable, are more "friendly" to play on.[10]

Table chairs—If you have brought the table, you must bring the matching chairs. Wrap each one in a pad and stack in pairs, seat-to-seat, one inverted over the other. Small things like record players and portable sewing machines can nest between the legs.

Table, Coffee or end—Like the other tables discussed previously, it would help if the legs came off these. You may have seen some take-apart designs that will do a better job for you. Some of these ideas include slot-together bases and removable tops. One interesting idea is to assemble a new coffee table every time you move. Obtain a really nice hardwood top surface, such as walnut or oak, and support it with materials found at your new location. So many support ideas are possible from native stone, sea shells, and tree branches to tiles, bricks, and even bent wire. Invent something nice; and when you move, pack the hardwood top in the truck and recycle the support back into its original environment.

Play structures: Play Specialties, Inc.

Table lamp—This is generally not much of a problem to move. The shade or ball should be packed well and supported in a B carton along with the bulb. The electric cord should be coiled and secured with a twist-tie, then taped to the column of the lamp. Wrap in plastic.

Television, Combination—This is usually a large TV combined with some kind of stereo system. It creates the same kind of moving problems as any other major appliance except that it is more delicate. Naturally, if you are thinking of updating to a newer component stereo and smaller, portable TV, now is the time to sell the console. If you plan to move it, you will have to treat it very carefully. Tape down all interior components as well as the control knobs. Likewise, tape all the lids or doors closed, then carefully wrap in a furniture pad. Put the unit on a platform dolly or carry it by hand. Do not put it on end or on its back.

Television, Console—Move this on the platform dolly. Keep all TV sets vertical, on their feet. Never pack them on their sides or back, and wrap them well with a pad.

Television, Portable—Obviously, this is not a major packing problem. One caution: never trust the handle on top. Always carry the set like a box, with both hands securely underneath. I'll never understand why units so big and heavy as to tax two men still have a dinky little handle. The best place for it is on top of the carton wall that you put into the truck first.

Toolbox—A tool box needs no special packing, but save it for near the end, since you never know when you'll need something from it.

Toy chest—Fill this with all those little bits and pieces from the kids' rooms. Stuffed animals and other light contents will keep it easy to move. It may be a good idea to buy a toy chest or footlocker for each of the kids just for your move.

Tricycle—This item is usually sold easily once your children have outgrown it. If you do move it, use it to fill in oddly shaped spaces near the top of the van.

Utility cart—This should be taken apart if possible. Put it near the roof of the truck, and pack soft goods into it.

Vacuum cleaner—Put all the hoses, parts, and spare bags in a B carton. Take the dirty bag out of the vacuum before you load it on the truck. It would be smart to buy some replacement bags for it before you move so that you won't be searching around for them at your new place.

Wagon—Not only is a wagon a great toy, but it can be very handy during the move. You may even consider buying one for your kids just prior to the move as a way of getting them involved in it. The neatest ones have the wooden-stake sides. The kids can use this to take charge of the plants or other gangly nonboxable objects and get them out to the van for you—a real help.

Wardrobe closet (armoire)—Victorian and earlier-period homes never had closets in the bedrooms. Instead, large cabinets were brought in for the storage of clothing items. Because of their size, they are very difficult to handle during a move; but for various reasons, you may want to take yours along. Empty it; then using the platform dolly, wheel it out to the truck. After it is in the truck, repack your clothing in it, secure the doors and drawers with tape, wrap it well with a pad, and slide it to face the wall of the van. Lash it to the truck with rope. As long as you store nothing heavier than clothes in it, you will probably find it movable. But before attempting to move it, make sure it will go through the doorways of your old home as well as those of your new one.

Washing machine—Like the dryer, it would simplify things if you made this part of your house deal. It may well be the heaviest (and most cumbersome) appliance to move in your house. However, if you decide to take it, disconnect it, wedge the tub and motor, and put the hoses in the basket so they don't get lost. Use the appliance dolly, securely strapped, to maneuver it out the door. Plan to put it on the truck right after the initial wall of cartons. Be sure to pack pillows and other soft items in it, then tape the lid shut. Cover with a pad.

Wheelbarrow—Like the garden cart, see if it can be dismantled. The handles and wheel can easily be stashed, and the shell put near the roof of the van. If you can't take it apart, save it for the end.

The following is a list of other household items that are commonly not included on an inventory list. Nonetheless, you should be familiar with the best method of packing and protecting them.

Air-conditioners—These are easier to sell and buy again later. One can usually find very good units by shopping around. In addition, the process of looking up ads and tracking them down is a good way to become acquainted with your new area.

Appliances, Small—Pack these into A or B cartons. Cushion the box bottom with newspaper. Pre-wrap white appliances with clean paper so that the newsprint doesn't transfer onto them. Pack the appliances into the box in an upright position, secure the cords with twist-ties, and wedge them with additional newspaper.

Books—Use only the A cartons, as books are very heavy. Pack them flat to the bottom and not on edge, as this will damage their bindings. As you add books, lift the box periodically to check its weight to prevent it from becoming unmanageable. You can always fill the gaps with other light objects, soft goods, or newspaper.

Clocks—Protect the glass and faces by wrapping well in tissue paper or towels. Pendulum clocks require the removal of the pendulum and weights. Pack these things separately, not inside the clock. Large clocks like a grandfather's clock should be crated. See the instructions for building a crate later in this chapter.

Clothes—Things on a hanger belong in the wardrobe carton. Make sure all the hooks on the hangers go over the bar from the same direction, which will make it easier to remove clothing later on. Items like hats and purses can be put on the bottom. Other clothing items should be packed in B cartons that have been lined with white paper to keep the clothing clean. Blankets, pillows, and towels should be used in various places to act as padding for other items. Be sure to leave out the clothing you will need for the move.

Dishes—Dish-paks are highly recommended, and many of them come with sectioned inserts and packing instructions. The heaviest items, such as platters and large bowls, belong on the bottom. Each item should be wrapped in white paper or tissue paper. Put them flat to the bottom, never on edge or upside down. Fill in the spaces with heavily wrapped small items like sugar bowls or knick-knacks until you have a level layer. Now start on the plates and saucers. Wrap each one separately, then group them into sets of five or six. Wrap each set in newspaper. Use the same technique as before to build up a level layer. Next, do the third, lightest layer of glasses and stemware. Wrap individually, and put the stemware upside down to take the pressure off their delicate bases. Plan to pack the silverware in a different carton. Remember to do the packing in layers, starting with the heaviest items and ending with the lightest on top. Use lots of crumpled paper for padding.

Explosives—Obviously, you don't intend to pack along some TNT, but many common household items can have the same damaging effect. Do not attempt to pack anything that is flammable, such as aerosols, paints, thinners, charcoal starting fluid, or even nail polish remover. Likewise, don't pack things that can spill or damage other articles, such as ink, bleach, chemicals, or medicines. Even syrup, catsup, or pickles in a jar may break and smell up your goods.

Foods—Canned goods as well as dry packaged foods can be packed in B cartons. Jars must be individually wrapped for protection. You may also want to put these into large Baggies before wrapping so that if they break, the spill will be isolated. It isn't worth packing boxed goods that have been opened because of possible spillage and spoilage. The canned goods should be packed on the bottom, the lighter foodstuff on top. Use paper to wedge everything and keep items from rattling against each other.

Glasses—Glasses are put on top of the Dish-paks. Another possibility for packing cups, glasses, and stemware is to secure a few heavy, divided cartons from your local liquor store. Wrap each glass in white paper, then pack one or two in each division of the box along with newspaper padding.

Lamps—Lamp bases, if small enough, can go into a B carton or even a bureau drawer along with some clothes for protection. Shades, however, present a problem. They are easily crushed, take up a lot of room in a box, and don't allow for anything else to be packed with them for fear of damage. It may be more practical to sell them and buy new ones later. If you pack them, be sure to wrap in white paper before wedging in newspaper.

Paintings, prints, and photos—These are best protected in a specialty carton such as the ones used for mirrors. Many of these items can go together in the same box with light paper and light cardboard as a separator. Measure what you have, and get a large carton for them all.

Pets—Pets go with you. Hopefully, your pet will be able to manage the long drive or flight. Be sure to keep some familiar things for the animal to identify and associate with home, such as a feeding dish or plaything. Pets in transit should remain in a carryable "home" for their safety. These come in all shapes and sizes, and are available everywhere; but you might consider saving some money by making one yourself. If the trip will be a long one, you may want to ask your vet for a sedative prescription for your pet, but use it sparingly. Be sure to let your pet get fresh air and exercise on occasion, and never leave it in the car with windows rolled up. Some motels and hotels allow for pets in transit. The AAA can supply you with a current list of these.

Pianos and organs—Moving these may not be as bad as you imagine. Grand pianos can be tilted over onto their spine (the longest side) and placed on the platform dolly. The legs come off and can be packed separately. You will need at least two people to horse a piano around; three are even better. After moving it out, rest it on its spine in the truck. Wrap it in a pad, and secure it to the wall with rope. Upright pianos or organs can be tilted into a two-wheeled truck and guided out the door by a single person. I wouldn't suggest trying this, however, since the platform dolly is still the easiest way. Tilt the piano and slide the dolly under it. Like the grand piano, wrap it well with pads after putting it in the truck, and secure it to the wall with rope. Also be sure to secure all lids and doors with tape or rope to keep them from opening while you ease the piano through a doorway.

Plants—Plants are almost like pets to some of us. They can also be the most difficult to move because of their delicacy and slow adaptation to climatic changes. The truck is no place for them, ever! They should go in the car, where they can receive daily care and sunlight. Otherwise, you should give them away. Find out if the place you are moving to (and any states you happen to drive through along the way) will allow your plants across their borders by writing to the agriculture department of each state. It is better to give any banned plants to a friend as a remembrance than to try to sneak them through. The border guys know what to look for, and you may find yourself in the unbearable position of having to dump one of your leafy friends by the side of the road before you can go through. Personally, I'd rather see a friend own the plant.

Pots and pans—Carefully wrap pots and pans in white paper and pack in a B carton. Heavy flat pans should go on the bottom with as many nested pans on top. Separate with wrapping and soft items. Don't pack glasses or other fragile kitchenware in the same boxes.

Records—Pack records in an A carton. Albums require no special padding; single records should be wrapped in white paper. Records can be packed on end in the carton, but be sure to handle with extreme care. Because records are very heavy, a full record carton shouldn't be placed on top of other, more fragile boxes in the truck.

Shoes—These are heavy enough to warrant an A carton. Don't stash them in the wardrobe carton, as their weight will push the bottom out.

Valuables—Pack jewelry, important papers, cash, and the contents of your safe-deposit box in a small container or lockbox, and keep this with you at all times.

Almost everything else you might have should fit into the above categories. It should be interesting to note how many of the items listed above are really needed and used by your family. The secret to a good move is the ability to look at your belongings with a clear mind and critical eye. Be willing to part with anything that does not serve a direct purpose. Unused items can be turned into usable cash, so liquidate anything of value by selling it. The more you sell, the less you have to move. Before examining the various ways of selling your household goods, let's look at some ideas for packing your belongings and loading the van or truck.

The best way to organize a move is to pack one room at a time. This keeps associated items together and allows for easy marking and identification of the cartons. To assist you in your packing operation, set up a "portable packing station," a work area you can take with you from room to room.

CHART 10.

THE PORTABLE PACKING STATION

A portable packing station might consist of the following:

☐ An *aluminum picnic table* or *card table* that is light and easy to carry and fold. Use this as a work surface for wrapping objects and sealing boxes.

☐ An assortment of *cardboard cartons* (see Chart 8). The number of cartons you need will depend on your personal inventory of household goods (see Chart 2). Buy the A and B cartons in bulk and folded flat. Overbuy if necessary; you will always find a use for them.

☐ *Packing materials* include a stack of newspapers, an ample supply of white paper (butcher's paper or drawing paper on a roll), and tissue paper. You may also want to buy a roll of heavy brown paper for wrapping rugs.

☐ *Tape:* the wide 3- or 4-inch *masking tape* for general purposes, and the 2- or 3-inch *wet tape* for sealing boxes. Test the masking tape before buying to assure that it will easily pull off your furniture. The wrong tape here could be very hard to remove and could possibly damage your belongings. The correct tape will easily pull from wood without leaving a residue or picking up the wood grain. For the wet tape you will need a *sponge* and a *dish*.

☐ A package of *twist-ties* to hold electrical cords together or tether small parts to an object.

☐ A box of *Baggies* large enough to hold a standard-size jar. Use in packing food and in storing nuts and bolts. The latter can then be twist-tied or taped to the object they came from.

☐ *Scissors* for cutting the packing materials and tapes.

☐ *Felt-tip markers* or *a small can of spray paint and stencils* for marking the cartons.

☐ *A notebook* and *pen* to itemize the contents of each box. Never itemize the contents on the carton itself, since an unscrupulous person may be tempted to abscond with your goods.

First, take a carton and put it upside down on the table. Tape the bottom with wet tape. Turn the carton over and place it on the floor next to the table. Then, starting with the heavier objects, wrap each one on the table and pack it into the box. When the box is sufficiently packed and cushioned, pick it up to test its weight. If it is too heavy, repack it. Don't worry if it seems too light. Place the box on the table and seal it with wet tape. (Seal heavier boxes on the floor to avoid lifting them.) Be sure that the box is not overpacked and bulging. As you pack each item, tally it on your notebook under the correct marking for that carton. After sealing, mark the carton with the marker or spray paint. If it is from the living room, for example, write (or spray) the letters *LR* on it along with the number 1. Your personal tally will keep track of the number of boxes from each room so you can account for them after the move. In keeping with the initials, the bedroom would be *BR*; the kitchen, *KIT*; the bathroom, *BTH*; the dining room, *DR*; and so on.

Do not pack any items you will need during and immediately after the move. These items can be tallied in a simple list and packed in a special carton. I like to call this the "survival carton," since you won't be able to survive without it.

CHART 11.

THE SURVIVAL CARTON

☐ *Toilet articles*—towels, soap, tissues, toilet paper, etc.

☐ *Tool kit*—for appliance connection. See Chapter 2.

☐ *First aid*—Bandaids, antiseptic, aspirin, etc.

☐ *Flashlight*

☐ *Spare light bulbs*—a few of different wattages to replace those that have burned out or mysteriously disappeared.

☐ *Eats*—plates, silverware, glasses, coffee maker, cereals, etc.

☐ And anything else that might make your situation more comfortable while you unpack.

If you are driving your own van, put these items in a carton and make sure it is the *last* thing on the truck, since it will be the *first* thing out at the other end. Items such as clothing and bedding are assumed to be separated out by now, so they don't appear on the list. If you are having a professional move, take the survival carton along with you, since there is the possibility that you will arrive at your new home before the movers do.

Now that we've discussed packing techniques, here are some simple rules for packing the van.

1. Load all the cartons first. Build up a wall all the way to the roof of the van. You will probably have enough cartons to fill the first quarter of the truck. When you have a neat, stacked wall of cartons, lash it to the walls of the truck with rope.

2. Next come the appliances—all of the heavies. Fit them as well as you can and fill in the remaining space with the leftover cartons and odd-shaped objects. Build up another floor-to-roof wall and rope it to the truck.

3. Now for the furniture and other items that are bulky but not too heavy. Furniture pieces can be stacked on top of each other, but keep in mind the rule of putting heavier things on the bottom and lighter things on top. Use lots of pads for protection and cushioning.

4. Last, tuck in all the odds and ends. This is often the hardest part, since none of this stuff will fit nicely together. Put the biggies like riding mowers and barbecues on the floor. Fill little things in between to wedge and secure objects from moving or rolling. Build up a deck and stack in the mattress boxes. Put the bikes and trikes on top. Finish off with Grandma's rocker, heavily padded.

When you are done, the front half of the truck should have all the heavy items in it. Pack the appliance dolly and platform dolly in with the last things they moved. Finally, load the hand truck along with the survival carton. Now you're all set to roll.

The last topic in our packing section concerns building a crate. Many of the precious and delicate items we own are too big and/or too heavy to be boxed easily. For their protection, you should build a crate in which to move and store them.

Building a crate is not particularly difficult; and you can save a tremendous amount over the cost of having a professional build a crate for you. You need only a hammer, nails, electric drill, wrench, and hand saw. The basic construction is of plywood and common pine 2 × 2's.

The first step is to measure the object you want to crate.

Use a good steel tape measure for accuracy, and measure the extreme points of each side. When you have the overall length, width, and depth, add 4 inches to each. This represents 2 inches of foam padding around the object. Now you know the interior dimensions of your crate. If your item has parts such as legs that must be removed to be packed, add additional inches to these dimensions to allow for storage of these items.

Next build a perimeter for the crate, comprising the sides. The depth of these four pieces is the same as your depth calculation plus the 4-inch add-on. Two of the opposing sides will also be the correct width dimension (plus the 4-inch add-on). The other two opposing sides must be longer to accommodate attachment of the other sides as noted in the illustrations. The formula for determining the correct length is as follows:

object dimension + 4-inch add-on + 2 times (the plywood thickness + the thickness of the 2 × 2) = the correct total length

When you have the perimeter measured, you can calculate the top and bottom by using the same formula. They will be the same size as the longest side and sufficiently longer than the other side to allow for attachment.

Let's say you have a grandfather's clock you want to crate, and it has a height of 8 feet, a width of 3 feet, and a depth of 2 feet. Here's how to calculate the dimensions. All the sides will be 2 feet 4 inches wide. The long sides can be the height of the clock plus 4 inches, or 8 feet 4 inches. The other two sides (at the head and foot of the clock) must be longer. Using the formula we get: 3 feet + 4 inches + 2 times (½ inch + 1½ inches) = 3 feet 8 inches.

Thus two of the sides are 2 feet 4 inches by 3 feet 8 inches, and the other two are 2 feet 4 inches by 8 feet 4 inches. The top and bottom lids are the same width as the perimeter assembly, 3 feet 8 inches, but they must be longer than 8 feet 4 inches to overlap. Using the formula again we get: 8 feet + 4 inches + 2 times (½ inch + 1½ inches) = 8 feet 8 inches. The top and bottom lids are therefore 3 feet 8 inches by 8 feet 8 inches.

You can get these cut for you at the lumberyard for a reasonable charge, or ask a friend with a hand power saw to help you cut up 4 foot by 8 foot sheets. When the plywood is cut, measure the perimeters and buy enough 2 × 2's to go all around. In the case of the grandfather's clock, the height requirement is greater than an 8-foot plywood panel, so the long sides and lids will have to be two pieces. Where the plywood is pieced together, you will need another 2 × 2, which you should be sure to add in. Cut the 2 × 2's with the hand saw. Glue and nail them to the edges of the cut plywood pieces.

Lay down the bottom piece, and set the item on top to assure that everything is going to fit nicely. Assemble the sides around the object to determine whether you have sufficient space for foam padding. The crate pieces are bolted together using stove bolts, washers, lock washers, and nuts. You should have a bolt for each 2 or so feet of length along a side. Have someone hold the pieces together as you drill clearance holes for the bolts; then immediately slide the bolt through and tighten by hand. You can build up the entire crate this way. When all but the lids are drilled, walk around with a socket wrench and tighten all the bolts.

Tape the seams of the inside with ducting tape to prevent dust from filtering in. Lay in 2 inches of foam, Styrofoam, or heavy rubber padding; then put the object in. Pack foam pads around the object to wedge it in place. It is sometimes a good idea to plastic-wrap the object before packing it. The 2-inch padding for the lid should be glued to it so that it comes off with the lid when you open the crate.

The illustration shows some simple rope handles you can install on your crate. You may want to bolt on heavy metal handles, or you may choose not to install handles at all.

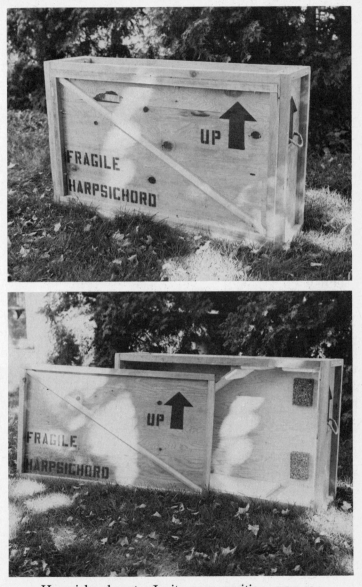

Harpsichord crate. In its open position, you can
see the foam padding and interior bracing.

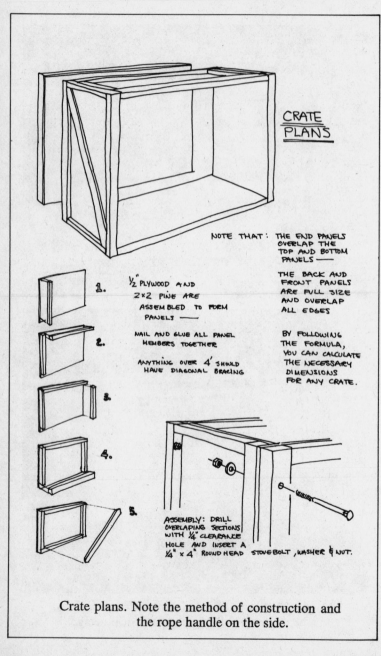

CRATE
PLANS

NOTE THAT: THE END PANELS
OVERLAP THE
TOP AND BOTTOM
PANELS ——

1. ½" PLYWOOD AND
2×2 PINE ARE
ASSEMBLED TO FORM
PANELS ——

THE BACK AND
FRONT PANELS
ARE FULL SIZE
AND OVERLAP
ALL EDGES

2. NAIL AND GLUE ALL PANEL
MEMBERS TOGETHER

ANYTHING OVER 4' SHOULD
HAVE DIAGONAL BRACING

BY FOLLOWING
THE FORMULA,
YOU CAN CALCULATE
THE NECESSARY
DIMENSIONS
FOR ANY CRATE.

3.

4.

5. ASSEMBLY: DRILL
OVERLAPING SECTIONS
WITH ¼" CLEARANCE
HOLE AND INSERT A
¼" × 4" ROUND HEAD STOVE BOLT, WASHER & NUT.

Crate plans. Note the method of construction and
the rope handle on the side.

After packing the object, secure the lid and spray-mark the crate to indicate which way is up. Do this on all sides, and put the word "top" on the top.

There is no better way of protecting your things than in a crate. If you are really ambitious and inclined to move a lot, build enough crates for everything in your household. (See the first alternative moving method described in Chapter 3.) In addition, the crates can be easily dismantled after the move and stored almost anywhere. However, I use my harpsichord crate as a convenient workbench down in the shop.

Selling

At least a month before you move, begin to organize your belongings, sorting those you want to keep from those you no longer use or need. To do this, take a tablet of paper and do a walk-through of your house. Objectively judge the utility of every item, then itemize those that are sellable. The more you sell now, the easier your move will be, not to mention the extra money you will earn. Some of the usual methods for selling household goods include newspaper ads, garage and house sales, flea markets and swap meets, and auctions. Let's take a look at each.

Ads

If, after you have taken your inventory, you discover that your list of things to sell is relatively small and composed just of major appliances and furniture, the best way to sell these items is to run an advertisement. There seems to be an unlimited number of places where you might put an ad, and the costs vary; some ads cost money, some are free, and for some there is a charge only if you sell the advertised item.

As a start, there is your local newspaper. Since you must pay for a newspaper ad, place it in the Sunday edition. Many people subscribe just to the Sunday paper, so that's the one that will reach the largest audience. It won't pay for you to run the ad for a week.

There are neighborhood newspapers into which you can place an ad at a reasonable cost. This is a good idea, as you want those near you to know about your items for sale.

There are specialized newspapers like the *Pennysaver*, *Buy-Wiser*, and *Shopping News*, which, in addition to local business advertising, carry private ads at a reasonable cost.

There are also publications that specialize in selling items. These swap sheets cost about 35¢ at the store, but they are free to advertisers. You are required to pay only if you sell any of your advertised items; they usually charge a percentage of the selling price.

Finally, there are many small publications distributed at work or church, as well as the student newspapers of the local colleges.

When placing an ad, list each item with a short but full description that includes your asking price. People are more apt to phone if they know how much you are asking. Go through the local papers for a few weeks before placing your ad to see how others have written theirs and to get a general idea of the market value of the items you plan to sell. If you are selling an appliance, be sure to mention the brand as well as the size or capacity. Furniture should be described by its function, style, design, or period. Most often four or five words along with the price will suffice for each item in your ad. Some sample ads might read as follows:

> White, 22 cu. ft. Hotpoint refrigerator, $150
> Green fabric, Contemporary couch, $50

Be sure to include your telephone number at the end of the ad, but it is best to withhold your address, which you can always give interested people when they call.

Keep an accurate and lengthy description of each ad item by the telephone so that as calls come in, any member of the family can describe the item adequately. This should cover age, condition, brand, color, and the reason why you are selling it.

The garage sale

If your list of sellable items exceeds twenty, an ad would be too costly, so try one of the next alternatives.

Garage and House Sales

Quite a large number of people sell their belongings at garage or house sales. An equally large number of people have found that garage sales are so infectious and profitable that they run one almost every week as a means of income. There is no question that the buying and selling of good used articles can be profitable.

One of the first things you should do is call your town hall to find out whether there are any restrictions in your area. Some towns require a special permit for which you must pay a fee; others have ordinances prohibiting the posting of advertisements or signs.

You might think about having a joint garage sale with your neighbors. Getting two or three families together greatly simplifies matters, as there are more people to share the setup work, gab with during the sale, and keep an eye on the goodies when there are lots of people milling around. In our area, there have even been entire neighborhoods that have arranged to have all of their garage sales on the same date. Needless to say, the appeal of being able to park on a street and catch as many as twenty sales can bring in quite a number of prospective buyers.

First decide where to have the sale. Most people set up on their driveways to catch street traffic, but you may not even have a driveway! There is certainly nothing wrong with a front yard or patio; and if an indoor location seems warranted by bad weather, there is always a clean basement or back porch. Some people decide to leave everything where it is in the house and invite the public in. This kind of house sale may not be acceptable to most people, since large crowds tramping through the house may be hard to control. In any case, there should be at least one person in every room to keep an eye on things.

Set the date and time of the sale, and stick to them. In all of your posters and ads, be sure that this information is clearly spelled out to prevent people from banging on your door at 6:00 in the morning—a week after your sale.

It pays to visit other garage sales in your area before you have yours. You will be able to see what things are selling well and what kinds of prices people are getting for items similar to those you wish to sell.

Your list of sellable objects should include anything and everything that is in reasonable condition. It is amazing what some people are looking for, and the most ridiculous items are the first sold, it seems. Put everything out, even things that don't work, but be sure to label these items AS IS. Also, don't sell anything that might be hazardous, such as broken toys with projecting parts, firearms, or firecrackers. Point out the frayed cord on small appliances or their tendency to blow fuses when plugged in.

You should make up an inventory sheet of all items and write your asking price after each one. Be fair in pricing your things; let your experience of other sales help you determine a reasonable price. Be realistic about what you have and the condition it is in.

Set up a place where you can prepare objects for the sale. At this time, it pays to clean things up, make minor repairs, sew on buttons, polish chrome, or do whatever else is necessary to make the item appear more pleasing. A little time spent here could mean the difference between a sale and a leftover.

As each item is prepared, place a price tag on it. Buy the small Avery self-stick labels to use as tags, since these can be taken off without damage to the item. Mark the prices with a ball-point pen or waterproof marker. Color code your tags if you have a combined sale with a neighbor.

Expect people to bargain for items. Be willing to drop a little in price for large, expensive things; 10 percent is a reasonable gesture. Ask interested people to make an offer and obtain their phone numbers. If the item doesn't sell for a higher price, you can call the people who offered you the lesser amount. Be willing to give a package price for a number of different items.

Advertise your sale a week before by running an ad in your local paper. The ad should be enticing and sound unique compared to the other ads in the paper. The phrase "moving sale" is better than just "garage sale" because you want people to know your sale is a one-time affair in which real bargains can be found and not a recurring sale that is held every week for profit.

Put up signs and posters around the neighborhood. These should be sufficiently large to be easily read from a passing car but should not block the visibility of street signs and traffic-control devices. They should contain a minimal number of words. The word "sale," the address, date, and time are all that is necessary. Plan to have a large sign in front of your house on the day of the sale.

If possible, set up the sale the night before. Otherwise, have everything ready to go early in the morning. You will need a number of table surfaces, such as card tables or folding picnic tables, for displaying objects. Borrow extras from a neighbor if you need them. Items of the same category should be grouped together—for example, kitchen items or furniture. Leave enough room between the tables for people to pass without knocking anything over. Also, arrange everything so that you have a clear view of all the surfaces from where you plan to sit.

It is a nice experience to get the whole family involved in your sale. The kids can be a great help by providing directions for parking, advertising the sale with placards, helping people carry things to their car, taking care of the "toy department," and keeping an eye on the sale area. Someone should be given the responsibility of being the cashier and minding the cashbox; it should never be left unguarded.

You should have a cash-only policy. Checks are too risky, unless they are from someone you know well. Post a conspicuous sign at your sale so that this policy is understood by your customers. If a potential buyer does not have sufficient money for an item, tell him you will be glad to set it aside for some kind of down payment. This deposit will assure that he will be back. Never hold an item for someone without a deposit.

Be wary of anyone who seems to be loitering, especially if they seem to be watching you. If they are not buyers, ask them to move on.

For the sale you will need a cashbox and a lot of change. A roll each of nickels and dimes and three or four dollars' worth of quarters is a good start. You will also need some singles and larger bills. Keep the paper money with you, not in the cashbox. Write down the amount you are starting with so that you can subtract it from the sales to determine your profit.

Also keep the tally sheet with the prices near you so that you can cross off each item as it is sold. Be sure to mark the sale price if it is less than the original asking price. A paper pad will be helpful for calculating multiple sales, and you should have some twine and tape for wrapping things up.

You will probably not sell all the items you had wished to. Small objects can be donated to charitable organizations, such as the Salvation Army and Goodwill, to church bazaars, and to schools. Donations to nonprofit organizations are tax deductible. Unsold large items can be advertised in an ad. By the way, remember to remove the signs and posters you put up all over town.

Garage and house sales are dependent on location for good sales. The more people that happen by, the better the chances of selling your wares. People who live out in the country and have relatively few neighbors will find it hard to attract customers to a sale. In fact, they may sit for hours without a single visitor. Obviously, a garage sale wouldn't work well for them. The next two alternatives may give better results.

Flea Markets and Swap Meets

If you are lucky, there will be a drive-in theater or large parking lot somewhere in your area where a flea market is held every Sunday. For a reasonable charge for the use of a space, you can haul in anything you want to sell and expect to see many more people than you would at a garage sale. The buying spirit of these markets is infectious, and people flock to them every week as long as the weather is good.

The only negative factor about a flea market or swap meet is that you have to lug all of your sale items to the place where it is held. As a result, you'll need a van or trailer. If you don't own one, plan to borrow one from a friend or relative.

Likewise, if all your items are large, bulky things like appliances and furniture, this is not a practical place to offer your goods, because most buyers are not prepared to afford or move them. But for many small items, the flea market or swap meet has much more potential than ten garage sales.

Most flea markets require that you reserve a space in advance. Really popular places often have two- or three-week waiting lists, so decide when you want to sell and reserve your space early.

Planning for a flea market is just like planning for a garage sale. The day before, clean and price all the items and pack them into the van. Bring along folding tables and other surfaces on which items can be displayed. Don't forget the cashbox and plenty of change.

A swap meet is an all-day affair, and you'll be up from 6:00 in the morning to 5:00 at night, so plan to be comfortable and bring something to eat (although swap meets have refreshment stands, they tend to be expensive). Also, dress appropriately, and bring along a hat in case of a scorching sun or an umbrella if it looks like rain.

If you have large appliances or furniture items to sell, make up a nicely lettered sign listing the items and their prices. This should encourage people to ask about them. You can always make arrangements to show these things to them later at your home.

If you don't want to make all the selling arrangements and wish someone else would, then the next alternative is for you.

Auctions

Auctions are a means of selling in which you consign anything from a few items to your entire household to an auctioneer who, in return for a fee or percentage, will sell it for you.

If you are selling just a few major pieces, the auction people will pick them up and take them to their auction house for the weekly sale. If you are selling the entire household, these people will come to your home to sell everything on the spot.

One of the negative factors about an auction is that it costs you money; but unlike any of the other selling alternatives, you can bet that everything will be sold. You will be sad to see some precious things go for a song; but at the prospect of not having to deal with leftovers as you would with a garage sale, you will not find this too disheartening.

More has been said about the auction as an alternative moving method in Chapter 2. For the person who wants someone else to take charge and is willing to pay for it, the auction is fun and a great solution.

All of these selling methods are available to you, and some work better than others for your particular situation. If you don't want to do the work of a garage sale but cannot afford to pay an auctioneer's fee, then hire some local high school students to run a sale for you; or ask a friend who is having a sale if you can throw in some items for a commission.

There are unlimited possibilities, and the best time to start getting rid of all your stuff is *now*.

Planning

This section provides a step-by-step procedure by which you can successfully arrange and plan your move. It combines the best and most important information from professional moving companies, rental agencies, and friends and associates who have moved. It not only covers known facts, but it presents a number of helpful hints and shortcuts.

There are two ways in which you can deal with this planning information: you can use the following countdown checklist as it appears in the book, making notations and checking off the steps as the days progress; or you can transfer the information from the countdown to a large, easily read calendar. I recommend the latter alternative. Write the steps directly on the calendar, starting with your planned

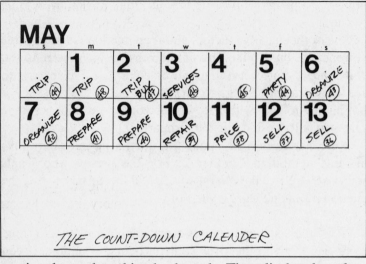

THE COUNT-DOWN CALENDER

moving day and working backwards. Then display the calendar in an appropriate place in your home. A day-to-day check of the calendar's visual array will make you aware of deadlines that are quickly approaching and things that must be done in order to keep up with the fast pace of planning and organizing the transport of your household.

Each countdown step is headed by a key word. You need only write this word on your calendar, since it is simply a reminder. You can always refer to the book for details about each step.

The countdown list is based on the assumption that you have two months of preparation time. Some of the steps will not pertain to your particular situation, so eliminate them from your calendar. If you are really short on preparation time, you can condense your calendar by eliminating unimportant steps and by combining two or three steps into one day.

You will have to adapt the countdown to your time schedule. This means that steps should occur on appropriate days. For example, days 35, 36, and 37 deal with having a garage sale. You should organize your calendar so that these steps fall on a weekend. Likewise, day 8 refers to the last-minute banking you will have to do, and it should fall on a weekday, when the bank is open.

This calendar will certainly help you to make an efficient, organized, and pleasant move.

CHART 12.

60-DAY MOVING COUNTDOWN

☐ Day 60—INVENTORY—Start by taking stock of what you plan to move and sell. (Use the inventory list in Chapter 2.)

☐ Day 59—INVENTORY—Determine from the inventory everything you do not really need and compose a second list of sellable items.

☐ Day 58—WRITE—Now is the time to send inquiries to moving companies for their information. Remember, you do not yet want an estimate.

☐ Day 57—LIST—Contact your favorite real-estate agency and put your house on the market. If you want to sell it yourself, use this day to place newspaper ads.

☐ Day 56—NOTICE—If you are renting, it would be a good idea to inform your landlord of your impending move. It will give him the chance to locate a new renter, which will assure you of a quicker return of your security deposit.

☐ Day 55—VISIT—Take this day to see an old friend or frequent a favorite spot. Enjoy the friendship and surroundings, as they will be your memories after you have moved away.

☐ Day 54—EXPLORE—Is there someplace in your area you have always wanted to see but have yet to visit? Well, you are going to be moving away sooner than you think, so hop in the car and explore those places you've put off seeing for so long.

☐ Day 53—PHOTOGRAPH—Set this day aside to take lots of photos of your old house, the neighborhood, and the town. It is so easy to overlook these in the rush to get moved, and you'll wish you had done it later.

☐ Day 52—GARDEN—Start spiffing up the out-of-doors. If your house is on the market, people will be coming, so cut the grass, trim the hedges, and prune the trees. Make your home look appealing and cared for. Those of you in apartments might start preparing your plants for the move. Get them accustomed to less light each day and longer periods without water.

☐ Day 51—REPAIR—Spend time around the house today fixing the screen door, repairing a window sash cord, or touching up the paint. The results may make your house more attractive to prospective buyers.

☐ Day 50—PARTY—Why not invite all the old friends over for a going-away party? It would give you a chance to say good-bye without rushing and to extend invitations for future visits.

☐ Day 49—CHOOSE—By now you have received information from various moving companies and can make a reasonable selection for your move. Call them and ask that a representative be sent out for an estimate. If you are moving yourself, you should be equally aware of the benefits and drawbacks of the local rental agencies. Make your choice and reserve the van today.

☐ Day 48—ESTIMATE—This is the day the estimator should come. Show him everything you plan to move, and point out the items you plan to sell, give away, or discard.

☐ Day 47—TRIP—If you can afford it, drive or fly to the
☐ Day 46—TRIP new city for your house-hunting trip. It
☐ Day 45—TRIP will give you an opportunity to become familiar with the area; and if you decide on a house or apartment, it will have been that much more productive. Besides, the trip may be tax deductible.

☐ Day 44—BUY—If all has gone well, you should be able to make a decision on your future home.

☐ Day 43—UTILITIES—Before you head back home for the packing, arrange with the local utilities to begin power, water, gas, fuel, and telephone service at your new home on the day you plan to arrive.

☐ Day 42—ORGANIZE—Garage-sale time. Plan your strategy for selling those unused items. Determine whether a garage sale, house sale, flea market, or swap meet would be best.

☐ Day 41—PREPARE— Have the family bring items down
☐ Day 40—PREPARE from the attic and up from the basement. Prepare for the sale by gathering together all sellable items and cleaning them up.

☐ Day 39—REPAIR—Work on items that need fixing.

☐ Day 38—PRICE—Make up an inventory list of all the sale items, and determine a fair price for each. Tag the items and arrange the sale area.

☐ Day 37—SELL—Open up the doors of your sale to all
☐ Day 36—SELL comers. Keep an eye on your goods and
☐ Day 35—SELL your cashbox. Hope for nice weather and lots of customers.

☐ Day 34—DONATE—After your sale, take a hard look at what's left. Donate small items to Goodwill or the Salvation Army. Be sure to get a receipt for tax purposes.

☐ Day 33—AD—You can now place a newspaper ad for those large or bulky items that have not yet been sold.

☐ Day 32—DISCARD—Throw out all junk from the sale. While you are at it, go through the basement and toss away any old paint or solvents, bleaches or dyes. Drain the gas and oil from all power equipment, motorcycles, and snowmobiles. Clean out the medicine cabinets.

☐ Day 31—INSURANCE—Arrange to have a sufficient amount of insurance coverage for the household goods that are to be moved. Both professionals and rental operators provide low-cost insurance options. Find out about them today.

☐ Day 30—MONEY—By now you have a pretty good idea what this is going to cost you. The professional mover has given you an estimate (which you can assume to be low) or you have calculated the size truck you need for a do-it-yourself move and have tallied the rental charges. If you are going to need a bank loan, now is the time to apply for one. In any event, get your money secured for the move.

☐ Day 29—CARTONS—Go to a supplier to buy the cartons you will need. Then go to a professional to buy used or new wardrobe, Dish-pak, and specialty boxes. Don't be afraid to overbuy.

☐ Day 28—RETURN—Return anything you have out on loan. Your neighbor will appreciate his tools, and your library would like its books.

☐ Day 27—PACKING—"Officially" begin packing. Start with the nonessentials of each room and do a little bit each day. If you are having professional movers do the packing, make the final arrangements today.

☐ Day 26—CAR—If you plan to drive to your new location, bring your car in for a maintenance check and tune-up. You certainly don't want to have any problems on the road.

☐ Day 25—NOTIFY—There are a number of people and agencies you must notify of your change of address. Start with the post office. Give them your new address to facilitate the forwarding of your mail. If you do not yet have your new address, give a temporary one (a friend's or that of your new place of employment). You can also ask that your mail be held until you send your new address. Talk with your postmaster and discuss the options. While you are at it, pick up a few change-of-address kits. They're free.

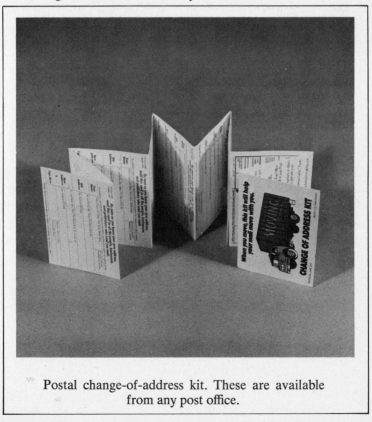

Postal change-of-address kit. These are available from any post office.

☐ Day 24—NOTIFY—Notify such persons as your doctor, dentist, accountant, lawyer, and broker.

☐ Day 23—NOTIFY—Notify business accounts you wish to cancel, or inform them of your new address. These include banks, finance companies, real-estate agencies, department stores, gasoline companies, bottled-water suppliers, the diaper service, the dairy, and the laundry and dry cleaners.

☐ Day 22—NOTIFY—Most of us have a number of insurance companies, so contact those which provide coverage for you: life, health, accident, home, hospital, auto, earthquake, flood, and so on.

☐ Day 21—NOTIFY—Notify federal and local government agencies: the Veteran's Administration, Social Security office, federal income tax and state income tax bureaus, the welfare office, and the motor vehicle office.

☐ Day 20—NOTIFY—Notify publications from professional and fraternal organizations, as well as newspapers and magazines to which you subscribe. The post office will forward magazines only if you sign a statement that you are willing to pay the additional mailing costs.

☐ Day 19—NOTIFY—Your closest associates will want to know where to reach you, so leave your new address with your church, business, and social organizations. Cancel the garbage pickup and request that the last pickup be made the day before you move.

☐ Day 18—SCHOOL—Contact the school the kids presently attend and have them forward their records to the new school. Also, contact the new school to pre-register your gang and get registration instructions.

☐ Day 17—RECORDS—Arrange for the transfer of your family's medical and dental records. Set aside your insurance records and arrange for their transfer on the moving date.

Have your bank records transferred and your safe-deposit box released. The box's contents and other valuables go with you, not on the van.

☐ Day 16—PETS—If you are going to transport a pet by air, make reservations now. Also arrange for your pet to have a physical, and ask your vet for a tranquilizer prescription if you think one is needed.

☐ Day 15—TRAVEL—Plan the drive to your new location. Contact the automobile club of which you are a member and have them send you a current road map with the best route indicated. You can also buy a good quality road atlas at an office supply store.

☐ Day 14—RESERVATIONS—Make your motel and hotel reservations for the drive. If you are flying, make your plane reservations. Plan what things you will need and pack them into suitcases to be set aside. Buy snacks for the trip, as well as some games the kids can play in the car.

☐ Day 13—CLEAN—Send clothes to the dry cleaners and laundry.

☐ Day 12—UTILITIES—Contact your gas, electric, water, fuel, and phone companies to arrange for shut-off on moving day.

☐ Day 11—ASIDE—Put aside things that you will be taking in the car, such as suitcases, plants, valuables, and important records and documents.

☐ Day 10—APPLIANCES—Call to have the appropriate servicemen come to disconnect and prepare your appliances for shipping. If you plan to do this job yourself, wait until Day 5.

☐ Day 9—SUITCASES—Pack suitcases now. Be sure they are set aside and not packed into the van.

☐ Day 8—BANK—Arrange to close out your bank accounts and have them transferred to your new bank. With-draw some cash or purchase traveler's checks to use on the trip.

☐ Day 7—KITCHEN—Clean appliances and work sur-faces. Dust and vacuum the motor compartments of the washer, dryer, and dishwasher. Wash and clean the floor where large appliances have been sitting.

☐ Day 6—SITTER—Call to arrange for a babysitter on moving day. Older kids should be put to work, but toddlers and infants will be a problem, so get someone to watch over them.

☐ Day 5—DISCONNECT—Today is when the servicemen (or you) will disconnect the washer, dryer, stove, oven, and dishwasher. Keep everybody out of the way. The washer and dryer should be prepared for shipping. You can do this job yourself with the help of Chapter 2.

☐ Day 4—SURVIVAL—Pack the survival carton so that the contents are fresh. Put it with the suitcases and other articles to be taken with you.

☐ Day 3—DEFROST—Unplug, empty, and defrost the refrigerator. There is no sense in keeping perishable or frozen foods, so give them to your neighbors. Make sure the water is mopped up from inside the unit and that the drip pan from underneath has been emptied. Keep the doors open so that the interior dries out.

☐ Day 2—PACK—By now almost everything should be packed. Attend to odds and ends. Leave out the alarm clock. Plan a simple breakfast for moving day. Set out minimal bedding and the clothes you will need for the next day. You can take all the items you plan to bring with you out to the car, and pack them in so they don't get confused with every-thing else. Put the plants in the car, too. Get plenty of sleep!

☐ Day 1—MOVE—Be up and around for the movers and

hope they arrive on time. If you are moving yourself, pick up the van and the equipment you will need for the move. Pack the truck as outlined earlier in this chapter. Since it will take you most of the day, take your time. Plan to spend the night at a motel or at a friend's, as your old house will be empty. Before you close the door for the last time, be sure that the water is shut off and no faucets are dripping, the furnace is turned off, all the lights are off, all the utilities are disconnected, all the windows are closed and secured, and all doors are locked.

With this kind of planning and careful preparation, you should find it easy to meet your deadlines and accurately schedule your move with a minimum of wasted time and frazzled nerves.

While on the subject of moving, there is the problem of easily carrying that pile of clothing, essentials, and important documents you will be taking with you. I have totally given

Totes: Uncommon Market. The Blow Works is for hair-care products; the Monks Bag is reversible.

up on suitcases. A hard suitcase is bulky and heavy, and it provides much more protection than is generally needed by clothing—after all, soft goods provide their own padding. I find that soft carrying cases are lighter to carry, easier to pack, and simpler to stuff and cram into those impossibly small spaces on an airplane. They can be folded down and stored inside another case on the way to someplace and will provide additional capacity for all those souvenirs on the way back. They are easily repaired and can be laundered with the dirty clothes. It is impossible for a rough baggage handler to break one, and I find them much more pleasing than any clunky suitcase.

Totes: Uncommon Market. The Schlep will carry just about anything; the Moving Van will take an entire family's clothing for a long trip and provide a big pillow in the car as well.

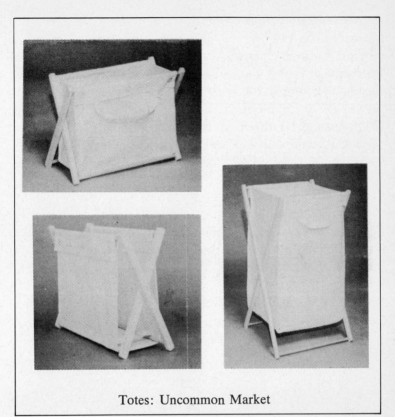

Totes: Uncommon Market

In our book *How Things Don't Work,* Victor Papanek and I discussed this subject of travel-transport and specifically mentioned Arnold S. Wasserman's TAG Modular Travel System. His designs are for the frequent traveler and are specialized to handle clothing items.

My favorite choice is the more universal soft tote, and the best are those made by the Uncommon Market. This remarkable company, founded by an equally remarkable mother of five, offers eight different canvas totes that can accommodate almost every carrying need. In addition to using them for travel, I've carried picnics, hauled laundry, and lugged books and a thousand other things in these (I've got an entire set), and it's this versatility that I admire and enjoy so much. Unlike the TAG Modular Travel System, these practical and far less expensive totes have many more uses and are still classy to carry around. The Uncommon Market distributes to stores all over the country; but if your neighborhood outlet doesn't have any, you can write to the company at: 227 South Bruner Street, Hinsdale, Illinois 60521. They can either sell directly to you or tell you who in your area carries their products. Better yet, clue in your local store and ask the owner to get some of these multipurpose totes in stock.

So now you've been given the best preparation advice. You know what to sell and what is going with you. You know how to pack and protect the things you move. You know how to pack the van. You have enough information to manage a garage sale, flea market, or auction, and you have a day-to-day calendar of events to help you move. You can do it!

Part II

THE
ACQUISITION

Probably the greatest concern of someone who moves, next to the transportation of a houseful of belongings, is locating and securing a new place to live. Those of us who can afford to do so visit the new location some time before moving day to look over the area, talk with real-estate agents, find out what is on the market, and ultimately choose a home to buy or rent. Those of us who are unable to do so have to wait until after moving day. Then, it's a race to find something so that the truck has a place to unload. In either case, there isn't much time to look for what very well might be an environment you'll have to live in for a number of years. So the acquisition of a home is as important to you and your family as the move itself.

This section will deal with a number of different methods of acquiring housing. Its purpose is to give you a broad account of the possibilities in both conventional and nonconventional housing. The four major avenues of renting, buying, adapting, and building will be discussed in detail; and hopefully you'll find a number of interesting alternatives that will meet the needs of your next move.

Chapter 5

Conventional Housing

WHEN WE MOVE, MOST OF US GO ABOUT FINDING HOUSING in a very conventional way, often because there isn't much time to explore other possibilities. Understandably, the realty network in this country is set up for conventional housing, and it is certainly the easiest and most direct method of finding a home. So, as a matter of review, let's cover the steps that are required when approaching housing in a conventional way.

Selling

In the early stages of your move, two months or earlier before the actual moving date, you should begin to think about selling your present home. This is a priority concern in any moving process because so many important decisions depend upon whether you sell your old house. Naturally, you cannot afford to buy a new house if your old one is still on the market; and you don't want to be caught in the position of having bought a new house while your old one is still up for sale. Unfortunately, this happens far too often, usually because the seller hasn't given himself or his real-estate agent enough time to sell the property. Never make your move before selling your old home. In fact, you may have to forestall the entire moving operation until a buyer for your old property has been found. Believe me, it's a pack of problems if you don't.

The sale of your old house will also clear you of mortgage indebtedness, as well as make you more acceptable to a bank for a loan. And it will give you an idea of how much money you can spend on your new home. You need to know all of this before you travel out to your new location to look for housing.

It is often difficult to determine whether you want to sell your house on your own or go with a professional. Understandably, you may want to save the 7–10 percent commission that many real-estate agents get these days; and many people discover that the job of selling their own house is not as overwhelming as it seems. The services the agent performs in selling your house cover advertising, posting signs, showing people through the home, and ultimately bringing forth serious offers to you. Certainly, these are tasks you can do yourself, but they require your time and commitment. Start early enough and give yourself a strict deadline. Beginning sixty days or more before your intended move, advertise heavily. Take the time to prepare your house so that it is neat and clean both inside and out. Give yourself a few weeks and stay near the phone. If by the end of a set time you haven't had any serious offers, you can turn to a real-estate agent.

When you list your house with an agent, he will require that you sign an agreement giving him "exclusivity," that is, the right to sell your house during a predetermined period of time. This means that no matter who buys your house within this time period, whether it be someone the agent brings forth or someone you find on your own, the agent will get his commission. Naturally, the agent wants you to sign for as long a period of time as possible, since this increases his odds of a sale. But it is to your advantage to sign for a short period, as your first-choice agent may be a dud and you'll want to be able to change agents if yours isn't doing much to "move" your house. Be aware that this agreement is negotiable and that you can set any of the conditions, as well as the commission, before you sign it. So read it through carefully and make sure that it benefits your interests.

Of course, you can pick-and-choose your agent, and the best way to do this is to invite a number of agents recommended by neighbors, friends, and associates to your home to give you an appraisal and discuss their services. You are under no obligation, so don't sign anything yet. Not only will you receive a number of estimates of the worth of your home, but you will be able to make a careful decision based on your impressions of their reliability, honesty, and enthusiasm. This enthusiasm assures you that the agent is positive about your home and its condition and will be aggressive in looking for prospective buyers.

When a legitimate bid is made, it should be done so on a legal purchase offer or sales contract form. If you are selling the house yourself, you can obtain copies of this document from a stationery supply store; then simply fill in the blanks. Typically, the sales contract contains the names of the buyer and the seller, as well as those of their respective attorneys, a description of the property, the type of deed that will be conveyed (see your lawyer about this), the date and time of the closing, and any other agreements that you and the buyer want to set down, such as the inclusion of appliances or the repair of certain things around the house.

You must have an attorney. While I personally feel that you can sell your house without an agent, I am adamant about the need for a good attorney. Because there are so many loopholes and problems that can be encountered in deed transfers and property disputes, having an attorney is essential for the sale or purchase of any property. Typically, the attorney gets only 1 percent of the selling price of your home, which means that, compared to that of the real-estate agent, his fee is a bargain. Besides, he's the one who works for *you* by figuring out your costs, searching for your title, making the transfer, recording the deed and the transaction, and meeting the other legal requirements with the buyer's attorney.

When faced with a move, it is obviously a lot easier to break away from the home or apartment you are renting or leasing, but there are some things you should pay attention to regarding your lease. The lease is the document you signed when you first moved in. Hopefully, you were aware of its conditions at that time, so they are of no surprise to you now.

You may find that you are going to have to do some clean-up and repair work before you can move away, especially if you wish to see your security deposit again. You may want to move before the termination of the lease, which would require finding someone to sublet the place for the remainder of your lease period. Sometimes the lease prohibits subletting, in which case you may have to offer the landlord some form of cash settlement.

All of these conditions should be clearly spelled out in your lease (if not, see a lawyer). So take it out and read it now to find out where you stand.

Looking in Advance

You need to know more about your new area in order to prepare yourself for your house-hunting trip. You can start by writing to a number of potentially helpful sources. First contact the telephone company in your new area and request that they send a current telephone book. Do this as soon as possible, since the directory will provide you with many important and needed names and addresses. The cost of having it mailed to you is certainly justified. While you are at it, write to the Chamber of Commerce and request information about the city, as well as road maps and guides.

Begin a subscription to the local newspapers. You will receive much needed information about the real-estate situation, as well as news about the town. Choose what appears to be the larger and better known real-estate agents and request information about their current listings. There may be one or two of sufficient interest for you to look at when you arrive.

In our 60-Day Moving Countdown (Chapter 4), we set aside four days for the house-hunting trip, although it would be better if you could extend this. However, since it is assumed that four days is about the maximum anyone can take, here is some advice on making the best use of that time.

Plan to arrive in your new location on a Friday evening. Make lodging arrangements in advance; and if you don't plan to drive, reserve a rental car. Spend Saturday driving in and around the area to find out what your new city has to offer. Be sure to drive through the areas that have good schools and shopping, as well as those areas that seem to match your interests and scale of income. If you are country-oriented, drive to the outskirts of town to see what is available. Note down those areas that most impress you, and plan to begin your house hunting there. The next day is Sunday, and the best way to spend it is by going through as many open houses and "open-for-inspection" listings as you can in the areas you liked. If you are extremely lucky, you will find the house of your dreams on this day and save yourself an incredible amount of time. In any event, as you go through each house, you will be confronted by the real-estate agent who is "sitting on" the house. He will undoubtedly tell you about other offerings he has, which might be more suitable for you. If you have toured enough houses on Sunday, you will have a pretty good idea which agents would be conscientious and helpful in locating *the* house for you, so plan to tour the listings of your first-choice agent on Monday. On Tuesday go through different listings with your second-choice agent. Between the two of them and the open houses you saw on Sunday, you should be able to make a reasonable decision on a house to buy.

If after four days of looking you haven't found anything to your satisfaction, then go home. Never feel obligated to make your house-hunting trip pay off because of the pressures brought about by the quickly approaching deadline of a move. You have a number of other alternatives at this point. You can arrange for another trip to the new location at a later time. If this is not feasible, then plan to rent a house while you continue to look for one to buy. While this may be more costly than buying a home at the outset, it will give you much more time to explore the area and discover where you really want to live, which in turn will enable you to make a better decision. I strongly advocate renting first as the best alternative. After all, there is always the chance that you won't like the new area and will decide to move back to your old one.

If your excursion to the new city has been successful and you've found a place you really like, then before signing a sales contract, go through the home with a tape measure and assure yourself that everything you own will fit inside. This will certainly tell you what household items you will have to sell before you move.

The calendar of days for your house-hunting trip may be summed up as follows:

CHART 13.

THE HOUSE-HUNTING TRIP

Day 48—Friday:	Arrive at new city; rent car, find lodgings.
Day 47—Saturday:	Tour entire area; make notes.
Day 46—Sunday:	Visit open houses; talk with real-estate agents.
Day 45—Monday:	Agent A, listings.
Day 44—Tuesday:	Agent B, listings.
Day 43—Wednesday:	Measure house; buy; obtain lawyer, banker; sign sales contract.

OR

Day 43—Wednesday:	No luck, locate rental property; secure lease.

Owning

The types of conventional housing that you can purchase are previously owned, older homes in established areas, new homes in subdivisions and tracts, condominiums and co-operatives, mobile homes, and distressed housing. Let's discuss each of them.

THE ACQUISITION 143

Previously Owned Homes

More than likely, most of the homes that you will see and like will fall into this category. They range in style and physical condition. Some may be in bad shape but provide tremendous investment potential; others may be crammed together into tracts or inner-city locations but have extremely reasonable prices; and still others may be veritable wrecks without windows or floors and listed as "handyman's specials." If the agent you've chosen has a listing like this, you can be sure he'll show it to you regardless of whether or not you are interested in it, since he is always hopeful that someone will fall for it. Real-estate agents also tend to show some of their listings which they know are not of interest to you just to impress the sellers with the number of prospective buyers to whom they are showing the house. This can be both annoying and a waste of time, so make it clear before you begin looking that you want to see only the listings of your own choosing.

The agent might also tell you about "private mortgage money," which he has available. Naturally, this is only for his exclusive listings; he won't offer it to you if you want him to share the sale with another agent. In any event, it pays to be cautious of private mortgaging, as it might get you in over your head. Ask your lawyer about it.

New Homes

In every city there are at least a dozen locations where new homes are being constructed. Unfortunately, in order to make a profit, the quality of these homes is inferior to those homes built a number of years ago. But because of the present state of mortgages and the financial bind the developer may be in, you can find yourself in one of these homes after having made a minimal down payment. If you can envision yourself living in a tract with neither trees nor grass nor perhaps paved roads, then the financial opportunity may intrigue you.

New homes. You have to be satisfied with sameness and be willing to wait for the trees to grow.

Condominiums and Cooperatives

A *cooperative* is a housing situation where everyone living in the same building has joint ownership of that building. Each party has an equal share of the whole, and decisions are made by mutual democratic agreement. In a *condominium*, each person owns his specific apartment and can do with it as he likes. Beyond that, these types of housing are about the same. It is like owning a house because of the investment opportunities and tax benefits, but it is also like living in an apartment, since each person's "property" is under the same roof. Unless you like apartment living, you may not want to invest in one of these. But some single individuals or people without children might be interested, and there are some fairly luxurious condominiums available in most cities.

Mobile-home park

Mobile Homes

Unfortunately, mobile homes are still far from being on a par with other conventional housing. They are cheaply made, incredibly ugly, and very often packed like sardines into a treeless sprawl. If they have any benefits at all these are that they can be bought "dirt cheap" and that most of them come already furnished (with furniture made from factory cut-offs). Obviously, you couldn't convince me to buy one of these things but I do see some nice trends coming in the future, a result of the efforts of new designers who are infiltrating the factory-built housing industry. See Chapter 6 for more about new design ideas for factory-built homes.

Distressed Housing

There is another area of housing that falls under the category of conventional housing but is not as apparent to the home buyer entering the market for the first time. It has to do with what I call distressed housing. These are homes, usually within the inner city, that are being sold or auctioned off at incredibly low prices by the city or the government to pay for delinquent taxes or abandonment. Almost every city

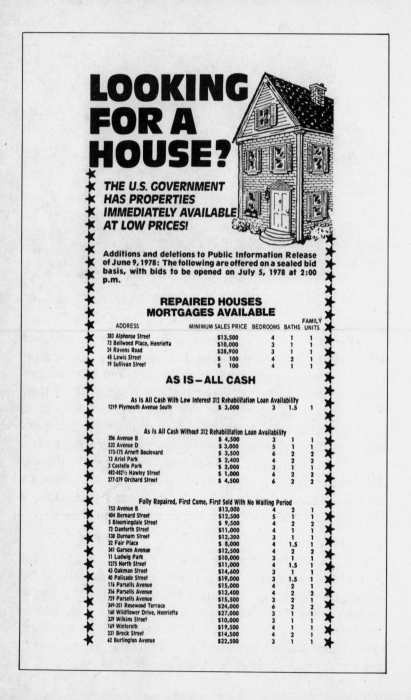

LOOKING FOR A HOUSE?

★ **THE U.S. GOVERNMENT HAS PROPERTIES IMMEDIATELY AVAILABLE AT LOW PRICES!**

Additions and deletions to Public Information Release of June 9, 1978: The following are offered on a sealed bid basis, with bids to be opened on July 5, 1978 at 2:00 p.m.

REPAIRED HOUSES MORTGAGES AVAILABLE

ADDRESS	MINIMUM SALES PRICE	BEDROOMS	BATHS	FAMILY UNITS
283 Alphonse Street	$13,500	4	1	1
73 Bellwood Place, Henrietta	$10,000	3	1	1
24 Ravens Road	$28,900	3	1	1
48 Lewis Street	$ 100	4	2	1
19 Sullivan Street	$ 100	4	1	1

AS IS — ALL CASH

As Is All Cash With Low Interest 312 Rehabilitation Loan Availability

1219 Plymouth Avenue South	$ 3,000	3	1.5	1

As Is All Cash Without 312 Rehabilitation Loan Availability

206 Avenue B	$ 4,500	3	1	1
532 Avenue D	$ 3,000	5	1	1
173-175 Arnett Boulevard	$ 3,500	6	2	2
12 Ariel Park	$ 2,400	4	2	2
3 Costello Park	$ 2,000	3	1	1
482-482½ Hawley Street	$ 1,000	6	2	2
277-279 Orchard Street	$ 4,500	6	2	2

Fully Repaired, First Come, First Sold With No Waiting Period

152 Avenue B	$13,000	4	2	1
404 Bernard Street	$12,500	5	1	1
5 Bloomingdale Street	$ 9,500	4	2	2
72 Danforth Street	$11,000	4	1	1
138 Durnam Street	$12,300	3	1	1
32 Fair Place	$ 8,000	4	1.5	1
341 Garson Avenue	$12,500	4	2	2
11 Ludwig Park	$10,000	3	1	1
1275 North Street	$11,000	4	1.5	1
43 Oakman Street	$14,600	3	1	1
40 Palisade Street	$19,000	3	1.5	1
176 Parsells Avenue	$15,000	4	2	1
356 Parsells Avenue	$13,400	4	2	2
729 Parsells Avenue	$15,500	3	2	1
349-351 Rosewood Terrace	$24,000	6	2	2
160 Wildflower Drive, Henrietta	$27,000	3	1	1
339 Wilkins Street	$10,000	3	1	1
169 Winteroth	$19,500	4	1	1
231 Breck Street	$14,500	4	2	1
62 Burlington Avenue	$22,500	3	1	1

As Is, First Come, First Sold

23 Rauber Street $ 2,000   4   1   1

Vacant Land

44 Alpha Street $ 4,000

273 First Street $ 100

208 Lyndhurst Street $ 100

68 Orange Street $ 100

619 Smith Street $ 100

Properties Sold Since June 9, 1978 Listing

78 Avenue B
1126 Bay Street
8 Bauer Street
139 Cottage

Canandaigua—39 Carriage Court

133 Ellicott Street
195 Gregory Hill Road
9 Quamina Drive
238 Roycroft

HOW TO BID:

- GO TO ANY LICENSED REAL ESTATE BROKER OF YOUR CHOICE.

- YOUR REAL ESTATE BROKER WILL EXPLAIN ALL DETAILS AND PROCESS YOUR BID APPLICATION AT NO COST TO YOU.

- THERE ARE NO CLOSING COSTS OR BROKER COMMISSIONS CHARGED TO YOU. HUD PAYS THESE COSTS AND WILL PROVIDE HOUSING ADVICE AT NO COST.

CALL HUD LINE

IN ROCHESTER, 288-2700 (or) 546-6289

U.S. DEPARTMENT OF HOUSING & URBAN DEVELOPMENT
Statler Building, Suite 800
107 Delaware Ave., Buffalo, N.Y. 14202

EQUAL HOUSING OPPORTUNITIES

Typical ad for distressed housing

with a reasonable population has housing like this available. Although most of it is in the central city, slum, or urban-renewal areas, some is situated in "face-lift" areas. These parts of the city are being turned around by professional owners who are investing in their property by restoring and rebuilding, which thereby creates new centers of historic interest and economic growth.

Above is an ad that appeared in my local newspaper, outlining the sale of housing by the U.S. Department of Housing and Urban Development. HUD is interested in as little as $100 for some of the properties they have listed. Many of the less desirable homes will go for that price to buyer-speculators because not enough buyer-homemakers exist who want them.

For people who intend to make the structure they buy their primary residence, the government will provide very low interest mortgages and home-improvement loans, which will get them off to a strong start on the necessary repairs and alterations these homes need. No one is pretending that these houses are in super shape, since most of them have been neglected for years and are a terrible mess. But for someone with ambition and not much money, any of these homes presents a stronger investment proposition than a mobile home or rental.

The way to find out about distressed housing is to subscribe to the local newspaper and keep your eye on the real-estate ads. You might also ask some of the real-estate agents in your new area if such housing has been advertised before. Call the town hall to learn whether such sales are run from time to time. Contact the area's federal government representative for HUD to inquire about government sales. Finally, give the landmark or historical society a call to see if anything of historical significance is available.

Cities have always been involved in urban-renewal projects; unfortunately, this sometimes means the destruction of a fair-sized neighborhood. Over the past years, however, some cities have offered the homes in these areas to buyers at outrageously low prices in order to dispose of them. One such sale in the city of Rochester offered houses at the price of $1.00. The catch? You had to buy a lot and have the house moved at your expense. But even at the cost of moving, these homes were a bargain. Many of them are now settled in fine areas and have proved to be tremendously successful investments as well as comfortable homes.

Renting

You may not be in the position of wanting to buy something now, so let's talk about renting or leasing. The main difference between renting and leasing is that renting is on a month-to-month basis, while leasing is for a specified period of time, usually a year or longer. These days, most of the nicer locations are leased; and there are a number of possibilities for renting or leasing apartments, houses, or mobile homes.

Apartments

Every city has a large number of apartment complexes in which there always seems to be available units to rent. They vary greatly in atmosphere and price, and many are exclusively for singles, retired persons, or families without children. Some are "no-frills," while others offer swimming pools, saunas, and gymnasiums. The Yellow Pages will indicate the addresses of these complexes.

Apartments are usually reasonable to rent, but they do mean a physical proximity that isn't for everybody. Apartment living can also be very difficult because of the peculiarities of individuals and the particular tastes of your neighbors.

Houses

If you are looking for a house to rent, you should first look in the local newspaper under HOUSES FOR RENT, SUBURBAN PROPERTY FOR RENT, and RECREATIONAL PROPERTY FOR RENT. The latter is extremely important because many beautiful areas of the country have incredible houses for rent during the off-months from September through May. Beyond the amenities that such property usually provides—large acreage, lake frontage, distant vistas, and beautiful forests—you can expect to find tranquility and privacy. If you are looking for something to buy, you can often locate a beautiful property to build on or one that has an unimproved cabin which you can expand and winterize. You may have to sink a well or install a septic system, but the inexpensive initial price will hardly dent your budget, and you can get home-improvement loans to subsidize insulation, drilling, or building. If you can't find what you want in the city and are willing to drive, perhaps a good distance, by all means look into this possibility.

Real-estate agents don't usually advertise their rentals in local newspapers unless they specialize in leasing homes, since most don't expect to make a large commission on rental properties. Just the same, call all the local agents to see if they have anything available. Some buy and sell properties in the speculative market and are interested in reliable renters to "sit on" their property while it gains in value for a few years. Others may have homes you can rent with an option to buy. If the house is something you might want to purchase but cannot presently afford, this would be a great opportunity. It may be more expensive than a straight rental; but if you ultimately buy the property in, say, a year, all the rental money will be applied to the selling price of the house.

Mobile Homes

Of course, there are always a few mobile homes for rent. If all else fails and you can find one in a nice location, you may consider moving into it as a temporary measure. Beware, however, that mobile homes rent for the price of a house and offer no more privacy than an apartment. Personally I would be reluctant to choose this option, but I might consider it if absolutely no other alternatives were open to me.

For all of these rental situations, you will be required to sign a lease or rental agreement. Before you sign, read the contract carefully. Also, remember that you have the right to make additions or deletions, as well as changes in the wording, with the mutual agreement of the landlord. Rents are not fixed but are, to a great extent, negotiable, as are the contents of the apartment. Furthermore, you can stipulate that painting or repairs be made before you move in. The landlord may not agree to any of these, but it doesn't hurt to try. If he is in a bind because the property has been vacant for some time, he most likely will not pass up a good prospect because of a small outlay for paint. Offer to do the work yourself if he supplies the materials. And ask that your security deposit be lowered in lieu of the repairs. Bargain!

As you can see, just within the realm of existing housing there are a great number of alternatives available to help you locate new housing for your family. The key to this whole operation is *time*. You must begin your search for new housing early enough to allow for travel, advertising, setbacks, delays, and the whims of everyone else involved. You need time to investigate your new town, discover its areas of interest, and make a reasonable housing choice. Too many of us make the mistake of buying on impulse from the pressures of a hectic move, and we live to regret it soon after. Give yourself adequate time, and the satisfaction of a beautiful new home will be the result.

NOTE: It should be noted that much information about selling and buying has been purposely omitted from this chapter. For the most part, intricate questions about buying and selling should be answered by your real-estate agent and attorney. To outline every possibility here would be time-consuming and quite dull. For further reading on the more complicated issues of housing, refer to the titles mentioned in the bibliography.

Chapter 6

Alternative Housing

To make our investigation of housing alternatives complete, we should discuss the types of housing that are regarded as unconventional or highly experimental. For the most part, these housing alternatives appeal primarily to people who are tired of renting, want an environment more suited to their interests and needs, and have the time to find a lot or parcel of land on which to arrange to have one of these structures installed.

Most of these homes are factory-built and shipped, either complete or in various disassembled stages, to the site; in that regard, they are portable. Some of them even have the capability of being moved more than once and can easily adapt to a nomadic way of life. Some are minimal structures that house just one individual, while others are as expansive and spacious as any conventional home.

These structures fall into two basic categories: factory-built homes and experimental or kit homes.

Factory-built Homes

The most common factory-built homes are mobile homes and modular homes, and there is quite a difference between the two.

Mobile homes are probably the least expensive full-size home alternative available to any buyer today, and one certainly gets what he pays for. The bulk of criticism lodged against the mobile-home industry maintains that the homes are minimally safe, minimally adequate, and minimally constructed. Assembly-line techniques at the factory involve the use of pneumatic staplers, and a good portion of the home is literally stapled together like sheets of paper. Even the term "mobile home" is misleading. "Mobile" derives from the fact that the frame which supports the floor is comprised of a chassis, wheels, brakes, and towing bar, so that the home can be towed from the factory to the site. This frame is a permanent part of the mobile home and stays with it throughout its life in order to qualify its owner for certain tax benefits, as it applies to the mobile-home definition. However, mobile homes are really mobile only once. They are purchased and moved to a mobile-home park, assembled onto a foundation of sorts, and remain there. As moving a mobile home a second time is usually extremely costly and can result in damage to the structure, most homes are never moved again.

Modular homes are also factory-built, but the emphasis here is on standard construction techniques, conventional building materials, and quality workmanship. The result is a product which is rather indistinguishable from a conventional home except that it has been produced indoors. Modular homes have standard floor construction (instead of I-beam chassis) and are shipped on flat-bed trailers. They are normally installed on full-basement foundations and provide basement stair locations in their floor plans. In other words, they are designed to be permanently installed. These homes are more expensive than mobile homes, since there is a higher quality of material and workmanship, as well as higher costs for shipping and installing the finished product.

Factory-built homes tend to have significant advantages over the homes being site-built today. Since all construction is done indoors under one large roof, there are no problems or setbacks due to weather. Likewise, stacks of lumber and other materials are not subject to shrinkage or warpage from heat or rain. Factory-built homes can also boast better quality control. If the worker finds a piece of wood that is bent or warped, he can easily discard it and get a better one from storage, whereas site-built housing relies on the materials delivered to the location, and there is little surplus to accommodate necessary replacements. It is understandable, then, that a carpenter might "force-fit" a warped piece into the structure to eliminate the delay it could take to replace it.

Factory-built homes are usually constructed in far less time than site-built homes; in addition, they can be built while the site is being prepared (during leveling, grading, and pouring of the foundation). Delivery dates as short as four or six weeks can thus be met without difficulty.

Mortgaging for these homes differs from that for conventional housing. Mobile homes are purchased much like automobiles and boats. Interest rates are figured on a straight yearly basis of somewhere between 11 and 18 percent, depending on the state law. The loan is arranged through the place of purchase, and it is usually held by some private financing company. The majority of these loans are payable at the end of ten years, so the monthly payments can easily be as much as those of a quality apartment or home rental. If the home qualifies, it might be possible to obtain HUD-insured loans through a commercial lender, but not all mobile homes can pass the strict government inspections.

Very few mobile homes are bought "off the lot," and you can expect to wait while yours is being manufactured and shipped. Most mobile homes end up in a mobile-home park, so if you have your eye on a particularly nice location, make sure there is space available there before you order your home. If you want to put the mobile home on your own parcel of land, contact your town hall to find out if there are any zoning ordinances that restrict mobile homes. Quite a few townships severely limit the installation of mobile homes in their areas. Often, to acquire zoning permission, you must convince the town that your home is aesthetic and permanent. Lots of luck.

I could go on about how mobile homes depreciate in value (it's about the only housing alternative that does) and how they are legally required to have elaborate tie-downs to keep them from blowing away in storms and how they are federally required to have smoke alarms and break-out windows because of the great fire hazard they impose, but I think I've made my point. If you are still interested in mobile-home living, talk with people who own them and live in them. It's your best way of knowing both the positive and negative aspects.

Modular homes are usually mortgaged through a bank or savings and loan institution. In some ways it is harder to find mortgaging for this kind of home than for a conventional home, since lenders tend to be dubious about homes that are not yet installed. But if the company from which you are buying the modular home is reputable and you can give the bank clear evidence of the design and construction of the home, you should be able to secure a loan for it.

It isn't surprising that the big turn-around in the factory-built home industry is being made by producers of modular homes. These homes are getting further away from the boxy single- or double-width mobile-home look and are beginning to take on the characteristics of custom-designed contemporary homes. These relatively inexpensive, modern homes are just the fringe of what will prove to be an incredibly large and successful industry. With the prices of conventional homes continuing to rise, it is understandable that people will want to seriously look into having something more special, spacious, and luxurious for their money.

Some of the most innovative and interesting design research presently affecting the mobile- and modular-home industries is coming from the frequent Reynolds Aluminum design competitions. Talented designers and architects have contributed to this series of competitions, which emphasizes the redesign of present mobile homes, with new directions in building techniques, materials, foldout rooms, and partitions, as well as a new consciousness of how people relate to these environments. Reynolds has received hundreds of encouraging entries, but unfortunately no manufacturer has picked up on these new approaches. Most manufacturers claim that these new designs wouldn't sell because of their higher manu-

Reynolds Aluminum Design Awards Program
mobile homes

facturing costs; they also contend that their marketing surveys of previous customers indicate no preference for change. But I feel there is a new market of people who desire better quality and design and are willing to pay for it. Why not see for yourself what the great potential is for mobile homes? Write for the Mobile Home Design Competition Portfolios from Transhelter Products Department, Reynolds Metal Company, 6601 West Broad Street, Richmond, Virginia 23261.

Probably the nicest designs available from a modular-home manufacturer I've seen are these from **Salem House.**

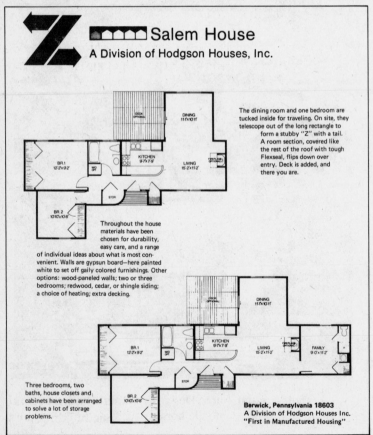

Salem House
A Division of Hodgson Houses, Inc.

The dining room and one bedroom are tucked inside for traveling. On site, they telescope out of the long rectangle to form a stubby "Z" with a tail. A room section, covered like the rest of the roof with tough Flexseal, flips down over entry. Deck is added, and there you are.

Throughout the house materials have been chosen for durability, easy care, and a range of individual ideas about what is most convenient. Walls are gypsum board—here painted white to set off gaily colored furnishings. Other options: wood-paneled walls; two or three bedrooms; redwood, cedar, or shingle siding; a choice of heating; extra decking.

Three bedrooms, two baths, house closets and cabinets have been arranged to solve a lot of storage problems.

Berwick, Pennsylvania 18603
A Division of Hodgson Houses Inc.
"First in Manufactured Housing"

The "Z" House and the Triad are both superior designs and innovative ideas in a relatively stationary industry.

The "Z" House is unique in terms of its foldout features. The dining room and one bedroom are shipped stored inside the bulk emptiness of the rest of the house. This eliminates the need for more than one flat-bed truck, thereby reducing costs. When the home is installed at the site, the two rooms "slide out" to add over 250 square feet of additional space. The interior is spacious and contemporary, with two wood-lined vaulted ceilings for warmth and visual interest. In addition, the home comes in a two- or three-bedroom version, with such options as wood-paneled walls (instead of gypsum); redwood, cedar, or shingle siding; and custom decks.

The Triad is ultra-contemporary and is shipped on two trucks. The four-bedroom two-bath version provides 1,328 square feet of living space, which is accomplished by installing the two sections of the home in a parallel position and utilizing the space in between. It's like making space out of nothing, and it's one of the most useful ideas to come along in some time.

Both homes are built well and finished well. You can even order them with wood-burning fireplaces. According to current base prices, the Triad can be yours for less than $30,000. These homes indicate a trend toward better and more responsive design. You can get more information about them from the manufacturer: Salem Houses, Ninth and Oak Streets, Berwick, Pennsylvania 18603.

Experimental and Kit Homes

Within this next section are structures that may be considered experimental or extremely unconventional. Tension-compression structures as well as inflatables are proven in concept and are readily available for industrial uses, but their application to living environments is still under current development by imaginative builders. Geodesic buildings and underground houses used to be considered experimental but

The Triad: Salem House (Tom Yee, *House
and Garden*)

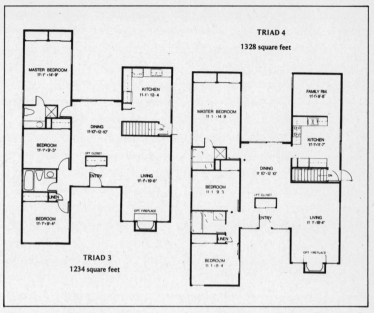

are now widely accepted, and examples are springing up in almost every part of the country. Greenhouses and boats are unconventional types of housing, since they were originally intended for other purposes; but some families have adapted these environments and found them to have far greater benefits than conventional housing. Log homes and other site-built kit buildings provide a tremendous selection of housing types from which the home builder/craftsman can choose. Altogether, this listing gives a comprehensive view of what is available in the area of alternative housing for those of us looking for something different and unique as well as affordable.

Tension-compression Structures

Back in 1967, the International Exposition in Montreal, Canada, was the site for many new and interesting architectural achievements. The United States pavilion was a large, ¾ geodesic sphere of Fuller's design. But equally exciting was the West German pavilion created by the famed architect Frei Otto. It was a tremendously large tension-compression structure in which a huge steel-reinforced canvas membrane was supported off the ground by tension much in the manner of a large circus tent. In addition to providing more than ample interior space for the pavilion's many exhibits, the Frei Otto structure was praised and admired for its sweeping forms and new architectural approach.

This same system of building components which undergo tension and provide compression to other components is certainly a feasible building technique for almost any purpose. Materials can be selected that have permanence, and a structure can even be assembled and sprayed with polyurethane, fiberglass, or concrete to give it permanent shape. Considering the simplicity with which a structure of this nature can be built, it is surprising that more experimentation hasn't yielded a more workable living environment solution.

For the most part, we still see tension-compression structures only in the area of tents and camping environments. While many of these use the principles of tensile construction, they retain a tent-like appearance and aura of impermanence.

Now, along comes one of the greatest innovators in the tent business, Bill Moss of **Moss Tentworks**. In addition to his wide variety of lightweight backpacking tents, Bill has created the Optimum 200, which can provide almost 200 square feet of space, making the tent a comfortable alternative to a recreation or vacation home. The design has an unusually pleasant free-flowing appearance, and its floor plan resembles a three-spoked wheel in that it allows for three ample alcoves. A unit such as this could provide accommodations for a family of three and for larger groups if several units were mounted together.

The entire structure, weighing forty-five pounds, has a framework of aluminum tubing and a membrane of cotton duck. Mounted on a deck or platform in the woods, the Optimum 200 would provide all the comforts of home for under $1,000.

Optimum 200: Moss Tentworks

If you would like to see the work of this top-notch designer, write to Bill Moss at: Moss Tentworks, Inc., **P.O. Box 309, Camden, Maine 04843.**

Inflatable Structures

One of the greatest areas still wide open to experimentation is that of inflatable housing. As the name implies, inflatables are structures that are supported entirely by air, and

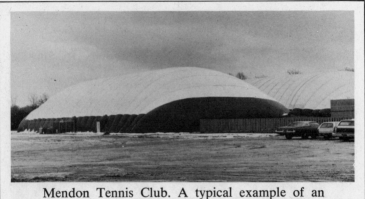

Mendon Tennis Club. A typical example of an air-supported structure that spans a large area.

there are two basic types. The first is the simplest kind of inflatable structure. It is composed of a single lightweight, airtight membrane that is secured to the ground in such a way as to prevent air from escaping. The doorway to this structure contains a fan that continually fills and replenishes the air inside the membrane; the air, in turn, fills out the shape of the structure and provides a habitable and protected environment. The doorway to such a structure is basically an air lock, so if the door were left open or the fan turned off, the volume of air would dissipate and the structure would slowly collapse. Of course, this could be a bit disconcerting should you be in the middle of an important dinner party, so not too many ·of these continuous-air structures have ever been adapted to use as homes. Instead, designers interested in living environments have developed a second system of inflatable structures in which the walls are double-thick and air is used to inflate just the space in between. The captive air provides the support necessary to keep the walls erect. In this way, the interior of the structure is unaffected by the air support system and can be maintained and controlled as a separate entity.

There doesn't seem to be any limit to the size these inflatables can take, nor are there any limits to shapes and contours the membrane can take when filled. Presently, these structures are used for commercial purposes, serving as warehouses, greenhouses, and even jet hangars. The military has developed quite a number of uses for inflatables and seems to be the only major researcher on the subject. Their emphasis has been temporary forms of shelter and special-purpose military applications, such as missile silos or tank camouflage. As a matter of fact, if you look around your own area, you will probably see some examples of air-inflated structures. They tend to be so common that we overlook them as pieces of industrial hardware rather than as potential housing alternatives.

It seems that the drawbacks presently inherent in inflatable structures concern the quality and permanence of suitable materials to be used as the membrane. Most of the lighter-weight materials have a very short lifespan; in addition, many of the plastics that fit this category are affected by ultraviolet penetration by the sun, which leaves them brittle and cracked in a matter of months. Heavier fabrics tend to be too weighty to be supported by a low-pressure volume of air. The industry is in need of a new material; and with the ever-growing number of technological developments, a suitable material won't be that far off in the future.

In the meantime, experimentation with inflatables goes on. Almost every major college or university boasting an architecture or design program has had a "quick city" weekend. The name is derived from the speed with which a group of students from various invited colleges can erect their own inflatable structures to form an "instant" city environment. Oftentimes the many unique structures are assembled in one Friday afternoon. They are then used as shelters for lectures and seminars on housing and design, and later, for parties or as living units for the visiting students. After the festivities, they are quickly deflated and stashed into vans or pickup trucks for the trip home.

With this kind of experimentation going on, one would

think that the inflatable home is just around the corner. It seems, however, that few people like the thought of living in a house entirely supported by air. We have a negative attitude about inflatable objects because so many of these products are cheaply made and short-lived. Until our attitudes change and better materials are found, inflatables have a long road to travel before they are accepted as a viable housing alternative.

On the other hand, with careful design and control, an inflatable would be a tremendously logical structure to use as a vacation home. Can you imagine buying a beautiful parcel of land and building a large wooden deck on it that takes advantage of the natural scenery? Something like an inflatable could be stored in a small space and brought out in the summer, when it is needed. In addition to providing a large one-room shelter, it would also be more durable than a tent, while possessing the same storage capabilities. At the end of the summer, the entire structure could be easily deflated and stored at the site for the next season. With no permanent structure, your land would still be considered "undeveloped," which should keep the taxes down. In addition, you would have no worries about vandalism or weather-related damage for the rest of the year.

It also surprises me that more hasn't been done in the area of tent campers and small trailers. As the size of our cars gets smaller and smaller in response to fuel and cost economics, so does the ability of the car to tow a heavy load. There seems to be a need for the de-emphasis of massive trailer homes and the resurgence of lightweight camping structures that can be easily erected.

A small, Volkswagen-towable trailer could contain quite a large inflatable structure and, like the tent campers currently available, could be inflated to yield protection from the elements and plenty of usable space. Its method of inflation could even come from compressed-air cylinders, thus enabling the entire operation to be totally automatic. So here

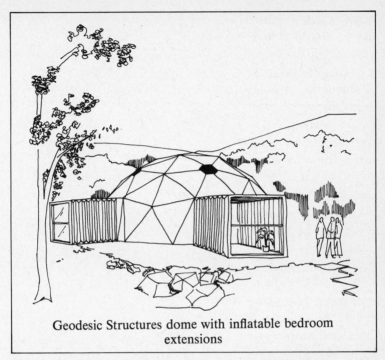

Geodesic Structures dome with inflatable bedroom
extensions

again is another strong potential market for inflatables.

As with the temporary housing structures developed by the army for use in Vietnam, there is a need for temporary housing to be used in all kinds of disaster situations. Currently, large mobile homes are brought into disaster areas. These are expensive to buy (states buy them with tax dollars) and expensive to transport. One truck brings one mobile home, which houses only one family. The same truck could carry five or six inflatable structures, which could cover the size of a football field and provide shelter for hundreds of people.

If you are interested in something unique and are willing to do some research, you might investigate this type of structure. As temporary housing for use as vacation or recreation homes, inflatables are obviously within the state-of-the-art. For more permanent structures, it would be neces-

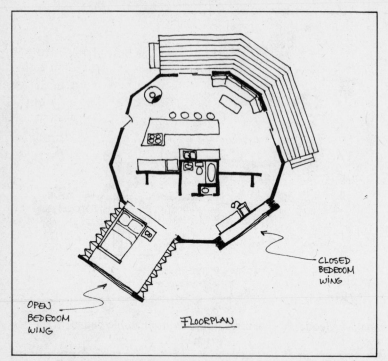

OPEN
BEDROOM
WING

CLOSED
BEDROOM
WING

FLOORPLAN

sary to find the perfect blend of shape and fabric. Perhaps the solution lies in gases other than air or in the use of water as the medium for inflation. It may be that inflatables would best function in conjunction with other types of conventional housing, perhaps as a means of expanding the structure for additional temporary uses. For example, a permanent structure might contain the living room, dining room, kitchen, and bathrooms; and all the bedrooms would be inflatable, foldout areas to be used only at night. During the day, these sections would be deflated and stored automatically, which would also decrease the amount of volume needed to be heated or air-conditioned. Such a combination of structures might even provide a new approach to energy conservation.

In any event, the rest is up to you. But I personally feel that air-inflated structures are bound to find a real place in the future of our living environments.

Geodesics

R. Buckminster Fuller gets the credit for bringing geodesic domes to our attention, but the basic principles of a dome structure go back centuries. Geodesic domes are far from experimental today; so many people have had them built or have built them themselves that all of the kinks have been worked out. Needless to say, domes are incredible structures. Not only do they contain far more square feet of area per building material cost than almost any other kind of structure, but they also have been proven to be stronger than almost any other kind of structure, since any force imposed on the roof is equally distributed by the network of linear members and hubs.

The skeletal system of the geodesic dome is achieved through a complicated mathematical formula, but the physical reality can be anything from simple electrical conduits with the ends flattened and bolted together to very sophisticated aluminum extrusions and trusses. In addition, many wooden-framed domes with welded hubs are produced in kit form for the do-it-yourselfer. Once completed, the framework can be covered with any number of different "skins," from plywood with shingles to fiberglass panels to clear glass. Domes can be constructed so that they are broad and flat, a hemisphere or ¾-sphere, and they can be built large enough to contain more than one story. Even the small domes have elevated loft areas for studios or bedrooms. Groups of domes can easily be clustered or added to when finances or needs dictate. Advocates revel in the simplicity, strength, and portability of geodesic domes. It isn't unusual for someone to sell his dome and have it quickly dismantled and carted away in the buyer's pickup truck.

Most domes that are intended as permanent structures are installed on full foundations of block or concrete and use the finest materials and best insulation. While most domes are intended as do-it-yourself projects, you can often find a builder-supplier who can do all the work for you. In either case, cost for cost, it would be very hard to beat this kind of housing.

One of the biggest suppliers of geodesic dome structures is **Monterey Domes** of Riverside, California. Monterey offers kits from 20 to 45 feet in diameter, at basic prices under $10,000. Their Alpine 45 series can provide as much as 3,600 square feet of living space at two levels, while their smaller 20-foot dome can be easily assembled by a husband-

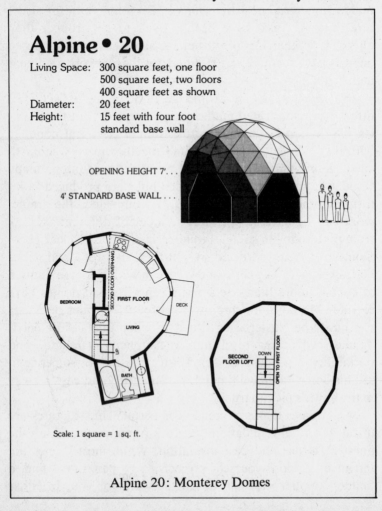

Alpine • 20

Living Space: 300 square feet, one floor
                500 square feet, two floors
                400 square feet as shown
Diameter: 20 feet
Height: 15 feet with four foot
                standard base wall

OPENING HEIGHT 7'. . .

4' STANDARD BASE WALL . . .

BEDROOM   SECOND FLOOR OVERHANG   FIRST FLOOR   DECK

LIVING

UP

BATH

SECOND FLOOR LOFT   DOWN   OPEN TO FIRST FLOOR

Scale: 1 square = 1 sq. ft.

Alpine 20: Monterey Domes

wife team and would be ideal as a summer retreat or vacation home.

Probably the most ingenious part of these homes is the simplified design of the hub system. The hub is a heavy piece of welded steel that is fixed at the correct strut positions, beveled at the correct angles, and pre-drilled. The color cod-

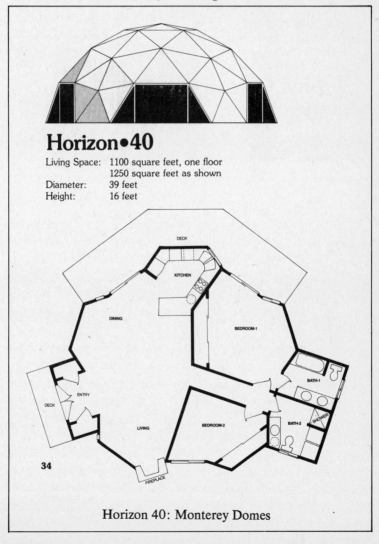

Horizon•40

Living Space:	1100 square feet, one floor
	1250 square feet as shown
Diameter:	39 feet
Height:	16 feet

Horizon 40: Monterey Domes

Geodesic Structures, Inc.

ings prevent any assembly mistakes and provide one of the simplest and quickest methods for dome assembly found today. The domes are also designed to use rigid foam insulation, which provides the greatest amount of R value for its thickness, making these dome structures 30 to 50 percent more efficient to heat than similarly sized conventional homes.

The company prides itself on the use of top-quality materials and superior construction aids in the way of professional assistance, working drawings/blueprints, and concise step-by-step construction manuals. If you live on or near the West Coast, Monterey Domes should be your source. They have a beautiful color catalog of their homes available for a $3.00 mailing fee. Write to them: Monterey Domes, 3777-W Plancenia, P.O. Box 5621-W, Riverside, California 92517.

A good dome supplier for people who live on the East Coast is **Geodesic Structures, Inc.** They can supply domes from 24 to 59 feet in diameter, in versions from ⅜-sphere to ¾-sphere. Their 59-footer supplies almost 6,000 square feet of living space on three different levels, at a price surprisingly under $30,000.

Geodesic Structures, too, is a company that takes its products seriously. The main difference between their kits and others on the market is that the triangular space frames which make up the dome are preassembled and insulated at the factory before being shipped to the site. On location, these triangles are bolted together to form the dome. Because of the preassembly, quite a bit of time can be saved.

Additionally, Geodesic Structures has innovated a series of modular opening options, such as single and double doors, double and triple sliding glass doors, and skylights, which can be chosen and substituted in any number by the potential builder. This allows for a custom approach to the site, the best winter and summer sunlight penetration, the best ventilation, the best view, and so on.

Those of you on or near the East Coast might be interested in their semi-modular approach to dome building. Write to them: Geodesic Structures, Inc., P.O. Box 176, Roosevelt, New Jersey 08555.

Because of the great interest in domes generated in the sixties, as well as the many writings of R. Buckminster Fuller, there are probably hundreds of books on designing and building geodesics. If you want to learn how, Mr. Fuller's writings would provide a basic understanding of domes, especially if you wish to design and create one from the complicated formulas. But if you just want to read more about domes and see what other types of domes have been created by do-it-yourselfers, get copies of *Domebook One* and *Domebook Two*, available through most bookstores and distributed by Random House.

For inexpensive and easily built housing, geodesic domes continue to provide one of the best alternative homes on today's market.

Underground Housing

One of the newest ideas in energy conservation is that of

underground housing. Its theory works like this. In the colder climatic areas of the country, there is a point roughly six feet below the surface of the ground that is called the frost line. No matter what the outside temperature, anything placed below this point will not freeze. This explains why we build our foundations and sink our water pipes below the frost line. Well, if that six feet of earth can insulate to such an extent, why not put part or all of a living structure underground?

If you are planning to install some kind of home on a parcel of land, you will have to provide an adequate foundation; and in the process, you could plan to construct part of your home underground in order to take advantage of this insulating effect. Since most of the kit homes discussed in this chapter can be installed on any kind of foundation, with careful land selection and house design, you could achieve a perfect blend of components.

Of course, we are all subject to great hesitation when it comes to putting our living environments underground. We have negative associations with subterranean places, and we tend to think of them as inferior or secondary spaces. Yet, there is no reason why an underground home has to take on these dark, dank images. Through a creative design it is possible to have all the light and space you now have and benefit from the earth's own warmth as well.

Consider the situation in which the "perfect" parcel of land is one that is on a continual slope of 30 degrees or more. In California, homes have been built on such parcels by using tall posts and projecting the homes out from the slope on a cantilevered basis. But, with the risk of earthquakes and land erosion, many of these homes could end up at the bottom of the hill. In order to take advantage of the incredible view that such property offers, one might consider burying a large portion of the house into the hill, while leaving the front to project slightly from the slope. This would allow the entire front of the house to be glass and balcony. The remainder of

UNDERGROUND HOUSE
BUILT INTO SLOPE

the house really doesn't need any windows, since the light penetration from the front can be assisted by carefully placed skylights in the roof. The lighting wouldn't be much different from the lighting of those apartments which have a single exterior wall.

Some thirty feet below the earth's surface the temperature is constant at around 50 degrees Fahrenheit. This means that should you build a structure that far down, the heat generated by lighting and human habitation might be enough to keep the space at a comfortable temperature without the need for any further heating or cooling equipment. But unless the environment can be made desirable, no one would want to live that far below the earth's surface.

Even buildings that are partially buried can command energy savings of 75 percent or more. In addition, heavy winds, sleet, and snow won't affect the structure. This means that some of the additional benefits of underground housing would be minimal maintenance (since so much of the building is protected from the ravages of climate and weather), stability with no vibration, operational savings (due to the stable temperature and humidity), and earthquake protection (a result of the muting of shear stresses, which often cause damage to aboveground structures).

Finally, the development of underground homes would be ecologically beneficial. As most of each living unit would be underground, large expanses of green area would be left free for trees, grass, and parks.

So it is indeed possible to have underground housing that is light and airy, with skylights and panoramic views and all the benefits of conventional housing without a bleak, dank atmosphere. The right location, coupled with careful planning and creative design, could make underground housing one of the most pleasing and energy-saving departures from conventional homes you can take.

Greenhouses

Once these structures were considered to be purely for the growing of plants and vegetables by commercial greenhouse establishments. Only a few well-to-do home gardeners could afford to have greenhouse additions to their home. But with certain new trends and advancements in greenhouse construction, these structures are now more easily available from a number of firms across the country.

Contrary to popular belief, greenhouses are not necessarily "hot" houses. Any structure that contains space which is not ventilated and allows sunlight penetration will heat up. (This "greenhouse effect" is also the basis for many experimental solar ovens.) But if the air within a structure is allowed to ventilate and fresh air is brought in, the air temperature can be controlled and normal temperature extremes can be maintained. So, just like any other type of structure, a greenhouse can be made ideal in temperature for everyday living. Combine this with the fact that a certain amount of solar heat penetration can be achieved during winter months to provide the basis for a very effective passive solar heating system (more on this in Chapter 7), and you can see why many people are exploring the possibilities that exist in adding a greenhouse to their present home or in choosing a greenhouse as the primary element in a vacation, recreation, or permanent home.

Greenhouse: Lord and Burnham

Greenhouses are available nationwide, but there is no company as grand or as old as the leader in the industry, **Lord and Burnham**. The product they manufacture is an almost indestructible greenhouse of top-quality components, and their method of construction has yet to be bettered by any other greenhouse supplier. They boast a totally unique, aluminum extruded glazing bar, which has the best design in the industry—their colorful and complete catalog does a persuasive job of convincing you of that. They also caution us against cheaper greenhouses which use self-tapping screws or pop-rivets to connect structural members; Lord and Burnham greenhouses use machine bolts. They tell us to be wary of greenhouse kits which must be totally preassembled before they can be lifted onto their foundations; their greenhouses, on the other hand, can be assembled one frame at a time di-

Greenhouses: Lord and Burnham

rectly onto the foundation for a simpler construction. They suggest that we avoid greenhouses with complicated assemblies of too many too-weak components, which add to the weight instead of to the rigidity. They further mention that some of the less expensive greenhouses ignore the importance of draining condensate (fog) from the inside of the structure to the outside. If this water is not sufficiently drained it will rest on the foundation wall, causing fungus, as well as deterioration and cracking.

The range of greenhouses available from Lord and Burn-

Greenhouse sitting room: Lord and Burnham

ham is spectacular. They have lean-to versions that mount to the wall of an existing building; these are available in models that have a 2-foot foundation wall and others that have glass to the ground. They also have full-span greenhouses, which either attach to other buildings or stand on their own. Their biggest greenhouse (that is in the catalog) is a massive 51 foot by 20 foot professional style, with an unbelievably low price of around $6,000. Their smallest greenhouse is an efficient little model designed to mount in the average window. This comes in six sizes, ranging in price from $185 to $227. In addition to their selection of greenhouses, Lord and Burnham has quite a number of special accessories, including benches and devices for heating, cooling, shading, and ventilating.

Their kits are delivered ready for installation. All the parts are numbered; the glass is precut to fit; and the doors are factory-preassembled, weatherstripped, and pre-glazed. Two people of reasonable skill can assemble a kit in a minimal amount of time. If you order a greenhouse from Lord and Burnham, they will supply you with installation and assembly plans ahead of time, so that while you are waiting for your greenhouse to arrive, you can begin preparing the site and laying the foundation. Another nice thing about this company is that they ship all of their large greenhouse kits freight-prepaid to any U.S. destination except Alaska and Hawaii. So it appears that there are no hidden costs and that the price you are given is the full price for your chosen greenhouse.

Considering the volume of business this company does and the spectacular custom installations they have achieved over the years, they are by far the best supplier I have seen. In addition to their main plant in Irvington, New York, 10533, they have representatives in California (3447 Investment Boulevard, Hayward, California 94545), Georgia (P.O. Box 47614, Atlanta, Georgia 30340), Illinois (2500 Devon Avenue, Des Plaines, Illinois 60018), Massachusetts (375 Concord Avenue, Belmont, Massachusetts 02178), New Jersey (Stokes Road and Schoolhouse Drive, Medford, New Jersey 08055), Ohio (P.O. Box 23, N. Ridgeville, Ohio 44039), Texas (4212 San Saba, Piano, Texas 75074), and Canada (325 Welland Avenue, St. Catharines, Ontario, L2R 6V9).

Without question, Lord and Burnham's chief competitor is **Janco Greenhouses**, produced by the J.A. Nearing Company, Inc. In many ways, these two companies offer the same top-quality product, but compared to the rest of the industry, they are miles ahead of everyone else. Janco likes to point out their advantages over other manufacturers, such as their fully rustproof aluminum frames and their beautifully prefabricated, pre-punched, pre-drilled kits. Like Lord and Burnham, they, too, have a special glazing-bar design made of extruded aluminum; and as with all quality designs, it includes a built-in condensation channel to drain out moisture from the interior. One of the little extras Janco supplies with their kits is bench legs and side supports, which allow you to build your own benches. They also have a simple 2 inch by 6 inch wood foundation system, which they claim will eliminate the need for costly masonry. Of course, any permanent housing structure would necessitate a solid, deep foundation, but some portable applications might be able to get away with the 2 × 6's.

Also like Lord and Burnham, Janco has a large, lavishly illustrated catalog and can supply just about any style or type of greenhouse you might consider. They offer curved-eave designs and freestanding lean-to models, all in a variety of sizes. While their catalog lists a mammoth 52 foot by 125 foot twelve-bay commercial greenhouse, more than likely your housing needs won't require this kind of space (6,500 square feet). But if you were thinking of designing a large, livable structure, Janco would be competitive with the quality and prices you can get from any other company. They, too, provide prepaid shipping to any point in the U.S. They make a long-lasting and well-designed product, and I would certainly consider their offerings. Their address is: Janco Greenhouses, J.A. Nearing Co., Inc., 9390 Davis Avenue, Laurel, Maryland 20810.

If your primary interest in greenhouses is in adapting them into a living environment for you and your family, you have just read about the two companies that can offer you workable versions. The next two companies do not sell a product that would be adaptable for year-round living in cold climates, but I am including them because they are unique in design, simplicity, and especially price. As simple home additions in temperate climates, as inexpensive recreation homes, or—as they are intended—greenhouses, their products might provide the solution to your needs.

Turner Greenhouses makes a number of different 8-foot- and 14-foot-wide freestanding designs and a 7-foot lean-to style. These greenhouses have steel frames which are factory-coated with a corrosive-resistant alloy of aluminum and zinc. This coating is hot-dipped (similar to the galvanizing process), which the company claims gives the frames long life and maintenance-free properties. Realize, of course, that a "corrosive-resistant" framework is not the same as a *non*-corrosive aluminum one.

Turner has some interesting ideas about simple foundations, from wood sills to combination wood and concrete block. All their greenhouses are designed in such a way as to be extendable in length at any future time. They sell two versions of their designs: one with fiberglass panels and the other with a polyethylene covering. Polyethylene is a thin, flexible, semi-clear plastic that has a somewhat short life span. Normally, it is replaced every season because of brittleness and eventual cracking. Even with repair, it will yellow in time and allow less and less sunlight penetration, so stretching it to last for two seasons is impractical. Fiberglass, on the other hand, is much more durable and has greater permanence, but it is not as transparent as glass or even polyethylene, which some people feel makes it less aesthetic. These Turner greenhouses are designed so that you can order them with the polyethylene covering and, at a later date, convert to fiberglass, which they guarantee for fifteen years.

Naturally, with all this simplicity and economy, Turner has a decided price advantage over many other companies. You might want to see their catalog. Write to: Turner Greenhouses, P.O. Box 1260, Highway 117 South, Goldsboro, North Carolina 27530.

Finally, there are the greenhouses you can buy from **Peter Reimuller**. I've saved him for last because his simple and straightforward designs are practical, inexpensive solutions. First of all, he has an interesting array of designs. The Crystallaire is a freestanding cathedral-shaped polyethylene-covered structure. The Handi-gro and Pearl Mist models come in both freestanding and attached versions, and the

Pearl Mist freestanding greenhouse: Peter
Reimuller

Pearl Mist can be ordered as a lean-to version as well. Inter-
estingly enough, Mr. Reimuller also has a geodesic dome
design, which is 15 feet in diameter and covered with flat
fiberglass panels.

The products this company supplies seem very honest, and
the catalog makes no attempt to mislead or deceive the buyer
about the quality of its offerings. All greenhouse frames are
of kiln-dried redwood, which is highly resistant to insects and
rot. The kits are carefully cut and pre-drilled. Doors, ridge
beams, and vent frames are preassembled before shipping.
The hardware is sorted and individually bagged. The instructions are direct and illustrated with large drawings. Larger
designs have corrugated fiberglass panels which, in addition
to providing necessary illumination, are structurally very

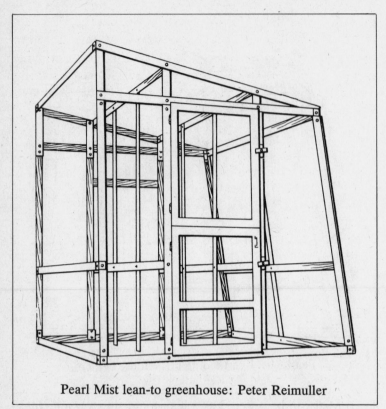

Pearl Mist lean-to greenhouse: Peter Reimuller

strong (in the direction of the fluting). Mr. Reimuller wisely mounts this material vertically to take advantage of the extra strength. His prices are extremely reasonable; and if I were interested in a hydroponic garden or other greenhouse application, I wouldn't hesitate to try out one of his designs. Write for his interesting catalog: Peter Reimuller—The Greenhouseman, 980 Seventeenth Avenue, Santa Cruz, California 95062.

Boats

This housing alternative doesn't usually come to mind when one is looking for a place to live, but surveys indicate that thousands of families live on sailboats, houseboats, cruisers, and yachts on a year-round basis. For some people, boating is a way of life, and their craft supplies the same comforts to them that a land-locked suburban ranch provides its owners. In addition, large boats can be purchased at only a fraction of the cost of a house. It is worth mentioning, too, that when moving time comes again, all you have to do is pull up anchor and sail to your new location. Your whole household of belongings will just go along with you! This is one sure way of simplifying your move. In any event, if your new location has any water near it and if you are the kind of person who would enjoy the boating life, you should certainly look into this alternative housing opportunity.

People who live in warm climates should find boat living appealing, since weather conditions are suited to permanent docking. Boat living in colder climates where the shoreline freezes is problematic, as boats have to be hoisted out of the water and dry-docked during the winter months. If these were to remain in the water, ice could form around the hull, imposing a tremendous force that could seriously damage the craft. However, many salt-water dock areas do not freeze, and boats in other areas can be protected by special anti-freezing devices, ranging from submerged heaters to products that create bubbles to prevent ice from forming. It is also possible to go through the normal dry-docking procedure and live aboard during the winter while the boat is out of the water. Your local marina may or may not have the means to accommodate this arrangement, so be sure to find out before you buy a boat.

People in colder regions also must consider the cost of heating their vessel, since most boats are not equipped for prolonged heating seasons. The exceptions are craft into which conventional heating systems can be installed. Some live-aboard families even use wood-burning stoves to heat the interior. There seem to be solutions to all the problems of docking and weather, and the amount of planning and effort involved is based on where in the country you plan to live.

Before you run out to look at the new- and used-boat markets, you should know something about the different boat sizes available. While boats come in a wide assortment of shapes and sizes, only the larger ones are really suited to full-time living. Generally speaking, this would mean a boat at least 25 feet in length, with those over 35 feet just beginning to provide comfort. However, many important marine maintenance functions are priced according to the size of the vessel. Docking space, hoisting fees, dry-dock rentals, and hull cleaning are just a few services that would be more costly if you had a really large boat. Therefore, plan to buy a craft that is just big enough to give family comfort.

If you have no previous boating knowledge, get hold of someone who does and who can advise you on your purchase. Be sure to visit boat shows and collect the literature offered. If possible, rent a craft to live on for a while. After all, you must be sure you can adapt to this way of life. In any case, gather as much information as possible, so you can base your final selection on good, strong fact rather than fanciful whim.

The best way to find used boats is to look in the newspaper. Any area bordering a large body of water will have a number of retail boat outlets, which you can find in the Yellow Pages. Visit these to familiarize yourself with what's available in your area. Ask to see used boats that were traded in. Used boats are the best boating buys, since a large number of people stretch themselves financially and find out too late that they cannot afford one. Also, there are those people who trade up in size because their family is larger or trade down because the kids have married and moved away. Boats have a much better life span than cars, and it doesn't take an expert to see what kind of care has been taken in the maintenance of a used boat.

In addition to the local newspaper, there are swap-sheet advertisements. For the sake of interest, I polled my latest copy of the local swap sheet and discovered twenty used

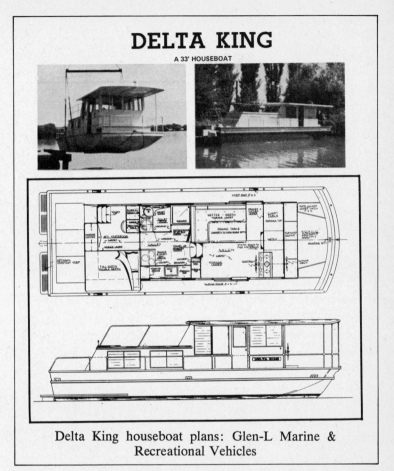

Delta King houseboat plans: Glen-L Marine & Recreational Vehicles

boats of sufficient full-time living size. Six were sailboats, ranging from 23 to 28 feet in length; and fourteen were cruisers, ranging from 23 to 36 feet in length.

Of course, another way to secure your own boat is to build one yourself. If you decide to do this, there are two companies you should know about. **Glen-L Marine & Recreational Vehicles** provides plans and, in some cases, full-size patterns for the construction of a vast array of boats. Their catalog starts with something as small as an 8-foot paddleboard and works up to a 49-foot Klondike cruising yacht.

Glen-L also can supply plans for houseboats up to 33 feet in length and sailboats up to 44 feet. The plans indicate that most of these designs can be built in plywood (Glen-L feels this is still the best and easiest way) or fiberglass. Fiberglassing involves the construction of a hull framework and the application of PVC Foam (Airex) or fiberglass planking (C-flex). Glen-L also offers a book on how to fiberglass, and some of their designs can be purchased as a frame kit to speed along hull construction. Their catalog of boat plans costs $1.00 and contains 129 pages of different designs. Before embarking on something as major as a "from-scratch" boat-building project, you should be pretty knowledgeable about machine tools and shop techniques. But for those who do have the time and know-how, this company can supply the ideas. Write to: Glen-L Marine & Recreational Vehicles, 9152 Rosecrans, Bellflower, California 90706.

One company that supplies top-quality kits is **Luger Industries**. They have precision-molded fiberglass sections that are factory-produced and can be assembled easily by the home builder. Their designs include cruisers from 22 to 24 feet in length and sailboats from 16 feet to their 26-foot Tradewinds Sloop. The Tradewinds has a sleeping capacity for four and includes a full galley and head. It supports 235 square feet of sail, which can be upped an additional 150 square feet by adding a genoa jib. The company indicates that the boat can be assembled in seventy to ninety hours. Considering the great savings in price and the fact that the Tradewinds is trailerable, you could expect the luxury of a large boat with the portability and convenience of a small one.

Luger's boat catalog is free, and you can write to them for it at: Luger Industries, Inc., 3800 West Highway 13, Burnsville, Minnesota 55337.

Log Homes

What with the current American interest in the "simple life" and the resurgence of early-American traditions and

Ward Cabin Company

crafts, it is understandable that people who want to build on a quiet and peaceful parcel of land imagine a log home as the solution to their nostalgic yearnings.

This revived interest in log structures has produced quite a few companies across the country that deal exclusively in re-creating these rough, sturdy buildings. Of the many companies manufacturing log homes, I've focused on five representatives which cover the distance from coast to coast and have their own unique approach to the art of log building.

On the East Coast, in the state of Maine, there is the **Ward Cabin Co.**, which has been involved in building log homes for over fifty years. The product they supply is a cedar log package prepared at their factory and shipped to your location. For some do-it-yourselfers, the ultimate challenge is to assemble one of these kits; but if that is not your forte, Ward also has a network of builder-representatives who are fully equipped to do the work for you.

Ward has twenty-six different floor plans, varying in ap-

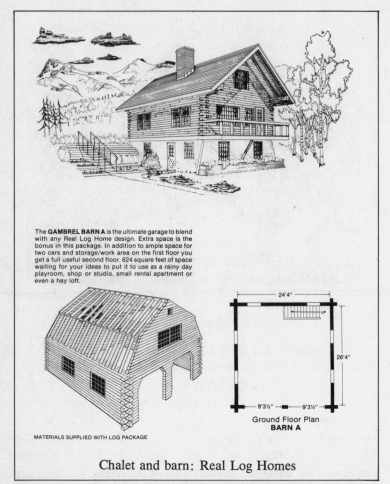

The **GAMBREL BARN A** is the ultimate garage to blend with any Real Log Home design. Extra space is the bonus in this package. In addition to ample space for two cars and storage/work area on the first floor you get a full useful second floor. 624 square feet of space waiting for your ideas to put it to use as a rainy day playroom, shop or studio, small rental apartment or even a hay loft.

MATERIALS SUPPLIED WITH LOG PACKAGE

24'4"

26'4"

9'3½"   9'3½"

Ground Floor Plan
BARN A

Chalet and barn: Real Log Homes

pearance from rustic log cabins to alpine chalets. Prices for starter kits go from $9,000 to $34,000; for complete packages, from $13,000 to $50,000. Probably their greatest asset is Ward's use of northern white cedar, which not only provides a strong natural insulation but is also one of the most durable woods known. The company takes the time to presand all interior surfaces so that the finished home can be stained, oiled, or varnished for a natural appearance.

If you are interested in log homes and live reasonably

close to their location, write to them for their current catalog of plans: Ward Cabin Co., Box 72, Houlton, Maine 04730.

One of the largest companies in the log-home business is **Real Log Homes**, with offices and factories in Vermont, North Carolina, Arkansas, and Montana, and franchised dealers in forty states and Canada.

Their homes are built of pine, and these logs are machine-stripped, dried, and treated against insects and fungus. Real Log Homes can supply kits for installation on your own foundation. These include 4,000-square-foot homes with two-car garages as well as 800-square-foot cabins. In addition, the company sells log garages and intriguing gambrel-roofed log barns. These barns are large enough to provide comfortable living space and should be considered as possible home alternatives.

Prices range from $1,300 for their modest 10 foot by 10 foot lean-to to $22,000 for their largest home. They have one of the best-illustrated and concise construction guides I've seen from any manufacturer, offering enough technical assistance to ensure that you can complete the building yourself.

Their well-designed graphic package of information is certainly worth getting. Write to the manufacturer closest to you:

Arkansas Log Homes, Inc., Mena, Arkansas 71953
Carolina Log Buildings, Inc., Fletcher, North Carolina 28732
Real Log Homes, Inc., Missoula, Montana 59807
Vermont Log Buildings, Inc., Hartland, Vermont 05048

American Timber Homes, Inc., of Escanaba, Michigan, is unique because of its collaboration with Solartran Corporation to create homes that are an interesting combination of the company's standard timber homes and the correct architectural and equipment considerations for solar heating. These were the first factory-produced homes to win a grant from HUD for their solar demonstration program and were

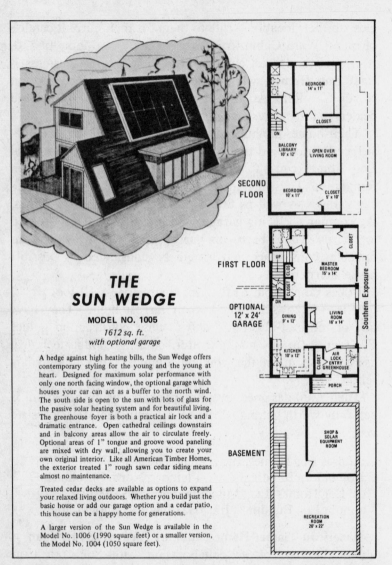

THE
SUN WEDGE

MODEL NO. 1005

1612 sq. ft.
with optional garage

A hedge against high heating bills, the Sun Wedge offers contemporary styling for the young and the young at heart. Designed for maximum solar performance with only one north facing window, the optional garage which houses your car can act as a buffer to the north wind. The south side is open to the sun with lots of glass for the passive solar heating system and for beautiful living. The greenhouse foyer is both a practical air lock and a dramatic entrance. Open cathedral ceilings downstairs and in balcony areas allow the air to circulate freely. Optional areas of 1" tongue and groove wood paneling are mixed with dry wall, allowing you to create your own original interior. Like all American Timber Homes, the exterior treated 1" rough sawn cedar siding means almost no maintenance.

Treated cedar decks are available as options to expand your relaxed living outdoors. Whether you build just the basic house or add our garage option and a cedar patio, this house can be a happy home for generations.

A larger version of the Sun Wedge is available in the Model No. 1006 (1990 square feet) or a smaller version, the Model No. 1004 (1050 square feet).

considered the product of the year for the state of Michigan in 1977. As far as I know, this is the only timber-home company that offers solar models. They can supply not only the entire kit for the home but also a complete package of solar equipment necessary to make it work.

In their brochure, Solartran mentions an interesting story about one of their employees who built a similar solar home in Michigan and for an entire year (April 1976–April 1977) racked up a heating bill totaling only $52.00. The company likes to point out that the employee and his wife spent more on birdseed than they did on heat, which underlines the economic viability of solar heating.

American Timber Homes, Inc., is not really a "log" builder, since they use logs only for the framework construction. Otherwise, they have panelized construction and conventional rough-sawn siding for the exterior finishes. They also have a broad spectrum of available designs, including some contemporary models. For an all-around home, and expecially for one that can be solar-heated, contact this company for their catalogs: American Timber Homes, Inc., and Solartran Corp., P.O. Box 496, Escanaba, Michigan 49829.

A company with a unique approach to log construction is the **National Log Construction Company** of Thompson Falls, Montana. Their fame is based on a specifically designed 6-, 7-, or 8-inch diameter log which is precut and hollow, and has a tongue-and-groove design, allowing for easier construction. The hollow space in each log enables it to dry more thoroughly and provides a channel for electrical wiring, a feature unique to the log-home industry.

The company has been in business for thirty-two years and has had extensive experience with this construction technique. Presently, it offers fifty-five different floor plans of log cabins, homes, lodges, and camps.

For more information about the company and their special approach to log construction write to: National Log Construction Co., P.O. Box 69, Thompson Falls, Montana 59873. Their book of plans costs $2.00.

Finally, there is **Pan Abode Cedar Homes**, the first company to develop a precut log system (1953). Pan Abode supplies 3- or 4-inch pre-formed retangular "logs" that have perfectly matched tongues and grooves for easy assembly.

Air-lock logs: National Log Construction Co.

The company uses western red cedar exclusively, and their special log design provides such a strong structure that only the first perimeter layer of logs requires nailing. They also have a double-wall construction, which is separated by a 4-inch air space to allow for insulation from R9 to as much as R27.

Pan Abode has twenty-five standard plans, ranging from a 320-square-foot cabin to one around 2,000 square feet; their prices begin at $13.50 a square foot for 3-inch logs, $15.50 a square foot for 4-inch logs, and $18.00 a square foot for 3-inch double-wall construction.

Because of their approach to log design and their contemporary plans, you might be in the market for what Pan Abode can offer. If you live near the Washington area, write

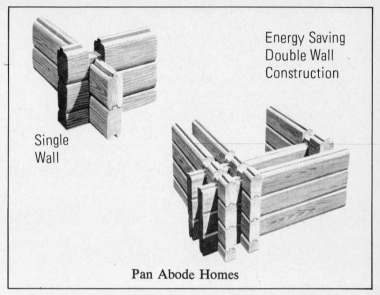

Energy Saving
Double Wall
Construction

Single
Wall

Pan Abode Homes

to them at: Pan Abode Homes, 4350 Lake Washington Boulevard, N. Renton, Washington 98055. They have a free pamphlet, but their complete book of plans is $4.00.

As you can see, the types and construction of log homes vary greatly from manufacturer to manufacturer. Of course, there are many more manufacturers producing log-home kits than I have had room to mention. Probably mixed in with those are some poorly designed and overpriced kits, so be very careful before you order anything; and by all means see a few of their finished models before you buy.

Site-built Houses

This last section deals with some ideas on site-built houses, those homes that are built on your land by either yourself or someone you contract. As more and more people are discovering lately, the finished cost of a predesigned, prefabricated kit home is not much more than the price of a new house in some suburban development. Although homes presently being built in tracts have such amenities as sewers and water lines, these may not outweigh a tract's negative factors, such as crowding and sameness. With careful land selection and quality installation of the septic and water systems, you will be far better off with a one-of-a-kind house which will appreciate as you enjoy it.

Home builders of tract developments are willing to pay the points required for HUD- and VA-insured loans so that they can offer no-money-down houses at apparently low prices. You may feel that you'll never be able to finance such construction, but don't underestimate yourself. People are able to find financing every day, and they do so by having a good credit record and by satisfying the bank that the construction is worth the investment. If you are using a contractor, his reputation should be good enough to impress a bank. If you are going it alone, be prepared to outline the house you intend to build, your qualifications as a "builder," and your ability to see the project to completion. Inform the bank whether other homes in the area have come from the same supplier, as these homes would be a barometer of the potential worth of your house. You may have to travel from bank to bank, and it won't be easy. But securing this kind of loan has been done . . . many times.

The different manufacturers presented here will offer a wide range of alternatives for a house built on your own property and, combined with the other nonconventional methods of housing, should give you a pretty good picture of what is currently available on today's market.

The first two companies are **Deck House, Inc.**, and **Acorn Structures, Inc.**, both from Massachusetts. They supply an extremely sophisticated and beautifully designed series of homes which are intended for contractors to install, and both companies have numerous representatives across the country who can supply such a service. As you might expect, their prices are in keeping with top-quality contemporary homes and include neither the purchase price of the land nor the cost of installing the foundation or well and water systems. But homes available from these firms are exquisite. For the

Various models from Deck House

Eagle's Nest: Acorn Structures

ultimate in contemporary designs, these two builders are on top of the current trends in architecture and design. Their homes are warm, comfortable, and humanistic in their approach.

Each company has a massive catalog of its designs, and one of the most beautiful graphic packages I've ever seen comes from Deck House, Inc. The designs are rich in natural woods, and many have decks, sliding glass doors, balconies, lofts, and clerestory windows. Acorn Structures can provide homes from 728 square feet to 2,358 square feet, and they are priced from just under $35,000 to over $70,000, depending upon the kinds of options you intend to include.

If you are truly serious about a luxurious contemporary design and you have the money to spend to buy the land, to hire a contractor, and to go through the process of having one of these homes built, then look through the catalogs these two companies offer. Write to: Deck House, Inc., 930 Main Street, Acton, Massachusetts 01720; and Acorn Structures, Inc., Box 250, Concord, Massachusetts 01742.

For something truly unusual, look at the products of **Yankee Barn Homes**. This company provides kits for do-it-yourselfers that allow you to create the scale and atmosphere of a traditional, massive-beamed barn. A number of the timbers used in this construction are actually recycled from old barns, mills, and warehouses that have been destroyed. It's a good way to encourage the re-use of many parts of these old structures, which are sometimes (believe it or not) burned down as exercises for firemen. Their constructions combine the unique aura of huge hand-hewn beams with the clean, crisp appearance of natural wood in a contemporary setting. The products have been applauded by many professional magazines, as well as receiving special coverage in *House and Gardens* (January 1978).

The designs are not cheap. Again, depending upon options, they range from $30,000 to $80,000, but the end result is so different and so appealing that you will probably

Recycled barn timbers: Yankee Barn Homes

find the expense worthwhile. All Yankee Barn homes are beautifully designed and executed structures. In addition, the company prides itself on their highly insulated roof design, which provides an R value of 30 that can be raised with additional insulation to R37. This is far greater than any conventional roof (the industry norm for tract houses is R20–25). So a Yankee Barn home would be an economical structure to live in and heat.

The company also offers a special opportunity for potential buyers who are not quite convinced about the value of their products. At their expense they will provide overnight accommodations in a Yankee Barn home at their New Hampshire location, as well as meals and recreation. You have to

Various models from Yankee Barn Homes

pay for transportation to their location, but they will deduct this price from the cost of any home you eventually buy from them. It is a hard deal to pass up. For someone who appreciates the old-time atmosphere and massive contruction of a barn, as well as the comfort and beauty of contemporary surroundings, these homes are worth considering. Yankee Barn will send their color brochure for $4.00. Write to:

Lindahl Cedar Homes

Yankee Barn Homes, Drawer A, Grantham, New Hampshire 03753.

My favorite company (because of the products they offer) is **Lindahl Cedar Homes**. These people have the most beautiful and varied selection of homes imaginable. As the name implies, they are designed and built of cedar for permanence and resistance to fungus, insects, and rot. Of the do-it-yourself home-kit suppliers, Lindahl has probably sold more houses than anyone else in the United States. The number of successfully completed homes is spectacular, and many articles have been written by proud home builders/owners.[11] After reading through their brochures and catalog, I don't think they missed a trick or technique. They appear to have better insulation than any other home, and they have optional extra insulation kits for really "tight" houses. For example, their standard wall insulation is rated at R14.9 (nearly 6 inches thick), and even their floors are insulated to R13.6. Their "polar-cap" roof insulations can create up to an R42, and all their windows are double-glazed, with triple glazing as another option.

Their very colorful book of plans costs $2.00 and is worth the price. It gives clear and concise information about the ease of construction and shows the great variety of designs and ideas offered by this company. The full-color photos are mouth-watering, and the practicality of building a home on your own land becomes more of a reality as you thumb through their outstanding designs.

Lindahl is a home that is designed to be built by do-it-yourselfers or to be contracted out (one of their representatives can do it). Even though based in Washington State, Lindahl has representatives all across the country, and they sell from coast to coast. Write to their main headquarters to find out the address of your local representative: Lindahl Cedar Homes P.O. Box 24426, 10411 Empire Way South, Seattle, Washington 98124.

I have included the **Hexagon Housing Systems, Inc.,** de-

signs in the book because, as far as I can tell, they have the only system currently based on the hexagon. The advantage of such a system is that modules can be added to any of the sides to form additional clusters, since, as we all know from our early geometry days, the hexagon is a close-packing polygon comprised of six equilateral triangles. This factory-prefabricated system is relatively inexpensive, and you can custom tailor it to your particular needs by ordering as many of the hexagons as you want to complete your design. The basic hexagon has quite a bit of space: 718 square feet. It contains two bedrooms, a full bathroom, kitchen, and living room; and because of the thinner interior wall design, it actually has more net living space than a conventional structure. It uses a unique post-and-beam construction; the posts are made of 2-inch steel pipe, and the beam is a 7-inch small-scale steel I-beam. This combination forms the framework which is imbedded in concrete piers. The wall system is pre-assembled and suspended into the framework.

This appears to be an interesting concept, especially in situations where modularity and the possibilities for exten-

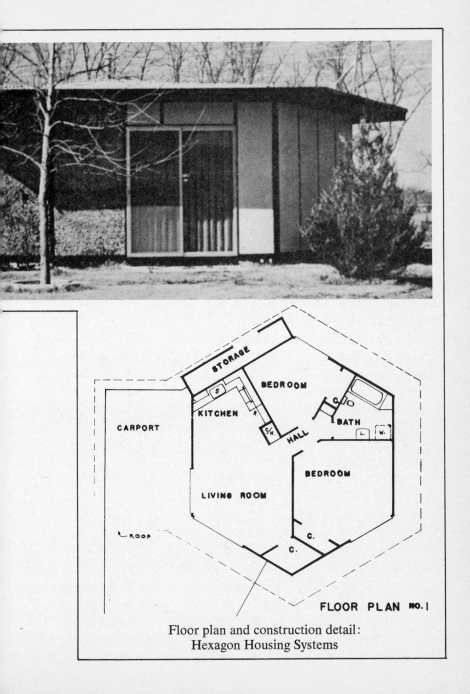

Floor plan and construction detail:
Hexagon Housing Systems

sion and variation are necessary. Some of the firm's plans are for multi-family or motel units, which may be extremely well suited to this type of design. Their package of information is $1.00. The prices are modest and range from $11,000 for the basic hexagon to $30,000 for a triple hexagon supplying 2,100 square feet of space. Write to: Hexagon Housing Systems, Inc., 905 N. Flood, Norman, Oklahoma 73069.

My favorite approach to modular housing is the one offered by **Shelter Kit, Inc.** This is the first truly modular, extendable housing system on the market; and because of the elegant simplicity of its module, the resulting single and combined units have a very nice contemporary flair.

The initial building block is called the Unit One, and it is a simple square module that is 12 feet by 12 feet in plan with a sloping roof ranging from 9 feet 2 inches at the peak to 7 feet 10 inches at the lowest point. The front is a full-width 12-foot sliding glass door, and the rear of the module has a 3 foot by 5 foot sliding glass window. To this can be added any number of other modules, such as the Porch Module, which projects 9 feet and has its own roof; Enclosed Porches, the same as the porch but with siding all around and additional windows; or Decks, wooden, slatted platforms. All their designs are combinations of these various modules, and it is surprising to see how different these structures can appear even though the basic units are the same.

Some of the real benefits of Shelter Kit's systems are that two people can easily assemble the Unit One in four days, even without building skills or blueprint-reading experience. The kits contain all the materials needed to build the module, with components quality-selected, precut, and pre-drilled. They take pains to keep each of the bundles of materials individually strapped to weigh around 100 pounds. This makes them easily lifted by one person and allows the structure to be carried to a site where there is no road. Other plus factors are that no power tools are needed to build the modules and that all the necessary tools are supplied in the kits. Shelter Kit even goes so far as to include two stepladders and two carpenter's aprons.

The modules use a post-and-beam construction, which puts the total support for the structure on six heavy beams. In this way, the walls are non-load-bearing and can be removed easily when more modules are added later. The heavy beam support is also the trick that allows for a full-front sliding glass doorway.

It appears this company has thought of everything, including shipment. They will deliver any of the modules within two hundred miles of their New Hampshire location. But for greater distances they will rent a U-Haul truck in your name, load it, then turn it over to you to drive to the site. After unloading, you just take the van to the closest U-Haul representative. As many as three Unit Ones can be put on a 16-foot truck, so this method of shipment can be really economical.

This small and conscientious company has had its products featured in many fine publications, including *House and Garden* (January 1976). The illustration I've chosen is their simple one-bedroom plan, which provides 450 square feet of space. It is comprised of two Unit Ones, one Enclosed Porch, and one Deck. In addition to the modules, it has a 12-foot sliding glass door, two 5 foot by 3 foot windows, three 3 foot by 3 foot windows, a junction kit, a set of tools, and construction plans.

I really admire this company's sensible approach to modular design, and I find their prices to be well within everyone's budget. This type of housing has numerous applications, from garden sheds to artist studios to small or large housing. For a system that you can build now and add to later, for a shelter that you can carry into remote locations, or for a serene little living environment that has a minimal effect on the ecology, this is the ultimate. Their kit of plans is $1.00. Write to: Shelter Kit, Inc., Franklin Mills, Franklin, New Hampshire 03235.

Building a Unit One: Shelter Kit, Inc.

Unit One with deck module (top) and porch module
(below): Shelter Kits, Inc.

The incredible array of ads for other do-it-yourself homes
suggests that the do-it-yourself home is going to be a strong
future trend, especially since we can all see the affordability
of professional housing slowly escaping us. It would probably be advisable to take a few night school courses in
woodworking techniques to prepare yourself for the next
eventuality: the home you build yourself.

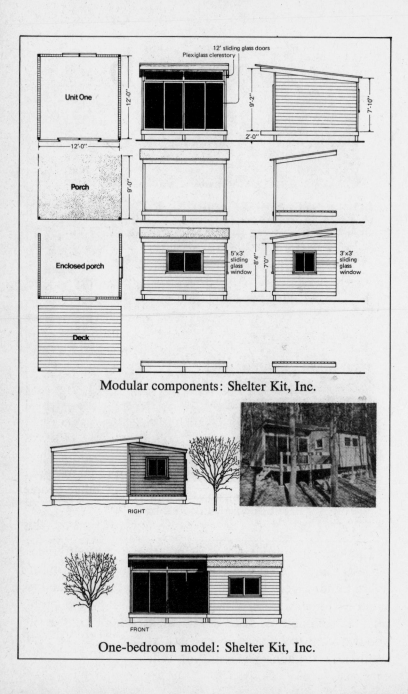

Modular components: Shelter Kit, Inc.

One-bedroom model: Shelter Kit, Inc.

Chapter 7

The American Dream

IT SEEMS THAT EVERYONE I SPEAK WITH THESE DAYS HAS a strong yearning for the time when they can cast aside the conventional life for a lifestyle specifically designed for themselves and their families. I call this longing The American Dream, and it can be summed up in a simple statement: "All I want is five acres of beautifully wooded land where I can build my own house, with a panoramic view and, perhaps, a pond or lake nearby." I used to think that *I* was unique in having this kind of a desire, but I've discovered that I'm just one of a great many people who view this goal as the one thing in life worth striving for. And, as I sit here on my own five and a half acres looking out upon the beautiful trees and rippling pond, I begin to realize that this dream isn't so far-fetched or unobtainable.

You've just been reading about the various types of site-built housing that can be put on your own piece of land and the booming market of kits available for do-it-yourselfers. The abundance and range of this kind of housing can make your American Dream a reality.

I feel that there is no "right time" to begin to pursue your dream, because while you delay, hundreds of other people are taking advantage of the economic situation and the current land market to buy up available land. If, indeed, this dream is a strong part of you, then there is no time like the present to start actively realizing it.

Buying Land

The availability and adaptability of land parcels depend on where in the country they are located. Beautiful, inexpensive parcels of land are hard to find in California, where the large population produces a lot of competition for anything of value that might enter the market. The only solution is to stay on top of the market and be prepared to spend a fair amount of money for that one special acreage you want.

In other parts of the country, especially toward the East Coast and outside the heavily populated big-city areas, there are tremendous land opportunities. The most beautiful rolling hills and wooded land can be found in areas of New York, Maine, and Vermont at prices as low as $100 an acre.

The first step is to be your own real-estate agent by constantly keeping abreast of all possible listings. In pursuing the land I now own, I was actively engaged in a continuous search for about a year and a half. It does take time for "all good things to come to pass," which is another reason to begin your search now.

Next, you'll need to find those listings. I have found listings for land parcels in four separate areas of our local newspaper. Land is a nebulous commodity in the real-estate business, and many people who are trying to sell acreage are not really sure where to list it. Try looking in such columns as SUBURBAN PROPERTIES, COUNTRY PROPERTY, FARMS AND LAND, or even BUILDING LOTS. Of course, the amount of land you buy is up to you. The American Dream of "five acres" probably evolved from the land being sufficiently large to "get lost in," while still small enough not to incur high taxes. But it is possible, especially in country areas where taxes are low, to have twenty or even forty acres and not pay that high a tax rate. Conversely, if you have your heart set on being near town, where the tax rates are higher, you might find that all you can afford is one acre or even less. For those who desire small parcels, you would probably find them listed under LOTS FOR SALE or SUBURBAN PROPERTY. The larger acreages would probably be under headings like FARMS AND LAND or even VACATION OR RECREATION PROPERTY. The latter seems to make a lot of sense, since panoramic vistas and large trees, as well as ponds, lakes, and streams, are all found in areas where people like to vacation.

There is always the local swap sheet, which often has a real-estate section where you can find inexpensive parcels of land being sold by private owners. My recent local edition listed twenty-one properties ranging in size from two acres to one hundred acres. Most of the listings advertised ten acres of land at about $1,000 an acre.

Another great way of locating land, especially in the area you plan to move to but are not presently near, is the seasonal catalog of the United Farm Agency. The spring catalog I have contains 288 pages of listings from forty states, from Andalusia, Alabama, to Wheatland, Wyoming. While it deals primarily with farms in rural communities, it does have a fair share of land and recreational properties, which would certainly give you a good idea of what is available at what price in your proposed area. The catalog, as massive as it is, does not contain all the listings that the United Farm Agency has, since there is not enough space to fully accommodate each of their customer-service offices. So, in addition to a copy of the catalog, it would be wise to contact the customer offices in your area of interest. It is possible to telephone the national headquarters in Missouri to request their general catalog and to tell them about your particular preferences. They would like to know, for example, the type of property you are interested in (farm, ranch, recreation), the number of acres, what your price range is, and what you can afford as a down payment. They need to know what state you are interested in and what region of that state (northwest, northeast, southwest, southeast, or central). Given this information, the national headquarters will alert all the representatives in your area of preference and will see to it that you receive their latest brochures, which will continuously keep you informed about all possibilities in that area. The United Farm Agency, like any other professional agency, does all this for free. If you want to write, their address is: United Farm Agency, Inc., P.O. Box 11400, 612 West 47th Street, Kansas City, Missouri 64112. They also have a toll-free telephone number, which certainly presents a quicker

214 THE NOMADIC HANDBOOK

way of getting a response. It is: 1–800–821–2599. (If you live in Missouri, call: 1–800–392–7790.) For those particularly interested in the West Coast, they have a special office at 681 Market Street, San Francisco, California 94105; phone number: 415–392–8831. The United Farm Agency has been in business for fifty-three years and has a nationwide reputation for honesty and integrity, so I wouldn't hesitate to purchase from them.

Finally, you can go through a local real-estate agency in your particular area of interest. If the area is "pure country," you may find that the only one is the United Farm Agency; but if the area has recreation or vacation interests, you will find quite a number of small-town agencies that deal specifically with local cabins, lake-front cottages, and other properties that continually come onto the market. Very often, a local person will list with his local agency, and the only way to find out about the listing is to contact the agency personally. Because many agencies are small operations, they don't have a multiple listing service, so they often don't know what their competitors are offering. This, coupled with the fact that they don't advertise much (advertisements take away from the profits), makes it necessary for you to spend a day with each one. In dealing with any agent, be explicit about your needs and interests. It does not help to be diplomatic about the properties you see, since the agent may get the wrong impression of what you like and dislike. You should, of course, be tactful about your comments in front of the seller, but do tell the agent in private exactly what you think. Unless you are as specific as possible about your needs, it will be hard for him to know when something you might like does come along.

Don't be afraid to purchase from a private party. Treat private ads in the paper as you would an agency's ads. Call, make an appointment, and talk with the owner. Look at the land with the same kind of concern you would show any other possibility, and be honest with the owner about your reservations. If you do decide to buy, have your attorney draw up a purchase agreement, which you can then sign. *Do not* sign anything or pay any money to the seller until after he has signed this agreement. The agreement should carefully outline the conditions of the sale as they were agreed to by you and the seller. Give him the opportunity to take the offer to his attorney; and if all is agreeable, he will sign in his attorney's presence, completing the contract. All of this is handled by the attorneys; they do all transactions and transfers, as well as the financial calculations. If you locate a private party and reach an agreement with him that results in a sale, you've not only done the real-estate agent's job yourself, but you've saved the seller the agent's commission (as high as 10 percent), which you might use as a bargaining factor in the sale. Besides, you may find that agents won't work hard for you if all you want is a parcel of land. Their commission is too small to justify their spending much time showing you possibilities, so you are better off doing the looking yourself. Be wary of agents who ask you to buy only through them. No one should ask you for that kind of commitment. If they have a listing you want to buy, they deserve the commission; but they don't deserve to step in on someone else's listing unless they've led you to it.

You may want to look just at land parcels or at parcels that have a cabin, house, cottage, building, barn, or whatever on them. In either case, there are some factors you should consider.

An undeveloped parcel of land is usually exactly that. It has no amenities on it: no water, no sewer, no well, no electricity, no telephone. In the real-estate market, this would be the least expensive kind of purchase; but you would have to do a lot of preparation and spend additional money before you could live permanently on the land.

On the other hand, you might find a similar parcel of land with a cabin on it. A waste disposal system and water well may have already been put in, and electricity may have already been run to the property, saving you quite a sum of money. Of course, a parcel of land with a cabin or cottage on it is much more expensive than undeveloped land, and you will have to determine whether the additional expense is warranted, given the condition of the building and amenities that are provided. But a small, simple cabin can be a smart purchase, since it gives you a livable shelter on the property while you prepare the land for your dream house. Even those of us who disdain mobile homes might consider a piece of property with one on it which could be used just as temporary housing.

Either situation affects your ability to secure a mortgage. As a rule, most banks do not finance undeveloped land. (It's almost impossible to find a bank that will do so.). For this reason, you have to be prepared to purchase your land with cash or, if you are lucky, to find a seller willing to hold a private mortgage for you. Most sellers realize the problems of mortgaging through a bank; and those who are anxious to sell will be willing to settle for a reasonable down payment in cash and the remainder plus the current rate of interest for a period of one to ten years. This is particularly true of older couples who no longer need a summer place and can use the extra monthly income for their retirement. In some ways, the fact that owners are willing to hold private mortgages makes it easier to buy property by eliminating the necessity of dealing with a bank. However, you must be cautious with a private mortgage purchase. Be sure that if the owner holds the mortgage, you get full deed to the property when you take possession. Too many people buy under a land contract, which maintains ownership of the property with the seller until the price has been paid by you in full. Such a situation is just too risky. Were the seller to die before your contract were up, who knows where the land deed would go. Some distant relative might even have the right to oust you from your land.

But for a piece of property with the most modest cabin, you might be able to find bank financing. If you intend to live in the cabin year-round while you are building, you'll find that the bank may indeed arrange a mortgage for you. You will also want sufficient funds to pay for your new house construction, so you may be able to work out a "package deal" with the bank in which a portion of the loan collateral would be the value of the land and the cabin on it. While this is not easy to do, it is still much easier to do than to secure a bank loan for an undeveloped parcel of land.

After what will seem like a long and tedious search, you will probably find the perfect parcel of land; but before you run out to buy it, read the next three sections on zoning, water, and sewage systems to determine whether the land will work as a year-round, habitable location.

Zoning

Every small area of every state has its own zoning ordinances that both allow for and prohibit certain types of construction. Before you buy a parcel of land, you should be aware of any zoning restrictions or requirements. You may find that the particular type of building you want to erect is restricted or prohibited. You may find that because of certain flood-plain conditions, you cannot install the well you need. You may find that your interest in a particular type of septic system or composting toilet is prohibited. Or because of improper drainage to a neighbor's property, you won't be able to direct your septic-leach lines as you had intended. So know the zoning ordinances before you buy your land.

You can obtain a copy of the zoning laws for your township by going to the local town hall. Most places charge a small fee to cover printing and handling costs. In addition, get a map of the zoning area so you can identify the location of your property. Each area on a zoning map represents a different zoning district, and each district has different regulations. For example, within my zoning area there are districts that require a minimum of five acres for lot sizes, a minimum of two acres, a minimum of one acre, and a mini-

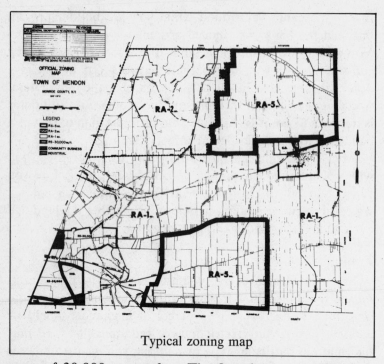

Typical zoning map

mum of 30,000 square feet. The first three are called agricultural districts; the last, a suburban-residential district. In
the five-acre agricultural district, it would be impossible to
buy a parcel of land less than five acres in size. If you
bought, let's say, six acres, you couldn't divide it and sell less
than five acres to someone else. So your first consideration
should be whether the zoning law allows for a parcel of land
the size you intend to buy and whether it could be divided up
later if you found it necessary to do so.

All zoning laws provide for careful scrutiny of any construction. Generally speaking, you cannot erect, alter, or
move a building without notifying the zoning board and
getting their expressed permission. While a zoning board
usually does not require a site plan except for large-scale
multi-unit developments, it does require that you submit a
written proposal detailing everything you plan to do on your

property. Of course, a carefully drawn site plan would help clarify questions of boundary lines and encroachment, so if you have the ability, draw one up.

Some of the other areas over which the board has control include limitations to the height or bulk of a structure; limits to the size and number of families that occupy any structure; specifications for the size of rear, front, and side yards; and provisions for how close any structure can be placed to the boundary lines of a lot. The zoning laws might severely limit your having an auto repair garage in your front yard or chickens in your backyard. The laws in my area, for instance, prohibit the installation of a mobile home but make an allowance for a mobile home used as a temporary residence while "construction is diligently pursued." This allowance has a two-year limitation and requires that the mobile home be removed from the property by that time. There are limitations to swimming pools and where they can be installed, as well as to the placing of fences and hedges. There are also "set-back" requirements, outlining how close your structure can be to a state, county, or town highway.

In the event that you find yourself in conflict with one of the zoning requirements, you can ask for a variance from the codes. You have to put this request in written form and submit it to the zoning board. They, in turn, will review it at one of their meetings; and you may be permitted to speak on your behalf. If you can make a clear enough case for yourself and if your changes will affect only you and your own land, then your request stands a pretty good chance of being approved. You could run into problems if your intended change might affect your neighbors or if the guy next door has already lodged a complaint against you. In these cases, you may have to forego your plans and devise new ones.

Some of the other important aspects of zoning affect water and septic or sewer systems on your property. These will be discussed in the next two sections.

Water Systems

If the parcel of land you own is in an incorporated area, you may have the benefit of an already installed water main adjacent to the road your property is on. With the permission of the local water authority, you can hook into this main to provide water for your new house. Normally, this necessitates hiring someone authorized by the water authority to install a valve at the main. This allows you to run a ¾-inch, 1-inch, or 1¼-inch-diameter copper line into the house, where a metering device and a shut-off valve will be installed. In addition to the labor costs for installation, you must pay for the materials necessary to run the line from the main at the street to the foundation of your home. (This procedure is very similar for a gas-line or sewer hook-up as well.)

Should you be building out in the country where the luxury of a water main at the curb doesn't exist, you will have to have a water well drilled. Depending upon how your land is situated, a well could become an expensive proposition. To get an idea what it would cost, poll your nearest neighbors on the depth of their wells. Since you pay by the foot to have a water well drilled, the depth of your neighbors' wells will be a good indication of how deep yours will have to be. On the average, water is normally found somewhere between 20 and 200 feet down. The really costly wells are those that must go deeper than the 200-foot level before water is found. Sometimes, if water cannot be found at this depth, another location must be chosen and another well begun. So up goes the cost. If you are lucky, however, you will have a water table not more than 20 feet down. It is conceivable for wells that shallow to be hand-dug. In the old days, a hand-dug well was wide enough (3 or 4 feet) to allow a bucket or container to be lowered into it to bring the water out, and was carefully lined with boulders to keep it from caving in. Of course, in this day and age, gasoline or electric pumps take over the task of bringing out water, and there isn't any need for a large and rather unsafe hole in the ground. While the well can still be dug by hand, after the insertion of a draw-pipe for the pump, it should be covered over. In addition to safety, another good reason to avoid an open well is that things can fall into it, contaminating your drinking water.

There are a couple of tests that should be performed as soon as water is located. First, send a sample of the water to the Water and Conservation Department for analysis. If the analysis proves the water to be clean and drinkable, then have a flow-rate test done on the well. This test determines how much water can be drawn from the well in a continuous manner without draining the well dry. Your flow rate will be very dependent upon the seasons. During the spring thaw, you will have a tremendous rate, but by the latter part of the summer, you may have hardly any water at all. For this reason, it is a good idea to have the well drilled as soon as possible so you can test it for a full year prior to building. If it dries up during the summer, you may have to sink a new or deeper well. Determining the flow rate will also help you plan your water system so that it contains enough storage capacity to accommodate your family's needs.

Before you actually get into the operation of digging a well, call upon someone in your area who has experience in this field and who can advise you on the best system of water delivery and storage for your location. In some rural areas, the best way to locate water on your property is to hire a dowser. This is a person who uses a Y-shaped stick, or divining rod, to sense vibrations from the earth where water is located. Such people may be ridiculed in some scientific communities, but their ability to locate underground water sources is unparalleled. I have heard of sophisticated, professional drilling firms that hire the services of a dowser to confirm the accuracy of their sonar equipment.

There are two types of well pumps. One is electric, looks like a long, metallic cylinder, and is submerged into the well head. Its outlet pipe and electric cable are buried below the frost line to provide a water service that won't freeze up during the winter. The only impact on the ecology of your lawn is a marker of some kind enabling you to locate the well head if repairs are needed. Other well pumps are designed to operate aboveground and can be either electric or gasoline, depending on your power situation. This type of pump is usually mounted above the well head on a concrete slab and protected against the weather by a small shed. To eliminate freeze-up in wintertime, however, the pump should be mounted in the basement and a water line run below the frost line from the well head to the basement.

An additional source of water is a pond. If the terrain and ground conditions on your land are suitable, a pond can be enjoyable to look at, pleasurable to swim in, a source of water for livestock and for fish breeding. If for no other reason, you should consider the addition of a pond for fire protection, especially where the flow rate of the water well is insufficient to provide abundant water on a continuous basis. The usual procedure is to have a gasoline-engine pump mounted in a protective shed near the pond with enough hose to reach from the pond to the house. In the event of a fire, you have an immediate source of water in great volume which will operate even if the electrical system cuts out (as is often the case in fires).

Ponds are made by simply scooping out an area and building up thick walls of dirt, which act as a reservoir or dike. There are local people who have the bulldozers and back hoes necessary to do this kind of work, and they usually charge by the hour. It would be good to have as large a pond as your land (and budget) will allow. For swimming, plan to have one end shallow. The pond should be around 6 to 10 feet deep, and try to locate it near some trees, since shading from the sun is good for limiting algae growth. Keeping the pond clean and clear of growth, as well as occasionally treating it with copper sulfate, will ensure a beautful pond and good swimming conditions. If you have live springs on your land, it would be wise to feed them into the pond to keep the water level up during the summer months. Otherwise, you can rely on natural water drainage from higher ground, along with occasional "boosts" from your well.

Waste Disposal Systems

Again, if your land or lot is in an improved area, then hook-up to sewer lines can be made at the curb. This was once relatively expensive, since heavy cast iron or steel pipe had to be laid. But most locations now allow the use of the large-diameter PVC plastic pipes, which come in 10-foot lengths. The only expenses you incur when hooking up to a sewer main are the cost of the pipe, the cost of having a trench dug from the street to your foundation below the frost line, and the cost of the plumbing work. This pipe must be placed so that it runs downhill from the utilities in your home. If you are constructing a prefab or kit home, most of this work has already been designed for you, and the sewer-line locations are indicated in the blueprints. But if you are building from scratch, you must make sure that every sink, toilet, shower, and bathtub, as well as the laundry drain, runs downhill to a central point in the basement and that this central point is a downhill run to the sewer main at the curb. The person you hire to dig the trench has probably done a number of these installations before and can advise you in your planning.

For parcels of land in undeveloped areas, the installation of a septic system can be quite costly, and this will depend entirely on the type of terrain the land is composed of. A correctly designed septic system has a number of components. The waste is collected from the house in a central waste pipe, which runs underground (roughly 40 feet from the house) to a large collection tank. This tank is buried below ground, and its size is determined by the number of people who will be using the system. If your soil is relatively soft, digging and installing this tank will be a less costly operation. The tank acts as both a settling tank for the collection of wastes that remain solidified or nondegradable and as a distribution center to a number of leach lines, which are perforated to allow the liquid wastes to leach into the soil. In some installations, it is necessary to go from the settling tank to a special leach distribution tank and then to the leach lines. This is particularly the case if the leach lines must be carried some distance from the house location. Since the settling tank is a collector for solid, nondegradable wastes, it must be cleaned out periodically. You should mark the location of the tank or provide an access hatch for the purpose of cleaning. Depending upon usage, the tank might have to be cleaned from every two to five years at an average cost of $60.

The ability of your soil to absorb water is going to determine the length and number of leach lines your septic system will need. Here is where septic installation can seriously affect the purchase of a parcel of land. I have heard of instances where people have bought a beautiful acre lot and discovered that because of the hardness of the soil, they would need at least four or five acres for effective leaching. Since they didn't own enough land to install an adequate septic system, the zoning board wouldn't allow them to build, and they were stuck with an unusable parcel of land. There are some areas in New York State where the soil, because of its clay composition, is so hard that zoning requires a minimum of *ten acres* for every single-family construction. So before you buy land, you must know how well it will absorb water. Fortunately, there is a simple test—called the percolation test—that you can perform yourself. The results of this test will tell you how many lineal feet of perforated pipe you will need for effective leaching. After determining the number of feet, you can do a rough sketch of a system for your land by drawing a plan view in an appropriate scale and trying to fit the correct length of leach pipes within your boundary lines. You must keep in mind that each leach line has to be at least 6 feet from the others. More than likely,

INSTRUCTIONS FOR DOING PERCOLATION TEST

(a) Dig or bore a hole with straight sides having a width of about 12 inches to the estimated depth of the proposed absorption trenches (not over 30 inches) in center of the proposed leach area (approximately 40 feet from house.).

(b) Prior to making the tests fill the hole with water and allow it to completely seep away. After the water has seeped away, remove any soil, etc. that has fallen on the sides of the holes.

(c) Fill the hole with water to a depth of 6 inches.

(d) Observe and record the time in minutes required for the water to drop 1 inch (from 6 inches to 5 inches).

(e) Repeat the test (as called for in c and d above) until the time for the water to drop 1 inch for two successive tests gives approximately equal results. (Within 10%) The last test will then be taken to represent the stabilized rate of percolation. The time recorded for this test will be used as the basis of design in determining the square feet of leaching or absorption area required for the subsurface sewage disposal works.

(f) Do not backfill test hole, cover with a board and mark with stake.

PERCOLATION TEST
INTERPRETATION TABLE
Lineal Feet of Tile or Perforated Pipe Required
in Trenches 2 Feet Wide

TIME FOR 1" DROP	FOR TWO BEDROOM HOME	FOR THREE BEDROOM HOME	FOR FOUR BEDROOM HOME
0 – 5	125	187	250
6 – 7	150	225	300
8 – 10	167	250	333
11 – 15	188	281	375
16 – 20	214	321	429
21 – 30	250	375	500
31 – 45	300	450	600
45 – 60	SPECIAL DESIGN REQUIRED CONSULT WITH COUNTY HEALTH DEPARTMENT		

MINIMUM DISTANCE BETWEEN LEACH LINES: 6 FEET CENTER TO CENTER

your zoning board will want to know the results of a percolation test before they grant you a building permit, so it pays to do this test as soon as you locate a parcel of land you're interested in buying. The results of the test could very well dictate whether or not you make that purchase. Of course, you can always buy a larger parcel or ask the zoning board about their attitudes toward a composting toilet or organic waste system.

To help you with the design process, contact the person who will do the excavating and installation of the system. He will usually provide free advice if he knows you are a future customer.

Another problem area regarding waste disposal is the possibility of contaminating ponds, streams, or underground water tables. Some people who have done their own installations and have tried to cut expenses through shortcuts have paid for it in the long run by contaminating their own water supply. This is bad enough; but there is also the risk of contaminating a neighbor's water system, in which case you could face a lawsuit from him. Since you will want to do everything you can (including spending a little more money if necessary) to preserve the ecology of your land, have the design and placement of the leach lines checked out by someone with expertise in those fields.

There is an alternative to a septic system and that is the use of the composting toilet. The composting system is not a new idea but an old one that has finally begun to find acceptance. Probably one of the largest suppliers of these types of toilets is **Enviroscope inc.,** which manufactures the Toa-Throne.

The Toa-Throne is a very simple and well-designed device. It is basically a large fiberglass container over which a conventional-looking toilet is attached. Toilet wastes, as well as kitchen scraps and other biodegradable material, are collected in the bottom of this container and begin a process of decomposition through the use of microorganisms, air, and

HOW IT OPERATES

1 . Body waste and garbage enter container through toilet stool.

2 . Electric blower draws in air to carry evaporated liquid from container (if electricity is unavailable, convection created by heat from process is used for ventilation). Gases are drawn off with air through ventilation pipe — no odor escapes into room.

3 . Longitudinal distribution conduits prevent waste material from packing together, insuring aeration of entire mass.

4 . Patented "air staircase" allows air to penetrate decay bed from below. Stairs incline downward and cannot be obstructed, permitting fresh air to circulate continuously through refuse mass.

5 . Waste is deposited on initial bed of starter material, prepared only once with initial installation. A new bed forms constantly as the waste decays.

6 . Micro-organisms decompose waste and transform it into humus at bottom of container.

7 . Humus is removed through access door one to three times each year depending on size of family. Humus has aroma of new earth.

8 . Inspection opening.

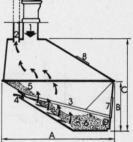

Figure 1

Toa-Throne composting toilet: Enviroscope inc.

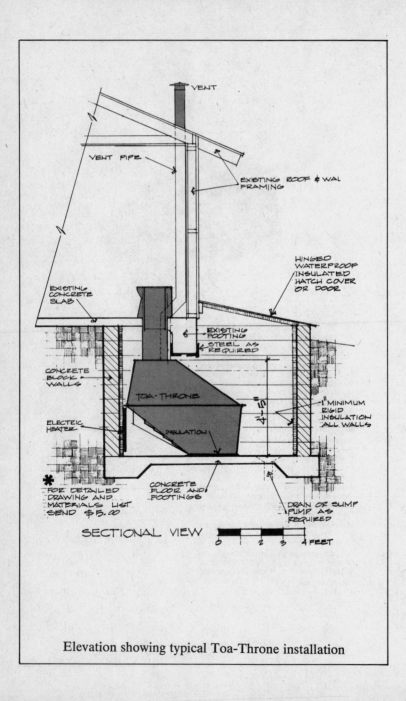

VENT

VENT PIPE

EXISTING ROOF & WALL FRAMING

HINGED WATERPROOF INSULATED HATCH COVER OR DOOR

EXISTING CONCRETE SLAB

EXISTING FOOTING

STEEL AS REQUIRED

CONCRETE BLOCK WALLS

TOA-THRONE

1" MINIMUM RIGID INSULATION ALL WALLS

ELECTRIC HEATER

INSULATION

* FOR DETAILED DRAWING AND MATERIALS LIST SEND $5.00

CONCRETE FLOOR AND FOOTINGS

DRAIN OR SUMP PUMP AS REQUIRED

SECTIONAL VIEW

0   1   2   3   4 FEET

Elevation showing typical Toa-Throne installation

heat. Liquids evaporate into the air, odors are vented through a special pipeline to the roof, and the remaining material is converted into humus (another name for clean dirt). Just like the dirt on your front lawn that derives from decaying leaves and other organic debris, humus derived from the Toa-Throne is tremendously rich in soil nutrients and can be used for all gardening applications.

At first, people seem taken aback at the thought of having a large container of decomposing human waste in their basement, but the hundreds of people who have installed these toilets in their homes can attest to the fact that not only are none of the negative connotations true, but there are incredible benefits to this type of waste disposal system. It doesn't use any water; it has no odors; it can use any organic or kitchen waste (which eliminates decaying garbage in your trash can) as well as human waste; it is sealed, so it won't attract animals or insects; it uses no chemicals or harmful products; it is environmentally safe and cannot pollute drinking-water sources; and installation is not difficult—in fact, it has been estimated that the average homeowner could install one of these toilets in a single day.

Although some people feel that the Toa-Throne is relatively expensive (it lists at a little over $1,000), when you compare its cost to that of a complete septic system (including toilet), you'll see that it will save you hundreds of dollars. But more important, for people whose property, because of its soil condition, cannot accept conventional septic systems, the composting toilet is the best solution. The only drawback of this system is that there may be problems getting the zoning board to approve it. However, because zoning laws do provide for individual sewage systems that are "approved by local health authorities," it seems likely that a homeowner could make a fairly strong case in favor of such a system, especially now that so many people, having installed and used these systems, have found them to be beneficial.

For more information, send $1.00 to: Enviroscope inc.,

2855 East Pacific Coast Highway, Corona del Mar, California 92625.

If you decide to use a composting toilet as the major part of your waste disposal system, you will still have to deal with waste water from sinks, showers, and laundry. It is possible to purify the waste water from these through the use of a trickle tank. The design is a simple fiberglass container of sufficient size that is buried in the ground. It contains layers of rock through which the water must drain before reaching the perforations at the tank's bottom. By the time the water has trickled through this rock layer, the soaps and residues have been eliminated, and the clean water is allowed to leach into the surrounding soil. The capacity of the trickle tank is determined by the number of sinks, baths, and showers in your home plus the number of occupants using them. One word of caution: the tank is not designed to deal with organic materials. As a result, it cannot be connected to a kitchen sink that has a garbage disposal. In any case, organic wastes should be put into the composting toilet. So, between the trickle tank and the composting toilet, you have a complete and efficient waste disposal system.[12]

The following is a checklist of questions you should ask about any parcel of land you intend to buy.

CHART 14.

LAND CHECKLIST

☐ 1. Can you secure a survey or tape map of the property?

☐ 2. Can you find a topological (terrain) map of the area?

☐ 3. What zoning clearances are necessary?
    a. Use permits?
    b. Height limitations?
    c. Set-back requirements?

☐ 4. Are there other review boards in addition to the one on zoning?
   a. Planning boards?
   b. Coastal commissions?
   c. Preservation committees?

☐ 5. What building codes are required?
   a. Road opening permit necessary?
   b. Septic system/leach field necessary?
   c. Percolation test necessary?
   d. Engineering plans and calculations necessary?

☐ 6. Questions for your lawyer:
   a. Can you acquire a preliminary title search?
   b. Are there any restrictions or covenants in the title?
   c. Are there any road easements over or through the land?
   d. Are there any utility easements on the land? Where?

☐ 7. Utilities?
   a. What will gas, electric, water, and sewer cost to install?
   b. If a well is already on the property, can you get a written guarantee of its year-round capability?

☐ 8. Dangers?
   a. Fire, forest-fire area?
   b. Flood-plain area?
   c. Earthquake area or fault line?
   d. Land erosion or slide area?
   e. Heavy snow or rain region?

After a run-through of these questions, you should be prepared to evaluate the land. Also find out the name of the local building inspector and ask him if any special conditions exist in the area. Everything you do will have to be approved by him, so you'll want him on your side.

Power and Energy

Your choice of a usable power source will depend on your location and the amenities available on the land. Of course, the easiest (although not necessarily the cheapest) method—if it is an option—is to bring electric power in from the road. This doesn't have to be very costly, especially if the distance between your house and the power source is minimal. The costs begin to pile up in remote locations, where the house is hundreds of feet from the power source. In this case, you have to pay the utility company either to install additional power poles and lines to your home or to have a heavy cable buried underground. Either way, you will be required to pay for whatever costs are involved: materials and labor, and even the electric meter on your wall.

Sometimes it is possible to work "deals" with the power company. If, for example, you and a number of your friends have purchased a large parcel of land and intend to build four or five separate homes on it, the power company may be persuaded to subsidize the cost of the necessary power-pole installations based on the projected income they will derive from the four or five homes. In any event, it is worth consulting the company to see what arrangement can be worked out.

However, you may be in a situation where no electricity is available, in which case a number of alternatives are open to you. You can opt to generate electricity from wind power, water power, or gasoline engine—or you may decide to live without it.

Wind Power

In certain areas, wind power is the most practical method of generating electrical energy. Typically, a tall tower is constructed with an efficient airfoil driving a direct current generator. This generator keeps a pack of wet-cell, automobile-type storage batteries charged to peak efficiency. Everything in the house is run from this bank of batteries, and the only requirement is that the appliances used in the home be able to operate on d.c. power. Fortunately, this is not too difficult, since the recent popularity of travel trailers and motor homes has brought about all sorts of lighting fixtures and appliances that run on 12 volts dc, not to mention all the conventional devices that can operate on 110 volts dc. (Most heating devices fall into this category, as well as a.c.–d.c. universally wound motors.)

Windmills can still be purchased new,[13] but one way to save some money is to scout around farming areas for an old unused or abandoned one to buy. Naturally, with the great interest in wind-derived energy, such "used bargains" are becoming increasingly hard to find, but there is no reason why you shouldn't give your area a close inspection before investing in a new one. Even if you are able to buy only the tower, you've saved quite a bit from the purchase price, since only the generator and airfoil will have to be bought new. It should be noted that some farm windmills were mechanical devices used to pump water up from a well to a storage tank. These old mills have the same type of design and construction, so if your land has a windy location, you might want to install both electrical and mechanical systems on your tower.

Water Power

If you are lucky enough to find land that has a stream that flows year-round, you may be able to build up enough of a head (pressure) to power a small turbine generator. The turbine operates in much the same manner as a wind generator: it spins at a high rate of speed and produces a direct current, which continually charges a bank of storage batteries from which the house derives its power. In addition to electrical power, it is also possible to derive mechanical power from a waterfall or water source. A simple mechanical hook-up could drive a water pump or ram, which could then bring the water from the stream to some uphill location for use. Given a stream of sufficient size, water can provide an ideal—and free—source of energy.

Gasoline Generators

For other remote regions or for areas where no other power source is feasible, there is the gasoline generator. These generators come in a variety of sizes, from small units producing only a few hundred watts to very large, electric-start units that could supply the needs of an entire community. Most of these devices produce 110 volts of alternating current, just like the voltage that comes out of the wall outlet at home. However, they are inefficient in terms of the energy they consume in order to produce energy. Likewise, the engine must run constantly, whether or not an appliance is drawing current from the generator. In addition, you have to provide a sufficient supply of gasoline (which can be quite a lot for a continuously running engine). For these reasons, some people have designed their own specialized systems which utilize a d.c. storage battery system that is periodically charged by a self-starting gas-driven generator. This eliminates the need to run the gas engine continuously, since the engine would start only when the batteries were low enough to warrant charging. Another benefit to such a system is that it could be added to a wind or water system as a backup for emergencies. Unfortunately, I don't know of any companies that presently produce a system like this, so you will have to take this idea and design around it.

No Electricity

There are many places in the United States where people still have no electrical power at all. Some of them live in rural regions where electric companies simply haven't installed poles and cables; but others have "divorced" themselves from these man-made luxuries because of religious or personal convictions. Somehow these people manage very nicely, and it makes one wonder what all the power we produce is used for and whether we really need it. For this group of people, lighting is accomplished through the use of oil or kerosene, which, because of recent safety developments, isn't as hazardous as it once was. Of course, entertainment like radio and television is out, as are a myriad of electrical devices that surround our lives, from blinking Christmas wreaths to electrically rotated necktie dispensers. Refrigeration isn't necessary, since the preservation of foods is accomplished through canning and conversion to food items with longer shelf lives. Treadle-powered machinery can perform sewing tasks and woodshop skills, while heating and cooking can be done on efficient wood-burning equipment. Needless to say, this is not an easy, luxury-ridden life. But the satisfaction of doing things by hand and not destroying the environment while doing so is attracting thousands of people to this way of life.

Alternative Heating Methods

Given the availability of electricity or natural gas, most people install conventional hot-water or forced-air heating systems. But what do you do if such sources are not available to you? More than likely, you would immediately consider heating with wood or, if you are technically capable, with solar power. Whether used as complete heating systems or in conjunction with conventional ones, these two alternative heating methods provide some down-to-earth and efficient solutions to thrifty, ecology-minded consumers.

Wood-burning Stoves

There seems to be a renewed interest in wood-burning stoves, which not only can heat your home but are energy savers as well. While many styles are currently on the market, most people unwittingly purchase some inefficient model, like the Franklin stove, which doesn't conserve enough heat to warm an entire home at a minimal expense. Efficiency is derived from careful control of the air that enters the stove to provide combustion. In this way, the rate at which wood is consumed is controlled, and thus the amount of heat produced can also be controlled. Because most inexpensive wood stoves have too many air holes to provide a controllable burning rate, you'll have to look at the more expensive and well-designed products from such foreign companies as **Morsø, Jotul,** and **Reginald,** and such well-known American manufacturers as **Fisher, Shenandoah, Stanley, Frontier,** and **Timberline.** Another feature to look for in quality wood burners is the weight of the cast iron used and the total weight of the stove. A heavy stove suggests the addition of internal baffles and ports that help to retain heat and disperse it into the room.

In addition to small wood burners, which are made for single rooms, there are units designed to be attached to conventional forced-air heating systems. These units yield heat throughout the winter and provide a conventional backup furnace for really cold days.

No matter what type of stove you buy, you should burn only good, dry hardwood. Pine, fir, and other softwoods, as well as freshly cut green wood (less than a year's worth of aging), will leave deposits of creosote in the chimney, which, if allowed to accumulate, could cause a serious fire. Likewise, it is important to keep the chimney spotlessly clean, and this is a maintenance task you should plan to do every autumn just prior to the heating season.

Solar Energy

People all across the country are developing their own solar systems, collectors, and other apparatus, some of which are ultra-simple, others ultra-complex. When we consider the amount of energy generated by that fiery orb in the sky and how little of it we are really able to convert and utilize, it makes us realize that solar power is still in its infancy. But every day there are more and more discoveries of better and more efficient collection methods, making solar power an increasingly viable source of energy.

The more complicated and technical solar energy systems use water as the heat-transfer medium, since it has very good heat-storage properties. Water is electrically pumped through large, flat collectors on the roof. As it goes through the col-

Energy House: Rochester Institute of Technology

lectors, the water absorbs heat and carries it to a number of storage tanks. From there it is distributed to radiant baseboard heating systems or hot-water outlets in the home.

Other slightly less efficient systems are based on the same principle described above but use air as the heat-transfer material. Here, air is blown through the collectors, where it is sufficiently warmed and blown back into the house. Very often, the heat from this air is transferred to a large bed of rocks, where it can be absorbed and stored. Both of these systems require a good amount of technical knowledge for design and some very expensive and sophisticated equipment for installation. In addition, the structure in which the system is installed must be adaptable to the large number of pipes and huge storage tanks necessary to make the system work. Simpler systems that work on the same principles can be purchased and retrofitted to older homes; and a number of these

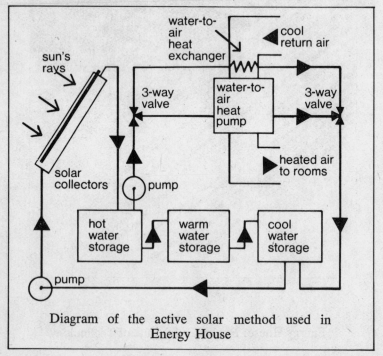

Diagram of the active solar method used in
Energy House

devices, from swimming pool heaters that mount on a garage roof to small water-heating systems to large solar collection panels that can be roof- or yard-mounted, are now available. However, there are a number of fly-by-night companies out to get into the solar market, so be very cautious before you buy.

I feel that passive solar heating systems are a better alternative. These systems are maintenance-free. They are developed through careful site orientation and placement, and a combining of various architectural elements to create a unique and purely functional form that will enhance the

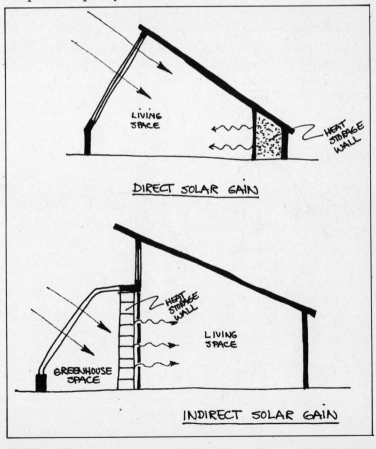

DIRECT SOLAR GAIN

INDIRECT SOLAR GAIN

absorption of sunlight on a year-round basis. The final result is not only an aesthetic place in which to live but an ecologically and environmentally integrated part of the land it occupies.

In these systems, solar heat is collected by sunlight penetration into a structure; heat movement is accomplished through convection and natural currents; and heat is stored in large thick walls of stone or walls comprised of water-filled barrels. The passive systems fall into two categories: those that are heated by direct gain, and those heated by indirect gain. In a direct gain system, heating occurs within the same living spaces the inhabitants occupy. In order to make such an environment bearable, the interior temperature must be regulated to the comfort of the inhabitants. The drawback, however, is that this doesn't allow heat to build up to its daytime potential, so that a maximum amount of heat to be used during the hours of darkness cannot be stored. In an

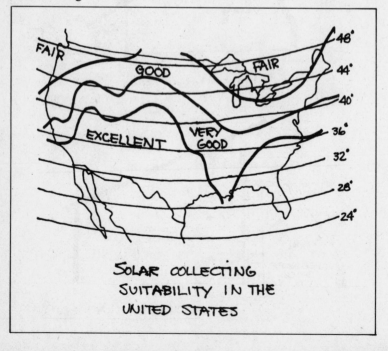

SOLAR COLLECTING
SUITABILITY IN THE
UNITED STATES

indirect gain system, a portion of the structure is set aside purely for the collection and storage of solar energy, and this area transmits its heat to the building (and its occupants) only as needed.

I could go on and on, as there is much to be said about the benefits of solar heat and the various types of equipment and systems that can be used or modified. I can only encourage you to look into the possibilities. The bibliography at the back of the book lists many books on solar topics, and a quick glance through some of them will highlight the benefits and perhaps convince you to adapt your housing so you can take advantage of them. These energy-efficient systems may be your first step toward the goals of energy independence.

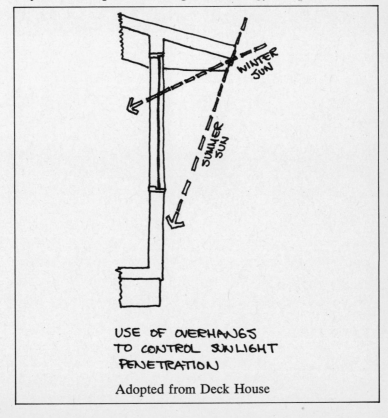

USE OF OVERHANGS
TO CONTROL SUNLIGHT
PENETRATION

Adopted from Deck House

Chapter 8

Adaptive-use Structures

IN THE PREVIOUS THREE CHAPTERS, WE TALKED ABOUT many of the ways in which you can look for and acquire housing in your new location. There is one other alternative worth discussing, since it can provide unique living environments. This alternative, which is ecologically beneficial and perhaps the ultimate in recycling, involves buying something in an almost unusable state and, with great creativity and imagination, turning it into a one-of-a-kind design showplace. What I'm talking about is the restoration and adaptive reuse of unwanted structures.

Spread out across the country are millions of structures that were originally designed and built for a multitude of commercial, business, and community purposes. Almost all of these structures have the potential of providing alternative housing. With the right kinds of additions and changes, old, drab, and awkward structures can be transformed into more spacious, comfortable, and elegant environments than you could ever afford to buy outright. In some cases, the structure may even have historic or nostalgic value to the community, and its preservation and redevelopment would be applauded as a way of preventing it from being destroyed or torn down.

Our discussion will begin with the more apparent adaptive-use buildings and progress toward structures that some people may not ever consider. At the end of the chapter, I'll give some examples in which agriculturally or commercially oriented structures can be combined with other architectural elements to provide solutions that are not only aesthetic and comfortable but energy-saving as well.

Barns

It seems to be of current interest to people who appreciate the rustic, "pioneering" look of buildings to adapt and live in old barns. As a matter of fact, so many people have taken on this type of reconstruction that old barns are becoming hard to find, although some areas have more than a fair share of barns available for adaptive reuse. Given the right geographic location, you could easily find yourself in a reasonably priced barn structure. (The barns shown in these photographs ranged from $10,000 to $24,000 and came with up to nine acres of land.)

So, what are the benefits of adapting a barn? To begin with, most barns are incredibly well constructed; and because of the massive beams and beautiful hand jointery, they greatly outlast the farmhouses with which they were once associated. They feature a self-standing post-and-beam construction onto which the siding is attached. Within the posts of the framework it is possible to have large areas of non-load-bearing materials, such as glass doors, windows, and other nonstructural components. By careful design, the barn could be constructed to have a great amount of light and window area. This type of construction also lends itself to partitioning interior space in any way you like and even to developing a modular grid partition system that could be altered as the needs of your family changed.

These structures also have enough interior space to accommodate almost any family need or function. Since many of the old gambrel-roofed barns soar four or five stories to the peak, there are so many opportunities for overhangs, lofts, balconies, and different levels that the interiors could become a veritable paradise for a designer or architect by offering more space and more alternatives for adaptation than almost any other type of structure.

Generally, barns are not insulated. A simple siding of some kind is nailed to the exterior. While at first this appears to be a negative factor, friends who have adapted these

Converted barn: Springwater, New York. This is
now someone's comfortable home.

structures tell me that this is the best way to start restoring an
old building, since it allows for easy electrical wiring and the
installation of superior insulation before interior walls are
put up. In this way, people who restore barns end up with a
better-insulated home than they could buy on the new-home
market.

Barns on a farm usually serve one of two functions. They
are used either to store hay or to house a dairy herd and
other livestock. Barns used purely for hay storage are often
located by themselves near the edge of a field, which can
make for a very pretty location. And, since the material originally stored inside was "clean," its restoration should be
relatively easy. A dairy barn presents a much greater clean-
up problem because animals were once kept in it; but it does
have some advantages, too. For example, the lower floor is
usually of poured concrete, which makes the barn much
stronger and weather-resistant. Additionally, a source of
water had to be nearby for the livestock, so most of these
barns had their own wells and pump systems. Adapting one

Barn and nine acres: Honeoye Falls, New York

of these could save some major expenses in terms of well drilling and water distribution. But either type of barn could be adapted to make a beautiful home.

Barns do present a wide range of interesting possibilities, and one can see why many people who cannot afford to buy an expensive structure might regard the reconstruction of a barn over a period of years as a better and wiser investment. Given some of the results I've seen, I must concur.

If you find yourself in an area where there are no barns at all, you can still have the charm and atmosphere of such a building by buying a Yankee Barn Home. (See the write-up on their offerings in Chapter 6.)

Railroad Stations

When I first began exploring adaptive-use structures, I realized that many people across the country were converting old train stations into homes. I assumed that very few such

And possible adaptation

buildings were still available. But I was in for a big surprise. A one-month search for these stations yielded *five* within a one-hour drive from my home, and all were unused and un-wanted. Apparently, these stations are just now appearing on the market as the railroad companies phase them out. I don't expect this situation will last very much longer once people find out about those that are available.

Train stations have tremendous appeal to some people. It could be that these structures evoke nostalgia for a once great American past. Many are historic and/or architectural masterpieces, with ornate trim and wooden carvings or flying-buttress supports. Some are wooden-framed with decorative clapboard, while others are made of brick. Some have shingle roofs; some, clay tile. Some are heated by coal stoves and some by hot-water radiators. But all are of a size adequate for housing and reasonably priced for reconstruction.

One of the problems with old train stations is their loca-

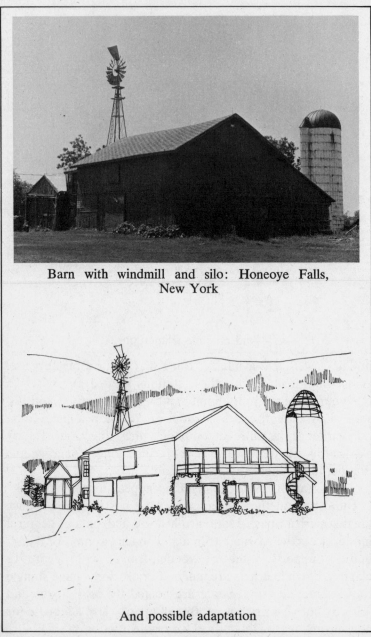

Barn with windmill and silo: Honeoye Falls,
New York

And possible adaptation

Train station, Honeoye Falls, New York. This one has been beautifully adapted for living by its owner.

tion. Because of their original purpose, they had to be located next to railroad tracks. While the trains were still running, these tracks and sidings were far too dusty and noisy to offer a pleasant living environment. Besides, the neighborhood aesthetics of railroad tracks and parked freight cars were far from desirable, which perhaps is why so many of these abandoned stations have remained untouched. Today, millions of miles of old track are being torn up for scrap, leaving these picturesque little stations to sit by themselves. Meanwhile, suburban developments, moving farther away from the city, are beginning to creep into the areas where these stations are located; and pretty soon these stations will be as much a part of a community as they once were. Location is, without a doubt, the only major stumbling block to adapting a train station; but if the future growth of an area can be anticipated, you might be the first one to recognize the potential of the old train station there.

Honeoye Falls Station. The kitchen. In the left-hand corner is the other side of the old ticket window, which now serves as a pass-through for food.

Most old stations relied on coal or wood-burning stoves for heat. Considering the high-efficiency stoves available today, this still seems to be a terrifically practical idea. Many are already plumbed with water and septic systems and have bathrooms, as well as electric power. A good number of these old buildings also have beautiful, natural wood wainscoting and seating for the waiting area; some have heavy oak counters and ticket windows; and many have high peaked roofs that can be turned into second floors or lofts with balcony overlooks. Because of these amenities, a train station might be a challenging yet relatively easy restoration to undertake.

When it comes to buying a railroad station, you are at the whims of the current real-estate market. Recently, I saw a small, totally undeveloped station in the Cape Cod area that

Honeoye Falls Station. The high ceilings and massive windows provide a light and airy environment.

had no water or septic systems, no electricity, and barely enough land to stand on, yet it was being sold for the hefty price of $40,000. I think you might find prices well above the $40,000 mark in other areas of the country as well, particularly the West Coast, while prices would be considerably lower in the more remote areas. But any old train station has the tremendous benefit of a great resale value; so no matter what you pay initially, there will always be someone who will pay top dollar for an already restored, tastefully designed home. There just aren't enough of these unique places on the market to satisfy the needs of this buying group, and I would consider a station a prime investment no matter where you live.

In addition to driving over the countryside and following old train tracks, you can find these stations by contacting the

Honeoye Falls Station. A large bedroom loft and beamed ceiling were created above this conversation area.

real-estate division of the rail lines in your community. These people can provide you with a listing of the available stations that are within a certain distance of your location and can tell you whether or not they are interested in leasing or selling them. Sometimes these structures go up for auction; but most of the time, they are purchased "behind the scenes" after an inquiry is made.

Finding these structures in an unrestored state will become more difficult as people pick up on the idea of buying and restoring them. So let this section be both an encouragement and a caution: if your interests are with one of these slices of American history, you had better get moving fast.

Honeoye Falls Station. In this view of the dining room you can see the old ticket window and original wainscoting.

Schoolhouses

One-room schoolhouses represent another quickly diminishing breed of structures throughout America. They were born out of an era when groups of neighboring farmers banded together to build a place where their children could receive an education. As the populations in rural areas increased, central school districts, with large, well-equipped school buildings, were created. This left thousands of one- and two-room schoolhouses abandoned across the country. A good portion of these were adapted into housing and are now almost indistinguishable from other homes in their areas; others were adapted into storage buildings for hay and equipment by farmers who owned the adjacent land. Unfortunately, a greater number have remained vacant and now exist in a state of ruin and dilapidation.

These old buildings have tremendous charm. Some have platforms and towers which once housed the old school bell; others have a double entrance, through which the sexes once passed separately. Most are situated in a quiet grove of trees, a location any homeowner would find enjoyable. Quite a few of these old schoolhouses have wells, and a large hand pump on the front lawn is not an uncommon sight. On the other hand, very few have indoor plumbing; and unless it has been vandalized, the old outhouse can still be found in some remote corner of the lot.

Most of the smaller structures were one-room environments in which all school activities once took place. The side walls usually have two or three windows each to allow as much natural light to filter into the room as possible. The front of the building has the entrance doors and is often windowless. Also windowless is the rear of the structure, since this was the area where the teacher sat and where the blackboards and map were hung. In one of the old schoolhouses I saw, the teacher's area was elevated on a step-up platform, creating an interesting change of level within the room. All of the old buildings have a tall peaked roof, which could accommodate the construction of a second level or loft and, with the addition of dormers, a second full floor. Somewhere within the interior is a brick chimney into which a large coal or wood-burning stove was once plugged for winter heat. None of these small structures has a basement, and some even lack a stone or concrete foundation. Many of the earlier ones were never wired for electricity, as they were closed at the turn of the century, before electrical power was widely used.

Finding an old schoolhouse involves long and tedious drives into the countryside and close inspection of every gravel and dirt byway you can find. If and when you locate a schoolhouse that appears vacant, contact the county housing department to find out if it is privately owned, publicly owned, or still part of the school district. If the school system has retained ownership, you must petition the school board to sell it. Barring any minor difficulties, most school boards recognize the benefits of selling buildings they no longer use and gladly welcome the profits from such a sale.

The schoolhouse may be owned by the town, county, state, or U.S. Government. It may be obtainable by paying off its delinquent taxes. These governmental divisions, wishing to reinstate unused properties on the tax role, are willing to offer great incentives to potential buyers. In some areas, for instance, they occasionally offer properties for $100 or $200 to potential "homesteaders."

A schoolhouse is an easy and fun structure to adapt. It offers quite a bit of design potential, yet its size is manageable in terms of reconstruction and expense. As a starter or investment home, it could be one of the best adaptive-use structures you can buy.

Churches

Not since Arlo Guthrie's "Alice's Restaurant" has there been such an interest in old churches for adaptation into private housing. For years people shied away from these fine buildings, convinced that it would be sacrilegious to alter their appearance or function. In the meantime, beautiful abandoned churches rotted to the ground, and vandals stripped their once-impressive walls and interiors of anything of value. This problem has been compounded by current economic trends. Today, all faiths are experiencing severe financial difficulties, and quite a few places of worship have been forced to close their doors. This, in turn, has brought even more church structures into the real-estate market.

In terms of adaptive reuse, there is one aspect of a church you cannot change, and that is its exterior appearance. After all, a church is a church, and many with tall towers and spires would be impossible to restructure except at great expense. So, initially, you and your family would have to be willing to accept and live with the architectural design of the church.

As a rule, churches have a tremendous amount of interior space. Many have full basements, which were used for church gatherings and social functions; and very often they come with a restaurant-quality kitchen. The main floor is a single, large space, usually without visible supports or columns, which, with the pews removed, provides a great square-foot area for living. Most churches have another level in the form of a choir loft toward the rear of the room. This loft could be continued all the way across the open area to make a full second floor; or it is possible to build a similar loft on the opposite end of the room. Most churches have such tall ceilings that an additional level could be built above the choir loft levels, so there is the possibility of having four floors of living space. In addition, the interior space of the towers, belfries, and steeples could be used for any number of purposes, such as a study, lookout, observation area, or even a "vertical" library. So the alternatives for interior development and design are endless.

Like barns, churches have a considerable volume of interior space that must be heated in the wintertime, making their energy consumption enormous. If you're living in a cold climate, one of your tasks should be to scale down the living area into something you can heat efficiently. This may mean partitioning off those spaces that are necessary to live in, and insulating and heating only those. Each successive year as you build onto that space, you can add another "zone" of heating until you have finally developed the entire building. This zoned heating system would provide separate heating for the different areas of the house. For example, the main body of the house—kitchen, dining room, and living room—could be heated by a hot-water or radiant system, with the thermostat set at a comfortable 70 degrees. Bedrooms could be heated by an electrical baseboard system, with each room controlled by its own thermostat. Heating in these rooms could be shut off during the day, when they are not used, and brought up to a cool 65 for nighttime use. At the same time, the main living area could be set really low until just before the family wakes up. The addition of efficient wood-burning stoves would also cut down on heating costs. But the time to plan and design this heating system is when you first begin the reconstruction of the building.

Because of a church's great interior volume and the fact that it has always been associated by the community as a "public" space, it can make for a successfully combined home and business structure. The layout is such that a store or crafts studio could easily be designed into the structure and still leave plenty of room for living quarters. Additionally, most churches have amenities that lend themselves to public access, such as easy-to-find entrances on main streets and ample off-street parking. Of course, re-opening the church for access by the public is another way of involving the community in your restoration project and dispelling the fears of those who feel that a church should be used only for religious purposes. This is true for the reuse of any structure that at one time served the community. The best approach is to take a positive and friendly attitude; a little P.R. will go a long way in helping the community accept you and your family.

If you can deal with and have the need for a large, well-built structure; if you are interested in combining your home and a business; if you want to live in something that is architecturally and, perhaps, historically unique, then a church will certainly meet your needs. In fact, a church structure may be so large that it would be more profitable to convert it into a two-, three-, or four-unit apartment complex as a means of recouping some of your investment and providing for the costly maintenance necessary for a building that size. Of course, such a multi-unit development has to be carefully designed to allow for the preservation of the structure, as well as for the privacy of its inhabitants.

The only way to locate churches that are for sale is to

check the newspaper listings and to drive through communities and become familiar with the churches that are there. You might also contact the local archdiocese of the Catholic Church to inquire whether any of their buildings are for sale. Follow through with similar calls to other religious organizations in your area. If your luck and your patience hold out, you will soon locate the ideal structure for you and your family.

Mills and Warehouses

Old mills and warehouses are prevalent in areas along waterways where water power was once harnessed to drive mill machinery. Small towns grew up around these enterprising mill structures, many of which now sit abandoned in areas of the eastern part of the country. It's not difficult to locate these structures. All you'll need is a good road map. Simply trace the major waterways to any town whose name incorporates the word "mills" or "falls." This doesn't guarantee that you'll find an abandoned mill in the town (nor does it suggest that mills are not to be found in towns with other names), but the chances of finding at least some old remains are pretty good.

In some towns, the mill has become a row of dilapidated warehouse buildings which have about as much appeal as a block of sleazy tenements. In other cases, the mill structure has been carefully preserved by the local historic group and now serves as the town hall, police or fire station, a restaurant, or some other business establishment.

But there is usually that one building that is apparently abandoned, unoccupied, and quickly deteriorating but has a good location and development potential. I imagined that, like so many other nostalgic buildings, it would be impossible to find examples of these structures for adaptive reuse; but, again, with a little effort in the right direction, I was able to locate a number of old mills, which by no means scratches the surface of those available. In the town where I live, there are two large mill buildings. The upper mill has been converted into a fine restaurant, and the lower mill was recently offered for sale by the town. A local developer is now carefully restoring the structure and creating a series of mini-shops and galleries, which are appropriate to this particular building. Not very long ago, a smaller mill, which had already been converted into housing and which sat right next to the picturesque waterfall, was sold for under $24,000.

So, these structures do indeed exist, and locating them involves weekend drives in the car, careful scrutiny of road maps, and letters to the town planning boards in those towns where you have been able to find old structures that appear unused.

Small warehouses fall under the same category, since old mills were usually stripped of their machinery and converted into storage structures years ago. Many people are now

Small mill, Honeoye Falls, New York. Now a lovely residence.

greatly attracted to warehouses because the venerable, oft-times brick, heavy-duty structures have a certain permanence and charm about them, as well as ample room for really spreading out. Old warehouse spaces for rent in New York City, Los Angeles, and San Francisco are fetching astounding prices as studios and lofts for designers, architects, and craftspeople. They offer not only room for a spacious apartment and a ceramic or weaving studio, but sufficient floor structure to support heavy machinery or large sculptural work.

The restoration of a warehouse is a simple process, as it is not architecturally necessary to hide the mechanics of the building, such as water and gas pipes, stove pipes, and other paraphernalia. Everything is usually run along the ceiling and brought down to the point where it is needed. Some studio owners mask this complex of pipes by spraying them

Grain mill. This is the home of furniture designer Wendell Castle and his wife, ceramicist Nancy Jurs. They have done a complete and extensive restoration.

Grain mill, conversation area

Grain mill. Floor-to-ceiling shelving brings continuity to the room and helps diminish the great ceiling height.

Grain mill. Loft space above the dining area provides a convenient location for projectors and a quiet, out-of-the-way location for reading or relaxing.

Grain mill. The living area viewed from the loft.

and the entire ceiling the same color, while other more out-going personalities prefer each pipe to be painted a different bright color. Old warehouses have high ceilings, which allow for the construction of lofts and multi-levels; multi-paned window areas; and impressive skylights. To the people who are presently paying dearly for them in the major cities, they are the ultimate in apartment living.

There is no reason why you shouldn't consider a mill or warehouse structure as a possible living environment. Even the larger warehouses could be converted into lofts and rented out for additional income.

The benefits these buildings provide in terms of their interiors are often enhanced by maintenance-free exteriors; flat roofs that accommodate sunbathing as well as repair (if necessary); and locations adjacent to streams, rivers, and waterways, which offer beautiful views. A warehouse in just the right spot makes an economical and wise investment, as well as a funky, low-key living environment with tremendous interior possibilities.

Storefronts and Firehouses

Storefronts and other small business buildings located on the main street of many a small community throughout the country provide a housing alternative of special interest to people who have their own businesses and want to combine their working and living environments. The first floor of the building could be made into a sales area; just behind it (perhaps partitioned from view), a small workshop could be set up; and the upper floor could be converted into a beautiful apartment.

These structures present a smart investment and ready sales clientele. There is a dream shared by many people, young and old alike, to return to a life of independence and being one's own boss. These people regard the prospect of owning and operating a small business as an ideal way of making a living, setting their own hours, and living close to

Residence: W. Bloomfield, New York

their work. For them, a small storefront or building in the downtown section of a town would be the perfect adaptive-use structure.

Almost every small town I've been through lately has at least one storefront for sale. This seems to coincide with statistics from the Small Business Administration that indicate that many new businesses fail after a few short months. While this is not particularly encouraging for people who want to start a business, it is encouraging from the standpoint of the availability of storefronts and buildings in the best market areas for one's product or service.

Other people buy these quaint little storefront structures with no intention of operating businesses from them. They simply want to convert them into living environments. They take advantage of the large front windows, which bring natural sunlight into their living areas, and they restructure the interior of the buildings into fashionable homes. One advantage to being situated right in the shopping district is that the needs of their families can be met within walking distance. This central location is particularly convenient in areas where heavy snowfall can prevent some people from getting out of their house. And, when the surrounding businesses have closed down for the night, their home is as tranquil and quiet as any house in suburbia.

Old firehouses also fall into this category; and believe it or not, these beautiful old structures do come on the market from time to time. What usually happens is that the community "outgrows" the firehouse because the fire district has been expanded, the number of volunteer firemen has increased, or the town has put through a bond issue for the purchase of a much larger fire truck. The next step in such a transition is the putting forth for a vote on a bond that will provide the funds for a new firehouse on the outskirts of town. This news is the signal to someone who is looking for an old firehouse for adaptive use to let his interest in the old building be known. With a keen buyer on hand, any town board will elect to dispose of the old firehouse before its citizenry has had a chance to vote differently. Keep your funds fluid, since you have to be prepared to move quickly when this kind of opportunity arises.

Most old firehouses had single or double garages on the street level, and living and eating quarters on the second floor. They are readily adaptable into housing because they have all the necessities: water, sewer, electric, gas, and heat. The conversions I've seen attempt to retain the charm of the building by keeping the brass pole, firebell, alarm boxes, hoses and nozzles, and anything else they could find on display. Such a building is easily renovated, and the results are worth tenfold the investment.

It isn't likely that you will find many of these buildings for sale any more. It will take much time to search, a great deal of persistence, and some good guesswork to keep you on top of the status of some of these old structures in towns near you. Needless to say, the waiting and planning are well worth it if you can land one of these for your own.

Railroad Cars

If the location is right and you have a railroad siding on your property, you might consider a slightly used passenger car, boxcar, or caboose as your next domain.

Passenger cars, especially those with rest rooms, make pretty good adaptive-use structures, and they boast some really exciting design features, such as folding racks for luggage, full-length hot-water baseboard heating systems, and folding drop-down sinks in the lavatories. Many an old passenger car was plushly appointed and adequately lit, and some even have beautiful hardwood wainscoting and seat framing. All have two doors and full-length windows on each side wall. Seriously, though, people have adapted these fine old structures not so much for their fascination and interest in trains but because they were able to buy them for next to nothing from a railroad that went out of business. Many a railroad passenger-car owner has gone through great pains to have the structure towed by train or carried by flatbed to its new location. Yet, given the great transportation expense, these adaptive-use homes were still a bargain, even if compared to other types of housing, such as inexpensive mobile homes.

Boxcars, while not very aesthetic, do offer as much latitude as possible in terms of adaptation. They have higher interiors than other cars and, because of their simple wooden construction, can be easily designed to accommodate windows and skylights, as well as lofts, decks, and porches. Recycled boxcars and a train station were nicely blended together at the Whistle Stop Arcade in Victor, New York, where they provide many interesting nooks and crannies for the arcade's unique stores.

Cabooses are great fun, but the railroad has more requests for these than they can handle. If you are on top of the situation, you might be able to get one; but like all else, it

Caboose: Schoen Place, Pittsford, New York.
Many have been adapted into houses.

takes a good deal of patience and being in the right place at
the right time. The caboose was the last car in a freight hook-
up, and it provided a comfortable bed and small kitchen for
the brakeman and signalman. People like them because they
have interesting interior spaces, with two elevated bunks and
a lot of beautifully engineered wooden bins and storage cabinets. As a small summer cottage or kids' annex—or even a
business office—they are quite in demand these days.

Call the main office of the railroad company to find out
who to contact about surplus or discontinued passenger cars,
boxcars, and cabooses. You will probably find the price quite
affordable. Now, if you can just somehow get it to your
property . . .

Silos and Towers

In addition to conventional, heavily constructed farm
silos, there are all sorts of observation and water towers that
have great possibilities as housing structures. Lighthouses fall
into the same category, but they are now so rare as to be
almost unobtainable.

This type of adaptation is for people who really like

heights and enjoy having a grand vista of the surrounding scenery. Living in a silo is sort of like living in a mobile home on end; each level has to be a well-designed and integrated area, with hidden storage and built-in comforts to conserve space. The top level is always a full-circle observation deck, with a commanding view at a dizzying height.

Silos are well-constructed structures built of special concrete staves, which are curved building blocks mortared together and banded for strength. Staves in new silo construction are designed to withstand the many tons of stress exerted by stored grain. A finished 20 foot by 60 foot silo will hold around 530 tons of silage, which is much more weight than any living environment would impose on the structure (even if you had a waterbed). For these reasons, silos are very solid structures in which to live, which is why you usually see the silo standing long after the house, barn, and other buildings on a farm have fallen down. A brand-new structure, including foundation, would cost around $15,000.

Many older silos were composed of beautifully fired red clay tiles; and because of appearance alone, these would be nice to adapt. Others were constructed entirely of wood. Because of the tremendous weight and permanent construction of silos, they are not movable once installed; but some, like the wooden ones, can be dismantled. Although tile silos can also be carefully taken apart, the resulting rebuilt structure will be shorter than the original, as many of the tiles will be damaged. The usable tiles can also be used to line circular stairways and to create roundhouse additions to other structures, as well as curved surfaces for fences or walls.

There are a goodly number of old silos around, and many are situated alone in the midst of a pretty field, a good site for a potential home. Old silos are practically worthless; in fact, I've heard of some cases where farmers have given away an old silo or barn just to have it dismantled and removed. But the land they are on does have value, so try to work out a package deal.

Silo: Farmington, New York. This little block silo is all that is left of a large farm that was cleared for a housing tract. Apart from the construction, this structure offers uniqueness in a suburban atmosphere.

You may look at a silo as temporary housing while you build another living structure on your property, or you just may want to live in a multi-level tower and explore the possibilities of a "vertical" life. In either case, a silo can provide a challenging and fun living space.

One might also find other types of towers as the search for housing and adaptive-use structures continues. I've seen some superb water towers with great potential. The one that comes to mind is a tall concrete tower that currently provides water to a small East Coast town. From its top you can see tens of miles of Atlantic coastline, and it sits in a beautifully treed area just outside of town. And when the town converts

Possible silo adaptation

to some other type of water system, you can bet I'll be there to bid on that exquisite tower! Other water towers (the ones on steel frameworks that are open and "skeletal") are perhaps less appealing, since they are really up in the air without a strong-looking support; but people who can adjust to getting up and down these structures will be glad to know that there are a lot of them around at reasonable prices.

In addition to that terrific view, a tower addition to your home could support wind-powered units for electrical generation and water pumping, giving the tower a utilitarian purpose as well as an aesthetic one. You could even ring your tower with balconies, decks, and catwalks so that each level has an outdoor area for sitting, sighting, and sunning. Silos and towers are remarkable structures with tremendous potential, and their somewhat limited space is a unique design challenge for the really creative person.

Barrels, Grain Bins, and Corn Cribs

These structures, generally cylindrical in shape and only one or two stories high, can be positioned in clusters to create another housing alternative. What makes adapting them such an intriguing idea is that they can be totally dismantled for transport and, like modular housing units, added onto as more space is required.

Wooden barrels large enough to contain an average room (10-foot diameter and up) are sometimes found in some industrial location. These barrels are made of rot-resistant cedar, redwood, or cypress and can be a great bargain if bought at a liquidation sale. Mounted on a concrete or pier foundation, these structures could make an extremely interesting group of forms and a very different style of house. It may also be possible to locate and buy an old wooden silo and section it to form one- or two-story units for clustering. Since silos are a bit more plentiful, this idea might be easier to realize.

Grain bins are also large, cylindrical structures that can be clustered like the wooden barrels. These bins are of a galvanized-steel construction and come in sizes up to 40 feet in diameter. Obviously, this is more than adequate space for a living environment. And considering this amount of space, they are really inexpensive. The grain bin just described runs about $4,500, including the roof.

After installation on a suitable foundation, the units can be sided or shingled like any other building. Cutouts can easily be made with a cutting torch and windows and doors installed using sheet-metal screws or pop-rivets and sealer. Protected from the elements, these large cylinders should last forever.

Another, even less expensive structure is the corn crib, a simple galvanized steel-mesh structure that comes with its own cone-shaped steel roof. A typical size runs 16 feet 6 inches in diameter and stands 23 feet high. Such a structure could contain two levels of space and be combined with

Grain bins: Palmyra, New York. Even these heavy, industrial structures have possibilities for adaptation.

others in any number of ways to create an exciting floor plan. At a cost of only $900 each, these cribs are hard to beat as a basic structure for a unique housing system.

Once the units are installed, they can be sided with vertical wood slats or their galvanized steel-mesh construction could be used as a perfect reinforcement for poured concrete walls. Even structural foam has possibilities when applied over this simple form. Windows and doors can easily be cut out and framed before pouring or spraying, and the finished product would begin to take on the appearance of a turreted castle or Spanish villa. The cribs can be assembled by a team of people within one day, since they are completely prefabricated.

There are probably other related examples of alternative-

Possible grain bin adaptation

use structures, but these are the only ones that came to mind or were available to me in the eastern part of the country. A quick look around the areas where you live might uncover some other tremendously adaptable structures or components.

Combinations

The combining of each structure or component just covered with every other could produce alternatives whose number would be far beyond the scope of this manuscript, so I'll gladly let you create these variations yourself. But before closing our discussion of adaptive-use structures, I'd like to present some of my current thoughts on combinations that could be used to create housing alternatives that would be both ecological and energy-saving.

Solar Heating

While a number of the newer concepts in solar heating use active systems, solar experimenters are finding that it isn't necessary to have so many pipes, pumps, and collectors cluttering up the usable interior space or altering the lines of the architecture. In a recent active solar house I toured, the designers were quite pleased that there was sufficient solar penetration through a huge bank of windows with a southern exposure (and enough insulation in the home) to keep temperatures at a comfortable range during daylight hours without the use of the collector system. (This system is used only for heat recovery and seems like a costly way to heat a structure.) If careful design of a building can provide for its own heat during the day, then a simple storage system and ample insulation to prevent the heat from escaping can heat it at night. For this reason, passive designs with neither moving parts nor high maintenance costs nor high installation expenditures seem a far better and more sensible idea.

The house I visualize is a combination of structures already mentioned in this chapter. *The core*, which could be any type of structure depending upon individual tastes, contains all the plumbing, most of the electrical system, and all kitchen and bathroom facilities. *The wings*, which are greenhouse structures, provide bedroom, living-room, and dining-room spaces, as well as playrooms and family rooms as needs and desires dictate. These structures are installed on deep beds of gravel over which a concrete foundation is poured and a final dark ceramic tile floor laid.

During the day, sunlight is allowed to enter the glass wings and heat the interior space. Heating is accomplished by the absorption of energy in the dark ceramic tiles, which as the day continues, transfer this energy to the gravel bed, where it is stored. Control of temperature for each wing is achieved

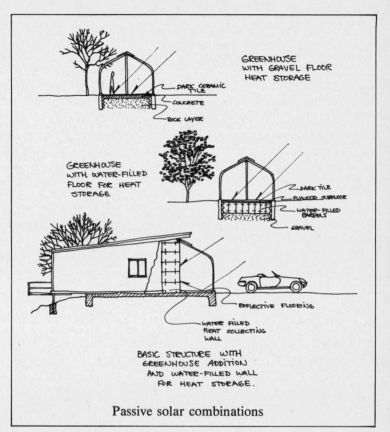

GREENHOUSE
WITH GRAVEL FLOOR
HEAT STORAGE

DARK CERAMIC TILE
CONCRETE
ROCK LAYER

GREENHOUSE
WITH WATER-FILLED
FLOOR FOR HEAT
STORAGE

DARK TILE
PLYWOOD SUBFLOOR
WATER-FILLED BARRELS
GRAVEL

REFLECTIVE FLOORING
WATER FILLED HEAT COLLECTING WALL

BASIC STRUCTURE WITH
GREENHOUSE ADDITION
AND WATER-FILLED WALL
FOR HEAT STORAGE.

Passive solar combinations

through the standard, automatic venting system that most greenhouses have. The venting system allows the hot air in the room to rise up to and out of vents placed along the entire length of the structure. This venting can be manually controlled or a thermostat can control a motor-drive assembly, which regulates the opening and closing of the vents. In the evening, interior insulating shades are used to keep the stored heat within the structure and to provide privacy for the inhabitants. The stored heat from the gravel bed will gravitate upwards into the room to give continuous radiant heating throughout the night.

During the summer, aluminum roll shades or reflective

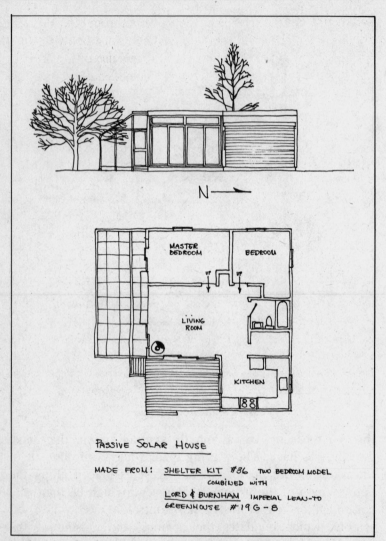

N ⟶

PASSIVE SOLAR HOUSE

MADE FROM: SHELTER KIT #36 TWO BEDROOM MODEL
COMBINED WITH
LORD & BURNHAM IMPERIAL LEAN-TO
GREENHOUSE #19G-8

mylar (and other mirror-like plastic) shading applied to the exterior of each wing limits solar penetration and keeps the building cool. During this season the gravel floor system will remain cool and act as a simple air-conditioner by absorbing excess heat from the structure.

The aim of any solar structure like this one is to maintain constant, comfortable temperatures throughout the year by absorbing the great temperature difference between night and day, winter and summer, through the use of a heat storage device, such as this bed of gravel under each wing. Of course, water has a greater heat-storage potential than rock, and it is therefore possible to alter this design somewhat to accommodate a great volume of stored water beneath each wing. Some systems presently use recycled 55-gallon metal drums for storage, which are stacked to form a wall. But given the natural convection of heat, I still think the floor is a better location and will more evenly distribute the heat throughout the structure by convection.

My interest here is *not* to attempt to heat entirely from the sun. In my area of upper New York State, total heating would be an unrealistic dream, so I would be extremely happy if such a system could substantially reduce my heating bills. Perhaps this system, in combination with a good-quality wood-burner, will completely heat the house.

I think the real advantages of this design are the availability of all the components and the fact that anyone could build it. The sketches show several other possibilities using various core designs and full or lean-to greenhouses.

Part III

THE
ADAPTATION

This last section offers some suggestions for the final step of the moving process: adapting your living environment to suit your needs, desires, and budget. The remaining three chapters discuss the unique situations of people who live in single rooms, apartments, and homes. Each of these living situations requires special design considerations, from interior design to architectural renovations.

Since the writing of the two *Nomadic Furniture* books, a great many books that offer further designs for portable furniture have come onto the market. People are now more aware of what kinds of things can be designed and created for their own "nomadic" lifestyles; and to my great pleasure, a growing number of furniture companies are designing and producing some terrific products in this area. But even with these types of furnishings available, many people still do not know how to adapt the places they choose to live in, even if just temporarily. I hope the following chapters will provide inspiration for adaptions that will enhance your living environment.

Chapter 9

Single-room Living

I SUPPOSE THAT AT SOME TIME IN OUR LIVES, WE'VE HAD to live in a single-room environment, whether as kids in our own (and often shared) bedroom or as students in a college dorm or perhaps now as singles in a studio apartment. With the exception of bathroom facilities, these studio efficiencies must supply all the facilities for food preparation, dining, entertaining, studying or working, and sleeping in a single room. As a result, the simplification of space is essential to comfortable living.

Space and Storage

There are many ways to simplify space. First, minimize the number of your possessions. The elimination of visual "clutter" is crucial, for not only does clutter make the room look unkempt, but it also makes things difficult to find. Clutter can also produce psychological effects on the room's occupant, sometimes causing confusion or even depression. One way to defeat stacks of clutter is to reduce the number of horizontal surfaces upon which things accumulate and provide some form of enclosed storage space as an alternative. If there is no convenient place to set things down, you might be encouraged to put them in a better and more out-of-the-way space. Clothing is the primary offender. With a clean, appropriate storage area that can be closed from view, the room will appear more organized and functional.

Probably the best way to simplify space is to consolidate several facilities into a single unit or area. This implies a number of self-designed and constructed items that can be easily moved and that can provide all the comforts of "home" no matter what single room you live in.

The food-preparation and dining areas are a natural

NOMAD

Mobility, versatil styling, Pletcher furniture that's f

Chair & Ottoman
$570
Nomad price

THE GOYA: A beautifully styled chair imported from the Netherlands. Made by one of Europe's leading contemporary manufacturers, the swivel chair features a laminated wood frame mounted on a chrome ball swivel base. Pre-formed latex cushions are covered in top grained Havanna leather. Matching ottoman (not shown) included. Delivered and assembled $680. Assembly rating: challenging.

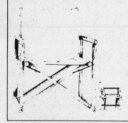

CANYON CHAIR: 1976 recipient of the International Residential Product Design Award from the American Society of Interior Designers. Hardwood construction features a hand-rubbed oil finish with heavy-duty canvas. Also features a swivel, floating back. 6.75 kg. (15 lbs.) Delivered and assembled $99. Assembly rating: easy.

Nomad price $83

BADGER DI CHAIR: Standard director's chair wi hardwood frame. yellow, pumpkin, lir plastic leg gli rust-resistant hardwa (13 lbs.) Delive assembled $33. rating: easy.

Nomad price $27⁵⁰

NOMAD

GULL ROCKER: The comfortable hardwood frame is covered in a one piece form fitting canvas available in chocolate brown. Hardwood frame is varnish finished. 8.1 kg. (18 lbs.) Delivered and assembled $88. Assembly rating: easy.

Nomad price $73

TEAK STRING CHAIR: This elegant teak chair beautifully compliments the teak tables shown elsewhere in this catalogue. Woven string seat. Delivered and assembled $95. Assembly rating: simple.

Nomad price $78

SOLID TEAK CHAIR: This handsome teak chair comes boxed and ready to bolt together into one of the most solid chairs available. Practical black vinyl seats. Delivered and set up $69. Assembly rating: easy.

Nomad price $57

FREE DELIVERY!

BAR STOOL: B compliments your entertainment center. foot rest wrapped ar maple finished leg covered seat swivel circle. 24"H. Delive assembled $25. rating: easy.

Nomad price $21

FOLDING STRING CHAIR: Fiber seat and back are woven onto a satin walnut finished frame. It's one of Pletchers most popular folding lounge chairs. 33" high. No assembly necessary. Delivered $42.

Nomad price $35

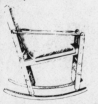

NOMA

, and ffers

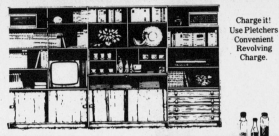

Extremely versatile and compact. Self contained leaves for full dining capacity. Delivered and set up $159. Assembly rating: easy
Nomad price $133

WALL SYSTEM: This three section imported system features several shelves, cabinets and compartments that adjust, mix or reverse to your own needs. Delivered and set up $699. Assembly rating: challenging.
Nomad price $560

TEAK BUFFET: This special imported buffet is expertly crafted in natural teak. Two sliding doors reveal ample storage space. Felt lined drawer for silverware. 58½" x 16¼" x 29¾"H. Delivered and assembled $310. Assembly rating: challenging.
Nomad price $257

R PILLOW SOFA: This 4 pc. pillow set provides ith loads of bold, bouncy comfort. Available in a ful array of serviceable fabrics. No assembly. ered $79.
ad price $66

THE GEO- SYSTEM: The perfect unit to add functional storage space or use as a decorator accent. Use your imagination, the possibilities are infinite. Delivered and set up, 9 panel in white $35. Also available in 21 and 50 panel sets (not shown). Assembly rating: challenging.
Nomad price $29

DECK ROCKER: It's uniquely designed natural hardwood frame provides comfortable seating plus rocking. Canvas fabric with headrest is available in natural or brown. Folds compactly. Delivered and set up $45. Assembly rating: simple.
Nomad price $37

CHROME PLANTER: Four styled ways to raise your plants to new heights over night. No assembly necessary. Delivered in box, 6" $9.95, 21" $17, 33" $25, 48" $27.
Nomad prices $8⁵⁰ $14 $20 $23

Is it a chair or is it a bed? Yes. This unique item can be used as a comfortable chair or it easily converts to a cozy bed. It has a monobloc mattress made of polyurethan covered in a removable machine washable nylon fabric. Available in yellow, orange, gold and green. Delivered and assembled $119. Assembly rating: easy.
Nomad price $99

TEAK DESK: Crafted from teak, one of natures hardest woods. You'll find years of beauty with a minimum of maintenance. Teak oil is all you'll ever need. Delivered and set up $129. Assembly rating: challenging.
Nomad price $105

DROP LEAF TABLE: The beauty of this table far exceeds the smooth, radiant graining of the walnut used in construction. Table opens to a big 64". Delivered and assembled $105. Assembly rating: simple.
Nomad price $88

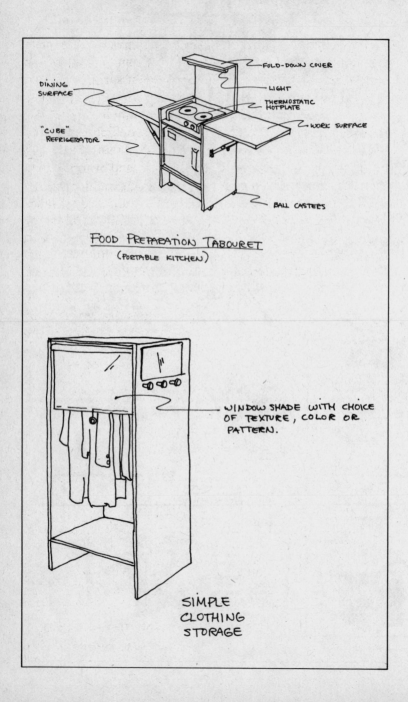

DINING SURFACE

FOLD-DOWN COVER

LIGHT

THERMOSTATIC HOTPLATE

"CUBE" REFRIGERATOR

WORK SURFACE

BALL CASTERS

FOOD PREPARATION TABOURET

(PORTABLE KITCHEN)

WINDOW SHADE WITH CHOICE OF TEXTURE, COLOR OR PATTERN.

SIMPLE CLOTHING STORAGE

combination. The "kitchen" usually comprises a hot plate and mini-cube refrigerator, which sit in some corner of the room. The "dining room" is any horizontal surface that can be swept clean for the purpose of eating. It is certainly possible to design a simple rolling cart that combines these elements in a unified way and provides both cooking and dining functions. Depending upon its method of construction and the materials used, it can add character and warmth to a single room, as well as simplify the room's appearance.

The biggest space waster in the room is the bed. It takes up precious space and is used (generally) only at night. A much more efficient setup would utilize the space the bed occupies in some meaningful way. There are three basic arrangements for bed storage: fold down, fold up, and elevate.

Fold Down

You have seen pictures of bunks in submarines. This method incorporates the same idea. The bed is mounted to the

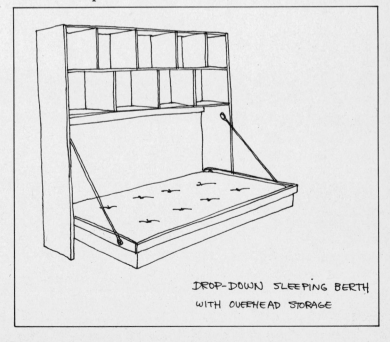

DROP-DOWN SLEEPING BERTH
WITH OVERHEAD STORAGE

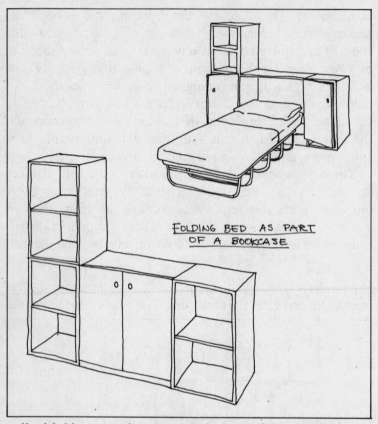

FOLDING BED AS PART
OF A BOOKCASE

wall with hinges, and rope or chain keeps it level. When you want more space, just fold it up to the wall. If your landlord (or school) frowns upon your drilling holes and setting anchors in their walls, you can design a freestanding version of the same concept.

Fold Up

Sofa beds are examples of the fold-up method; and of course, they provide a couch when not in use as a bed. Although the couch takes almost as much space as the bed, unless you do a lot of entertaining, it may not be necessary to have one. Besides, many of those on the market weigh a ton, and I wouldn't venture to move one.

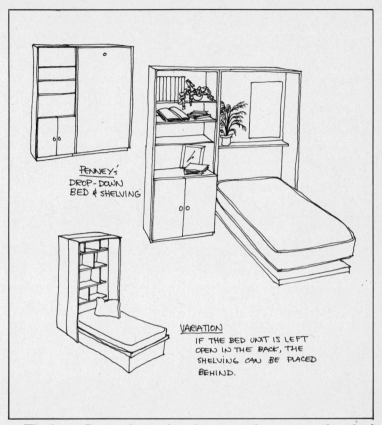

PENNEY'S
DROP-DOWN
BED & SHELVING

VARIATION
IF THE BED UNIT IS LEFT
OPEN IN THE BACK, THE
SHELVING CAN BE PLACED
BEHIND.

The latest Penney's catalog shows another approach, a bed
that folds up into a storage box. It can be coupled with another unit to make a clean, efficient work and storage area. It
appears to be a vinyl-clad particle-board construction (which
is a bit tacky), but the idea is a good, functional one that has
been around since the advent of the Murphy bed in the late
nineteenth century. One could easily take off with this idea
and create a more meaningful and personal design.

Elevate

You can also elevate the bed. In this case, the mattress and
bedclothes must be simple and lightweight so that they can be
stored or moved when the change is made. Beds that use

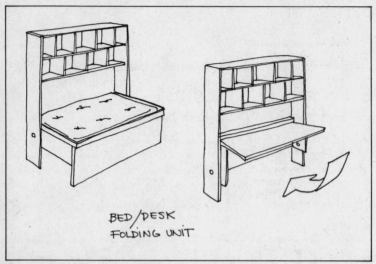

BED/DESK
FOLDING UNIT

doors as a base can easily adapt to desk or writing surfaces during the day. By continuing to elevate the bed through the use of supports from the floor or even ropes from the ceiling, you can take it to a height that is out of the way, allowing for other uses of the space.

Raising the bed to the ceiling introduces the idea of a loft or elevated bed design that provides for a second level. Simple structures can be designed that will support a bed up far enough to allow for other activities to be performed beneath it.

Other Alternatives

A platform bed can also provide storage, thereby conserving space. The bed portion could be hinged like the lid of a big footlocker to allow storage inside. For compact size when moving, the storage part of one of these bed/storage combinations can be a canvas fabric or plastic vinyl. Beds that fold up can have storage behind them or even in the bed section that folds up.

Beds and worktables are great combinations. Worktable height makes for a tall bed, and bed height makes for a low worktable, so some sort of compromise will be necessary.

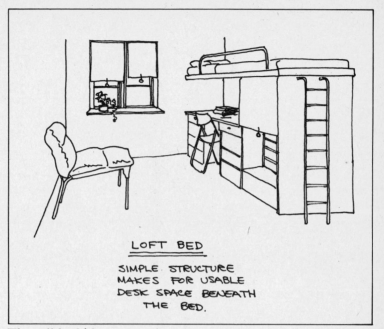

LOFT BED

SIMPLE STRUCTURE
MAKES FOR USABLE
DESK SPACE BENEATH
THE BED.

The tall bed idea seems the most popular, since it also allows for storage underneath.

Other more airy and less bulky-looking arrangements involve beds that can be flipped over and tilted, mattresses that can be stored easily, and bed platforms that can divide to provide half-width seating or even a worktable with a bench.

The Simplification of Space

In the previous section, we discussed the three basic ways of simplifying space: the minimizing of your personal possessions, the elimination of clutter, and the consolidation of interior spaces. In keeping with the goal of consolidation, a really well integrated room might contain a *single* structure that combines all the elements of living in one. Such an idea was presented, in part, in *Nomadic Furniture 1*. The idea is to create a simple structure that can be assembled inside a room and that replaces numerous separate-functioned products. This "box-inside-a-room" might contain all the func-

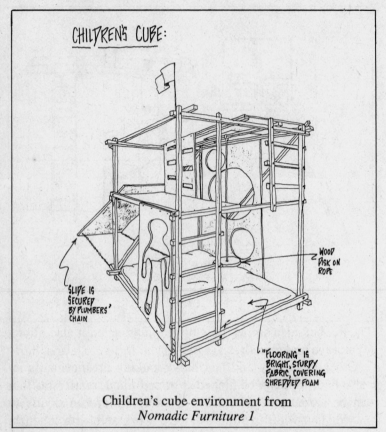

CHILDREN'S CUBE:

SLIDE IS
SECURED
BY PLUMBERS'
CHAIN

WOOD
DISK ON
ROPE

"FLOORING" IS
BRIGHT, STURDY
FABRIC, COVERING
SHREDDED FOAM

Children's cube environment from
Nomadic Furniture 1

tions of cooking, dining, working, entertaining, and storage within a single design. Living becomes associated with the structure and not with the room it occupies. When moving time comes, it is easily disassembled and transported to the new location where, erected once again, it becomes "home," eliminating drastic changes and acclimations to a new environment. Other people have continued to develop this idea, but none quite as well as Ken Isaacs, who has published a number of books on his innovative structural designs. (See the bibliography.)

Having discussed the box-inside-a-room idea, I now offer another concept called the "room-inside-a-box." This is the

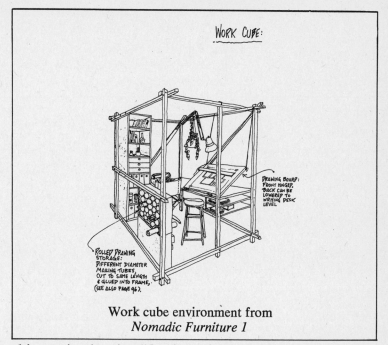

WORK CUBE:

DRAWING BOARD: FRONT HINGED, BACK CAN BE LOWERED TO WRITING DESK LEVEL

ROLLED DRAWING STORAGE: DIFFERENT DIAMETER MAILING TUBES, CUT TO SAME LENGTH & GLUED INTO FRAME. (SEE ALSO PAGE 96).

Work cube environment from
Nomadic Furniture 1

ultimate in the simplification of space because everything
you need for day-to-day living is combined in a single storage
structure. When this design is moved from place to place, it
resembles a well-made, sturdy crate of large proportions. It is
carefully designed to be carried by two people and will fit
through standard doorways. When placed in a room, it can
be taken apart, unfolded, and hinged into all of the necessities of life. Desk surfaces fold down, beds slide out, doors
open to expose storage or kitchen appliances, and the crate
itself becomes some useful item, such as a closet, couch, table
—even a darkroom if you like photography or a soundproof
environment if you are into meditation. The illustrations
only hint at what can be accomplished. Your own imagination and consideration of past needs and wants will provide
the necessary research and motivation. Just remember the
limitations in size and weight, and be sure to measure everything carefully.

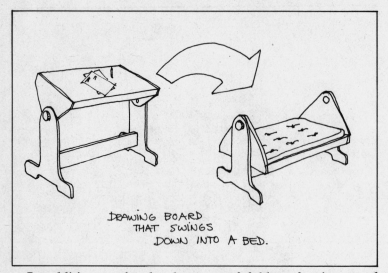

DRAWING BOARD
THAT SWINGS
DOWN INTO A BED.

In addition to the development of foldout furniture and nested designs, a careful choice of furnishings and accessories for the room-inside-a-box will have to be made. The array of things from Faye Noon's **Uncommon Market** offers exactly what someone with limited space needs: practicality and portability. Everything from this company comes knockdown. The line includes magazine, record, and wine racks; pocket wall organizers; hamper and duffel bag combinations; hanging shelves; and the Crash Pad, a wall-hung mattress that can be put on the floor for guests. The racks have their own natural wood frames that fold up. So does the hamper, and the duffel bag doubles as a tote with handles when taken from the frame. The wine racks hold colorful placemats, as well as silverware or weaving yarn (in addition to wine bottles, of course). The two hanging shelves are ideal for small spaces, since they allow for vertical storage. The 5-foot unit is just like the expensive imported ones from Denmark (but a lot less expensive); and the Shelf Help system, when combined with wood of your own choosing and length, will give a maximum of space with a minimum of materials. A wall can be filled up with the pocket organizers, and the wall-

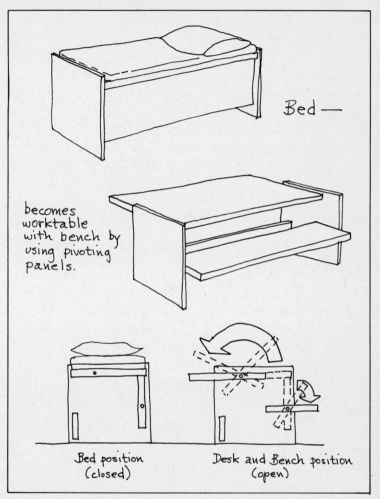

Bed —

becomes worktable with bench by using pivoting panels.

Bed position (closed)

Desk and Bench position (open)

hanging Crash Pad not only covers dingy walls but is an art form in itself. Each of these products shows great imagination and ingenuity. The quality is superior; everything is carefully sewn and double-stitched with buttons as fasteners, which means that all of them can be taken apart and tossed into the washer. You should be able to find these products in stores around your area, or write to: The Uncommon Market, 227 South Bruner Street, Hinsdale, Illinois 60521.

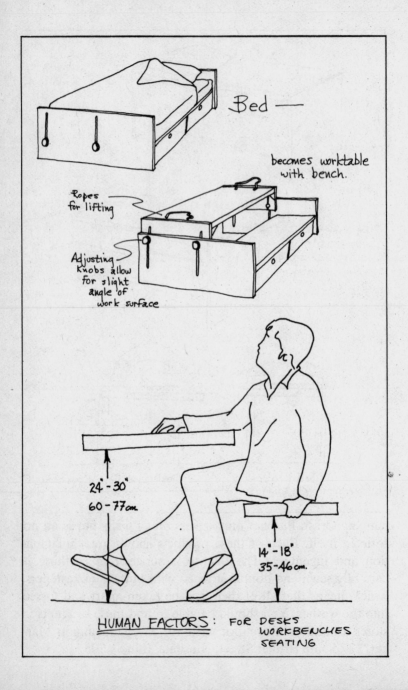

Bed —

becomes worktable
with bench.

Ropes
for lifting

Adjusting
Knobs allow
for slight
angle of
work surface

24" - 30"
60 - 77 cm.

14" - 18"
35 - 46 cm.

HUMAN FACTORS: FOR DESKS
WORKBENCHES
SEATING

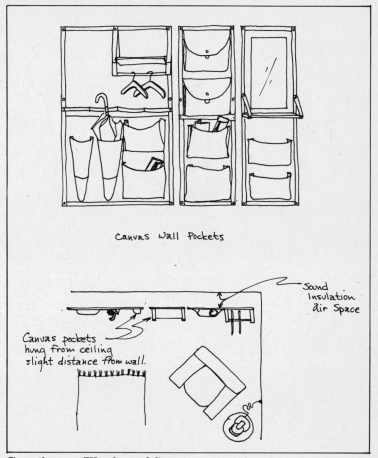

Canvas Wall Pockets

Sound Insulation air Space

Canvas pockets hung from ceiling slight distance from wall.

Creating an Illusion of Space

Living in a single room can be difficult. The walls seem to crowd you in and appear to get closer each day. There are ways of dealing with small rooms that can help you overcome "cell fever." One method involves the liberal use of mirrors. One wall, covered with panels of mirrors, will make the space seem double its actual size. Even a door-sized panel of mirrors will create the appearance of another room connecting to yours. All of this, even though visual trickery, will make your single room seem to have more space than it has.

Wine rack: Uncommon Market. We use it to hold decorative place mats. It has many other uses as well.

You might also look for boxes of 12-inch-square "wall mirrors" at a discount store. These are designed to be glued to a wall, and some brands are even self-adhesive. But rather than gluing them (which is permanent) and thereby defacing the walls of the room, mount each panel in a wooden frame. When the frames are hung together, they have the appearance and effect of a multi-paned window or door; and when moving time comes, you can easily remove the squares for your next place.

Discount stores also have inexpensive mirrors which are designed to be mounted to bedroom or bathroom doors. Although they are very thin and fragile, they are large; and when joined together, they can cover a large area.

Mirrors are fragile and expensive, but there are other alternatives. Any large plastic supplier has Plexiglas mir-

Crash Pad, Shelf Help, and Pocket Organizer: Uncommon Market. Together, they make for a very clean and utilitarian contemporary environment.

rors which, although expensive, will not shatter so readily as glass ones. This makes them easier to drill and lighter to mount. Many large plastic outlets also have scraps that can be purchased by the pound and pieced together to form interesting designs. Mylar, other mirror-like plastics, and even industrial metal scraps present further possibilities.

Another way to make a room appear to be larger than it is involves the selective use and control of lighting. The idea here is to light the environment in such a way as to prevent any light from striking one particular wall. If the wall is not illuminated, it will seem to be black and will "disappear"

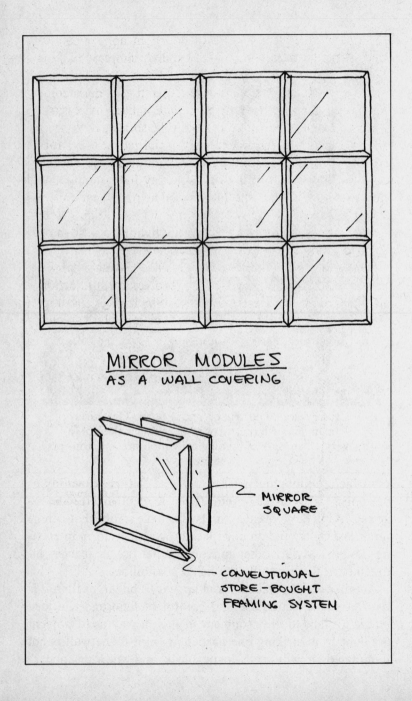

MIRROR MODULES
AS A WALL COVERING

MIRROR SQUARE

CONVENTIONAL STORE-BOUGHT FRAMING SYSTEM

from view. This tends to make the room appear endless in that particular direction. While it sounds simple, this kind of lighting control can be difficult to achieve. To help the wall "go black," it may be necessary to paint it a dark color or hang a dark fabric in front of it. The lighting necessary for the room should originate *at* this wall, so that it shines into the interior from the dark area. Specialized lighting for the worktable or kitchen should be spotlighting, which casts light only on the surface that needs it. Stray light falling on the dark wall could ruin the effect. To help prevent this, you might partition off the kitchen area with a folding screen. You will have to play around with the lighting a little in order to achieve this startling and dramatic "black wall" effect.

One other way to create "false space" is the opposite of the selective lighting method. It involves the projection of images, colors, or scenes on a wall, which gives the impression of added space. Since it is a projection, you can change

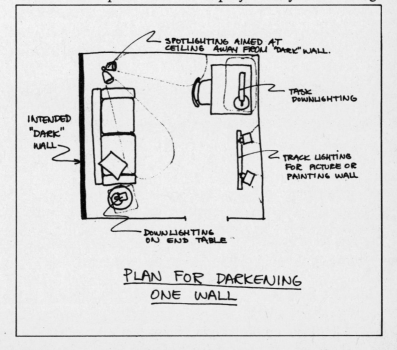

PLAN FOR DARKENING
ONE WALL

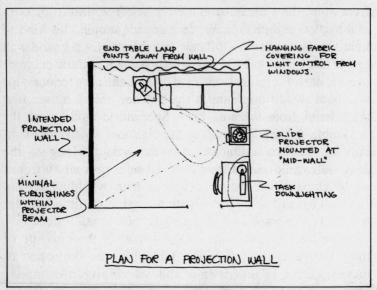

END TABLE LAMP
POINTS AWAY FROM WALL

HANGING FABRIC
COVERING FOR
LIGHT CONTROL FROM
WINDOWS.

INTENDED
PROJECTION
WALL

SLIDE
PROJECTOR
MOUNTED AT
"MID-WALL"

MINIMAL
FURNISHINGS
WITHIN
PROJECTOR
BEAM

TASK
DOWNLIGHTING

PLAN FOR A PROJECTION WALL

it at your whim. To achieve this effect you have to set the room up, as in the previous lighting method, with as little light falling on the projection wall as possible. The projection wall, in this case, must be white for a brilliant image. From the other side of the room, elevate and install on a simple shelf a single-slide 35mm projector. Choose one that has a cooling fan, since it will be operating for long periods of time. Buy an appropriate 35mm slide (or shoot your own), and you're in business. You will want to play around with the image size and intensity to suit your perception of "realism," and you might even frame the final image to look like a window view.

Of course, if you cannot afford these alternatives, you can always buy an inexpensive but good-quality color poster. These can be purchased to cover an entire wall, and there are even companies that will reproduce your own negatives for this purpose. Such a poster, if correctly mounted and lit, will give some impression of spaciousness or, at least, be a focus for daydreams.

While we are on the subject of covering walls, there is an

interesting way of controlling sound. Large, fabric storage pocket walls,[14] which are suspended in front of a room's wall, can serve as great sound absorbers. Two such designs, large enough to cover the two shared walls that connect your room with your neighbors', will tremendously reduce the decibel level in your environment. They may even enable you to make more noise or play louder music without bothering those adjacent to you. Plain heavy fabric of interesting colors and textures will yield the same results. Though initially an expensive investment, the fabric can be easily transported and will give years of welcomed privacy.

Chapter 10

Apartment Living

WHAT IS SAID HERE ABOUT APARTMENT LIVING IS TRUE
for house renting as well. Apartments offer much more space
and, certainly, greater comfort than single-room dwellings.
Some apartment complexes offer three- or four-bedroom
apartments with floor space equal to that of many a large
home. Unlike the space-utilization and congestion problems
of one-room living, an apartment contains at least two rooms
or more in which to spread out and organize. Many of the
adaptation suggestions outlined in the previous chapter are
applicable to multi-room apartments and house rentals. The
need for appropriate utilization of space, the design of multi-
functional units, and the selective use of lighting are equally
important in all types of living environments.

Probably the greatest problem associated with renting an
apartment or house is that the structure belongs to someone
else. Just the same, people try to make it "home" by modify-
ing and adapting the living space. The people who get into
trouble are those who make major modifications to the structure or spend large sums constructing beautiful and elaborate
built-in systems for the kitchen or living spaces. Some people
install expensive and permanent lighting systems. Some
modernize the kitchen or bathroom. Some even install appliances and disposal systems. The sad part is that most of these
alterations become part of the architecture and have to be
left behind when the inevitable move comes. The only one to
really benefit from this modernized apartment is the landlord,
who can now charge a higher rent for it. Alterations to the
interior architecture of an apartment or rental house are the
responsibility of the person who owns it, not the person who
rents it.

The renter is required to pay rent on time and to keep the apartment clean and hygienic. Further, it is the renter's responsibility to inform the landlord when repairs need to be done. The repair of heating, electrical, and plumbing systems, as well as of appliances, must be done by the landlord. Of course, this kind of maintenance takes a slice out of the rent, so it is very unlikely that, above and beyond the necessary maintenance expenses, an owner would be willing to do any modernizing or updating of the conveniences in an apartment. There is always a strong desire on the part of the renter to make these kinds of changes, with the rationalization that "We'll be here for a long time." But it never happens that way. All too soon you will be moving out and leaving behind a lot of work and money.

There are some things to expect in an apartment in terms of living conditions and repairs. You have the right, according to the law, to withhold your rent payments if the apartment you are renting can be considered "dangerous, hazardous or detrimental to life, health or safety." Before determining if your apartment is a hazard, contact your lawyer to help you judge whether you have the legal right to complain. Landlords who allow unsafe conditions, such as sagging floors, blocked plumbing, crumbling plaster, or exposed wiring, should be reported to the buildings department in your town, since these are building-code violations. The landlord also must supply heat to your building, and he can be arrested for purposely shutting it off. He can also be arrested for evicting you and securing your belongings without an eviction order. In any event, your recourse, with legal advice, is to withhold your rent until repairs are made and the apartment brought up to livable standards. I have included a chart outlining places where renters can go for help. Locate the appropriate phone numbers in the telephone directory and insert them into the chart. In this way you will have a handy reference for any problems that might arise.

What possibilities exist for people in a rental situation who

CHART 15.

HELP FOR RENTERS

IF YOU NEED A LAWYER:
    The legal-assistance corporation
      for your county   _____
    The Legal Aid Society   _____
    Lawyers' reference service   _____

IF YOU HAVE UNSAFE CONDITIONS:
    Department of buildings and property
      conservation, compliance division   _____

IF YOU HAVE NO HEAT:
    The department of health for your
      county   _____

IF YOUR LANDLORD LOCKS YOU OUT:
    City police department   _____
    County sheriff   _____

IF YOU ARE ON WELFARE:
    The department of social services for
      your county, housing unit   _____

OTHER AGENCIES THAT PROVIDE HELP:
    The housing council for your county   _____
    Community dispute service   _____

IF YOU HAVE BEEN DISCRIMINATED AGAINST:
    The division of human rights for your
      state   _____

want to liven up a dingy apartment and surround themselves with a pleasant and modern environment? There are a number of solutions to modernization problems and apartment updating that can be implemented and then taken along when moving time comes. They involve a concept which I call change without permanence, through which you can find ways to alter your rental environment without altering its architectural design.

Let's start with the basics. One of the first things most people notice is that their apartment needs a good coat of paint. No landlord is going to repaint an apartment at his expense just because you want it done. However, many are willing to supply the paint and materials if you are willing to do the work. This turns out to be a good barter. At his expense you can buy the best-quality paint, brushes, and other materials necessary to do a superb job; and even if you stay only a year, you will have a beautiful, freshly painted place in which to live. In addition, you can keep the leftover materials for future jobs. This turns out to be a good deal for the landlord, too, since you are saving him a considerable amount of money, and your willingness to have a clean apartment is an indication to him that you will be a good tenant.

Apartment painting is where I draw the line. It is the only task I am willing to perform without some form of compensation. Interior maintenance is the landlord's responsibility; but if you are a skilled mechanic or decent handyman, you may be able to bargain with the landlord, exchanging the periodic maintenance of your apartment for a rent deduction. For example, I found that replacing a defective oven element once was a lot easier and faster to do myself than if I had to rely purely on someone the landlord hired. Besides, with me doing it, I was able to get the materials at a much lower cost than a repairman would have charged, so the landlord ultimately benefitted, too. In this instance, we agreed on a cash amount, which covered the parts as well as my labor. A good rule to follow is not to make any repairs, alterations, or additions to the structure unless the owner both approves and is willing to pay you or deduct the costs from the rent.

Let's say the landlord is a cheapskate and refuses to finance the cost of materials for painting a drab, discolored apartment. Don't be tempted to paint it at your expense, as this is money totally wasted. Besides, if the landlord sees the beautiful job you've done, he might raise the rent! Instead, "mask" the offending walls and ceilings by using partitions, coverings, panels, and lighting control.

Partitions

You can make a partition out of almost anything. I've

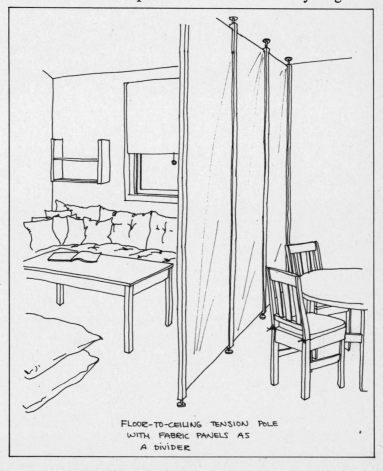

FLOOR-TO-CEILING TENSION POLE
WITH FABRIC PANELS AS
A DIVIDER

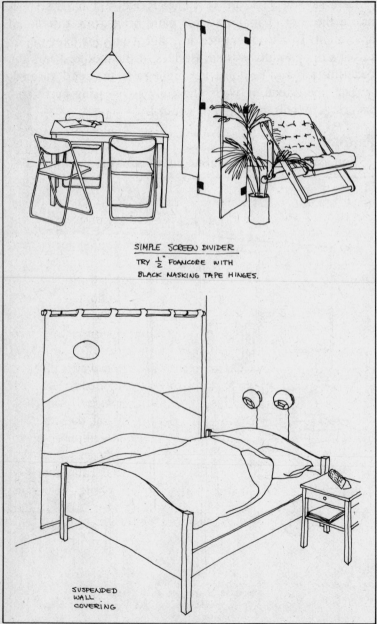

SIMPLE SCREEN DIVIDER
TRY $\frac{1}{2}$" FOAMCORE WITH
BLACK MASKING TAPE HINGES.

SUSPENDED
WALL
COVERING

seen great examples that were made of delicate wood lattice, commercial paneling, colorful fabrics, and even aluminum cans. Partitions can be installed from floor to ceiling using a simple screw-compression system or telescopic-spring system such as the type used in pole lamps. It is easy to make these[15] and support the partition material between them. Other types of partitions include hinged panels or screens that are self-standing and can be opened to block off an area from view. Construction varies with the degree of permanence you intend the partitions to have; but on the temporary side, some really nice ones have been made with large panels of foam-core board (available from art supply stores in sizes up to 4 feet by 8 feet), which are simply taped together.

Coverings

Coverings are usually made of fabric or wallpaper that has been directly attached to the offending wall. Panels of fabric are suspended on a wooden rod, which hangs on nails driven into the wall. Another interesting covering uses ordinary wallpaper. A pleasing and appropriately designed wallpaper can be purchased at any store and the paper attached to the wall with a very thin mixture of cornstarch and water. You must be careful to apply only a thin mixture so that the material can be easily removed later. Vinyl-laminated wallpaper holds up even better; and of course, fabrics like burlap work very well. When moving time comes, the material can be gently pulled from the wall and used in your next home. The walls can be washed with clear water if necessary. In this manner an entire wall of offending color can be hidden from view.

Panels

In Chapter 9 we talked about the use of paneled mirrors to give the appearance of space. For hiding blemished, cracked, or other unsightly surfaces, the panel approach can be effec-

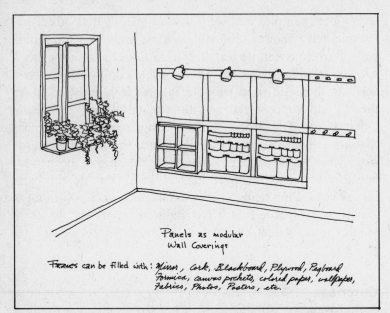

Panels as modular
Wall Coverings

Frames can be filled with: Mirror, Cork, Blackboard, Plywood, Pegboard
Formica, canvas pockets, colored paper, wallpaper,
Fabrics, Photos, Posters, etc.

tively used here as well. Any number of materials, from wallpaper to fabrics to mirrors to hardwood paneling to real wood veneers to large posters and photographs, can be mounted in simple frames and joined together to create a covering for an entire wall. For covering entire rooms, fabrics are the most practical.

Lighting

I mentioned lighting earlier in terms of creating an impression of spaciousness in a single-room environment. The same effect of making one wall disappear can be used to conceal *more* than one wall and tone down the walls' colors or blemishes. With the correct lighting, it is possible to conceal not only the four walls of an apartment but the ceiling as well by allowing only down-lighting to illuminate the interior space. Lights mounted on the ceiling, as well as freestanding lamps within the interior, should be arranged to illuminate only the needed areas and to cast shadows on everything else. The darkening of the rest of the room surfaces that

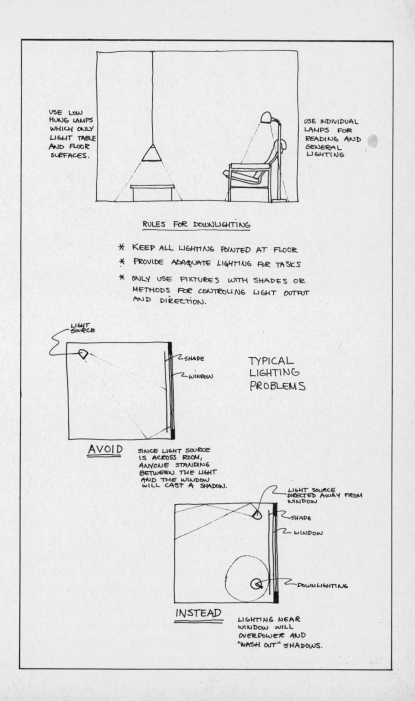

USE LOW HUNG LAMPS WHICH ONLY LIGHT TABLE AND FLOOR SURFACES.

USE INDIVIDUAL LAMPS FOR READING AND GENERAL LIGHTING

RULES FOR DOWNLIGHTING

* KEEP ALL LIGHTING POINTED AT FLOOR
* PROVIDE ADAQUATE LIGHTING FOR TASKS
* ONLY USE FIXTURES WITH SHADES OR METHODS FOR CONTROLLING LIGHT OUTPUT AND DIRECTION.

LIGHT SOURCE

SHADE

WINDOW

TYPICAL LIGHTING PROBLEMS

AVOID

SINCE LIGHT SOURCE IS ACROSS ROOM, ANYONE STANDING BETWEEN THE LIGHT AND THE WINDOW WILL CAST A SHADOW.

LIGHT SOURCE DIRECTED AWAY FROM WINDOW

SHADE

WINDOW

DOWNLIGHTING

INSTEAD

LIGHTING NEAR WINDOW WILL OVERPOWER AND "WASH OUT" SHADOWS.

results will mask them from view. You must also be sure to supply sufficient lighting to meet the necessary work or reading requirements. So there is a delicate balance that must be experimented with between the desired effect and practical needs.

More often than not, ceilings will become badly cracked long before the walls show signs of wear. Many of the above-mentioned methods can be used to conceal an unpleasant-looking ceiling. The lighting method can be the simplest and most effective; and in addition, all sorts of hangings, such as canopies and fabric arches, can be suspended from the ceiling to hide it from view.

These methods can also be used to block out window areas. Most people I know are tired of drapes and curtains, which gather dust and are a pain to alter, as well as to design and make. The trend seems to be toward simpler, flat hangings that cover the window. For these, people are willing to invest in more expensive and colorful fabrics like Marimekko which, in turn, add even more elegance and style to an apartment. Sliding panels, which can be moved in front of the window for privacy in the evening, are another option. It is also possible to make a panel that fits over the window and hangs on hooks. During the day, it becomes a beautiful graphic piece by hooking onto the wall next to the window. Such panels look especially nice if they allow the sunlight to illuminate their colors from behind. In this same category are brightly printed bedsheets, which can be cut into panels, or one-of-a-kind batiks, depending upon your preference and budget. A well-crafted batik can look like a stained-glass window when backlit by the sun. It's even possible to hand-paint a white shade to create something truly unique.

These partitions and coverings, like those mentioned in the previous chapter, can also provide sound insulation from adjoining apartments, as well as reduce the noise level emanating from yours.

FRAMED CANVAS PRINT
SLIDES OVER WINDOW
AT NIGHT.

A space of great size in which a number of isolated activities must take place demands some kind of partitioning. For example, a kitchen may be part of or next to a dining area. When guests are over for dinner, you may want to limit their view of the preparation area. A sliding partition of some kind can seal off the area, effect the necessary concealment, and contribute to the room's decor. Similar dividing can separate the dining area from a large living room, a hobby or craft area from a large family room, and even a baby's sleep or play area from another bedroom.

Partitions and dividers can take many forms. Almost anything that is extendable and sufficiently high can create a boundary. Bookshelves and couches are obvious solutions, but you can also use planters or plant walls, which create a humanistic and pleasant divider. One of the most effective dividers is probably one of the simplest to build. It is composed of flat panels of colorful fabric suspended on a rod and

Window coverings need not be fabric. Here, maize straw floor squares are hung over the windows for a very special effect.

hung from the ceiling by hooks. It is even possible, through a pattern of these hooks, to move or add these curtains, thus altering space for rooms with multiple purposes.

Sealing off or partitioning spaces also helps conserve heat energy. For example, if you are renting a large studio or loft space and don't want to heat the whole area, partitions or suspended panels can isolate a smaller living space to be heated. For this purpose, you might choose rigid foam as a panel stiffener with some aesthetic covering over it. In this way you will gain the greatest insulation possible. Heavy carpeting used in conjunction with this panel will further add to the heat retention of any specified area, as will a suspended ceiling of insulating tile or heavy fabric. Likewise,

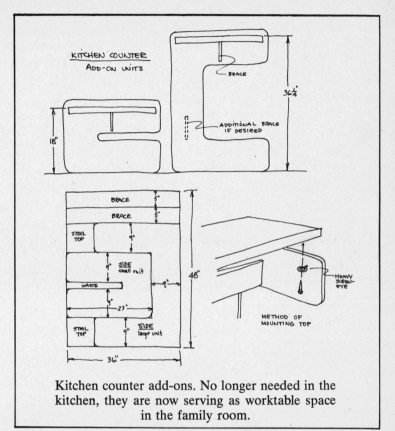

Kitchen counter add-ons. No longer needed in the
kitchen, they are now serving as worktable space
in the family room.

heavy fabric panels installed over windows will keep out
winter chills and drafts, and function as heat insulators as
well.

Some apartment kitchens are so small that it becomes
difficult to find enough area to prepare a large dinner or
party. There is often room set aside for a kitchen table; but
since all the dining is done in the dining room, there isn't a
need for one, and the space is wasted. Rather than buy a
kitchen table that isn't needed, why not build additional
counter space that can be integrated into the kitchen and
moved with you when you leave? One such simple design involves the use of heavy particle board and an old door topped
with a Formica laminate. The counters provide an additional

Kitchen counter add-ons

work area at the same level as the built-in kitchen counters and a small table for the kids. These portable tables can be taken with you to different locations, where they can serve as breakfast counters, hobby tables, and work surfaces.

Many apartments offer you the room and opportunity to experiment with space-expanding designs that make lofts out of high-ceilinged areas and multi-levels that provide storage. Any of these can be an interesting departure from four square walls. Units that stack, that are movable, and that combine many functions will continue to offer greater flexibility and ease of transport. It won't take superior imagination or tremendous building skills to design items that will provide "change without permanence" for your next apartment or home rental.

Chapter 11

Home Improvements

WHEN WE FINALLY MOVE TO A HOME WE CAN AFFORD TO
own, we can make any improvements we want to. Most of us
regard a move into a house as permanent but find out, sometimes too late, that a change of jobs or some health problem
can necessitate an unwanted move. If we have simply spent
our time enjoying and maintaining the house we bought, we
can expect to make some profit on its sale. After all, the value
of homes is going up at an unprecedented rate, which, in some
areas, is almost triple what it was a decade ago. But what
about those of us who have invested large sums of money in
improving our homes? If the market has not gained enough
between the time we bought the house and the time we are
forced to sell, we may not be able to recoup our investment.
For this reason, it is important to know what home improvements will ultimately increase the market value of the house
and consequently bring a reasonable return on our investment. The pros and cons of various improvements will be the
point of discussion in this chapter.

Walls and Floors

The first thing to do when you move into a house is what I
call "neutralizing." It involves the removal of all "secondary
ornamentation," that is, ornamentation that has no relationship to the architecture or the structure of the house. All
kinds of things fall into this category: gaudy and peeling
wallpaper, colonial towel racks, decorative curtains, shades
and mounting hardware, worn carpeting, inappropriate lighting fixtures, and shoddily constructed built-ins, to name but a
few. Once these accessories have been removed, carefully
prepare and paint the walls white or off-white. If the house

has natural woodwork, do everything you can to preserve and maintain the wood in its natural finish. If some has been painted, consider stripping the paint so that the woodwork can return to its natural state. Painted doors should go to the local furniture restorer for stripping. If *all* the woodwork has been painted, it becomes impossible to do anything but re-paint it, since the cost and time involved to strip it would be too great. But never paint natural wood otherwise, for it's a sure way of devaluating your home. Once the secondary orna-mentation has been removed, the natural woodwork has been restored, and all the walls have been stripped, repaired, and painted, the job of neutralizing is complete. You'll be surprised at how easy a neutralized structure is to maintain and keep clean. In addition, your furniture, hangings, paint-ings, and other belongings will stand out much more and will add color to the rooms. And when moving time comes, the house will present a neutral appearance, enabling prospective buyers to more easily visualize their belongings in it.

This process holds true for the floors, too. At one time, quality carpeting was in vogue, and everyone wanted Persian carpets for their homes. The first linoleum flooring was even designed to imitate Persian rug patterns. Then along came wall-to-wall carpeting and shag rugs, under which all sorts of unfinished, rough plywood floors could be hidden. While most new homes offer wall-to-wall carpeting today, the cur-rent trend is beautifully finished hardwood floors. If you don't have hardwood floors in your home, you can purchase planks, tiles, and strips of hardwood flooring designed for do-it-yourself installation. These come in a variety of patterns, from random strips with walnut pegs to herringbone pat-terns. Usually, the investment is justified by the current popu-larity of this kind of flooring and the added value it places on your home.

The greatest number of worthwhile improvements are made to bathrooms and kitchens. Most home buyers want these rooms to be fresh and modern, so money invested here will indeed pay off in the long run.

Bathrooms

First, you'll want to buy and install new toilet seats in all the bathrooms. This may seem unimportant, but old and cracked toilet seats are a hygienic hazard as well as an eyesore. You'll next want to purchase and install a hand shower for the shower stall or tub. It can be adjusted for tall or short people by being plugged into various sockets on the wall, and it is unbeatable for families with small children.

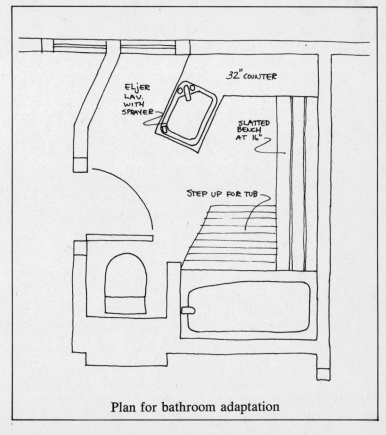

32" COUNTER

ELJER LAV. WITH SPRAYER

SLATTED BENCH AT 16"

STEP UP FOR TUB

Plan for bathroom adaptation

Bathroom. Framed, angled mirror gives a better view. Sink extends out on a peninsula for access all around. Natural pine was installed below the wainscoting, and Shaker pegs hold the towels.

The next step is updating the bathroom fixtures. You may have an original Victorian bathroom whose fixtures are still in good shape, in which case, leave them where they are. But if you have something from the 1930s that is old, cracked, or stained, consider replacing it.

Should you decide you want an old-fashioned bathroom, you'll want to stay as much in keeping with original designs from that era as possible, so read up on the decor of that period. Some companies produce replicas of tubs and faucets, as well as fixtures, for just such purposes.

Most old bathrooms contained lots of wood: wooden mir-

The cabinet over the toilet provides storage, ventilation, and indirect lighting in one simple design.

ror cabinets, wooden toilet seats, wainscoting around the room, and wooden towel or toilet paper holders. Because designing to this kind of style is very difficult and more expensive than modernizing,[16] you'll want to choose accessories that are simple and in keeping with the architecture and mood.

I would replace any old, rusty metal shower stalls with one-piece fiberglass units. Tubs that are cracked or chipped can often be repaired by professionals without having to be re-

A slatted bench fits over the room heater. It makes
for a warm place to sit after a bath.

moved. Check on this first before deciding to replace them.
Other alterations include replacing the medicine cabinet with
one that has better lighting or a larger mirror; installing a
one-piece vinyl floor, which is easier to clean and maintain;
painting the walls with a humidity-proof off-white paint; and
installing a better ventilation setup. You can save a great
amount of money if you are able to do these tasks yourself,
since professionals are expensive. Because much of this hardware is designed for owner-installation, you don't have to be
a genius to do it correctly. In fact, one major plumbing fixture
company not only offers a complete step-by-step guide for
amateur installation but also supplies a phonograph-record

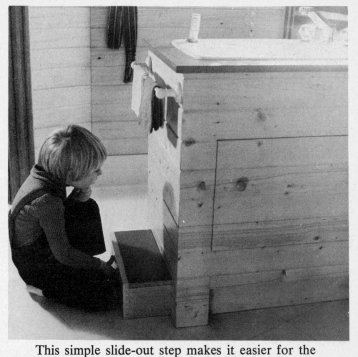

This simple slide-out step makes it easier for the kids to reach the sink.

narrative of easily understood instructions. Whatever you do, don't take any shortcuts. You don't want to be in the position of having to tear up a new floor to get at a leaky joint that was incorrectly installed. If you do not yet have the skills required, read some of the do-it-yourself books and manuals on the market or take an evening course offered at your local high school.

The Kitchen

Kitchen renovation is another wise investment. If your kitchen is old and awkwardly arranged; if it lacks sufficient storage and preparation areas; if the flow pattern of the house tracks people through the preparation area while you are trying to cook; if the room fills up with odors or gets

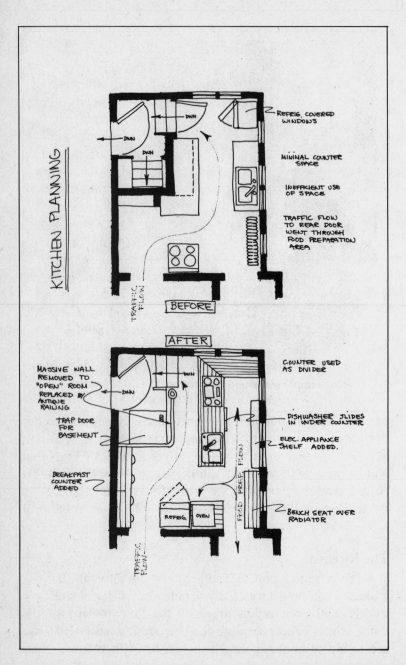

KITCHEN PLANNING

REFRIG. COVERED WINDOWS

MINIMAL COUNTER SPACE

INEFFICIENT USE OF SPACE

TRAFFIC FLOW TO REAR DOOR WENT THROUGH FOOD PREPARATION AREA

DWN

TRAFFIC FLOW

BEFORE

AFTER

MASSIVE WALL REMOVED TO "OPEN" ROOM REPLACED BY ANTIQUE RAILING

TRAP DOOR FOR BASEMENT

BREAKFAST COUNTER ADDED

DWN

COUNTER USED AS DIVIDER

DISHWASHER SLIDES IN UNDER COUNTER

ELEC. APPLIANCE SHELF ADDED.

FOOD PREP. FLOW

REFRIG. OVEN

BENCH SEAT OVER RADIATOR

TRAFFIC FLOW

unbearably hot to work in; if you can't see what you are doing because of inadequate lighting, then it's time to redesign and rebuild your kitchen. This can be done in various stages so that the kitchen remains usable even while the work is going on. If you have to remove the sink, rely on some other sink area (in a nearby bathroom or downstairs basement) as a water source. If you have to remove a stove, barbecue for a few days or plan meals that either require no cooking or can be made in an electric fry-pan. Such upheaval is never easy on the cook; but the end result makes the inconvenience worthwhile. Some of the illustrations show the ways in which I redesigned my kitchen.

If at all possible, plan to strip the room of everything: counters, cabinets, sinks, and appliances. Then begin neutralizing the floors, walls, and ceilings. When you redesign the space, try to eliminate any traffic that might flow through the preparation area. One way to accomplish this is by creating a central counter, with preparation on one side and traffic on the other. The rest is a matter of looking at the interior designs of other kitchens and talking a lot with the cook. What appliances are used the most? What needs to be near the sink? How large a counter is needed next to the refrigerator? Are preparation areas needed on both sides of the range? How much cabinet space is needed and where? All of these questions will help determine the arrangement and placement of objects in the room. The ultimate design should be simple and efficient. Choose good-quality solid-wood cabinetry, name-brand appliances, and sinks with single-handle washerless faucets. Accents like a single color for the sink, which is repeated in window coverings, can be very effective. Avoid using wallpaper, since it makes the room look too busy and can absorb odors and grease. Wainscoting, paneling, or off-white walls seem to work much better. A carefully designed plan, along with built-ins such as oven, range, dishwasher, refrigerator, and adequate storage, will really sell your house should the time come to move.

Counter peninsula separates the work area from traffic to the back door. Antique railing replaces what used to be a wall. Cork was installed below the wainscot, and natural oak was used for the counters.

There are other areas throughout the house where some investment can pay off. In the basement, prospective home buyers look for a modern and efficient furnace. They prefer homes which have been converted to all-copper plumbing and those with circuit breakers instead of fuses. Again, unless you can do this work yourself, this kind of updating can be expensive. Perhaps you have a skill that you can trade for this labor.

View from the other side. The dishwasher can be
pulled out to create more counter space.

The Exterior

The location of your house, the condition of its exterior,
and the beauty of the landscaping will attract people to look
inside. For this reason, it makes sense to invest in painting
and repairs, as well as roofing. This kind of maintenance
should be your primary concern during the summer months.
(You can always attend to interior renovations during the
winter.) In terms of painting, a body color with another
color for trim is much more appealing than a house painted
one solid color. Trim paint can be used to accent certain
architectural details and bring the uniqueness of your home
into view. New roofing should be installed only if the old one

Old architectural cornice supports are used to create the breakfast counter. All the counters in the kitchen are recycled oak flooring and cost $24.

The appliance shelf exhibits as well as organizes those electrical items used everyday.

The laundry was brought up from the basement and adapted to fit the pantry. Old homes have many such spaces that lend themselves to unique adaptations.

leaks or is badly damaged. The installation of new roofing alone will not be a strong selling point for your house; new paint has a much greater impact. People tell me that aluminum or galvanized siding creaks from temperature differences and that the vinyl siding is easier to install. But, if the wood siding on your house is in good condition, paint it instead of installing a fake covering. A few people I know are tearing off their old asbestos and stone siding so that the

Elevated Dining Area

nice old clapboards can show—a reflection of the current trend toward a return to things as they originally were.

Money invested in landscaping is also well spent. A clean and well-kept lawn is quite attractive, and the addition of a few trees would certainly help. Be sure to prune and protect the trees you already have.

Other exterior "improvements"—such as aboveground and belowground swimming pools (in cool climates they are too hard to maintain, and in warm climates people *expect* houses to have them), tennis courts, and basketball courts— do not seem to have the selling points to warrant their construction. If you happen to find a buyer who is an enthusiast for the sport, fine. But more often than not, this is seldom the case; and the "improvement" may, in fact, deter potential buyers. Realize that such luxuries have purely personal benefits and may not add to the value of your home.

The Interior

There are a number of interior alterations that can enhance the value of your home. Almost anything in the built-

To turn another attic space into a bedroom, Don
Bujnowski designed and built this circular stairway.

in category, as long as it is well constructed of good materials
and has an obvious utilitarian function, would be a wise alteration. An example of this is the removal of an awkward,
add-on closet and the construction of a storage wall in the
master bedroom. This kind of totally concealed storage for
clothing eliminates the need for dressers or additional closets
and would be welcomed by a prospective buyer. The same
kind of storage wall could be created for the kitchen as a dry-
and-canned-food/utensil storage area, much like the old
pantry. Such a wall could also be installed in the living room
as a bookcase/stereo unit, or in the bathroom for storing
linen and medicine. In addition to providing ample and clean
storage space, this kind of design can also hide old, cracked

While restoring their farmhouse, the Bujnowski family opened up an attic space to expose the beams and installed a bridge across to connect two opposite areas.

walls or pipes and plumbing. The possibilities are endless.

Another interior alteration that makes for a wise investment involves the construction of multiple levels and lofts within a room. One such example is an elevated dining area. This kind of step-up platform visually divides the room, provides a unique and specialized area in which to dine, and can be either surfaced in beautiful hardwood or plushly carpeted. Such an addition to your home would be simple and economical to build, and very appealing to future buyers. Platforms for the sleeping area in a master bedroom and play areas in the children's bedrooms are other alternatives. Traffic, con-

Adam Bujnowski looks down from the bridge into
the dining area.

venience, and safety should be considered before building a platform; but if you have no reservations, then an elevated platform is an alteration you should definitely think about.

Loft areas are a bit more difficult to construct and should be the result of careful planning and design. The most likely locations for these high-up places are the children's bedrooms and play areas. Since lofts involve some sophisticated attachment to the house, it is unlikely you would want to take them along when you move. So plan a permanent installation. First, inspect the room for any depressions or corners where a loft would be a natural addition, such as the area between a closet wall and opposite bedroom wall. Make the structure

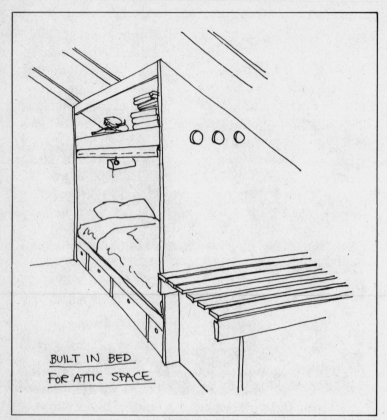

BUILT IN BED
FOR ATTIC SPACE

sturdy by anchoring it to the studs of the house, and finish it
to match the color and decor of the room. In some cases, it is
even possible to remove the ceiling in a peaked-roof house
and expose the beams and a portion of the attic space. A loft
can be built in this area and the interior of the roof finished
with natural wood planking. Such unique spaces are a pleasure for the inhabitants, a surprise to visitors, and a way to
greatly increase the value of your house.

Other major architectural changes involve putting additions of some kind on your house. Naturally, any add-on
construction is fairly expensive, and you should consider
only those additions you can build yourself or that are economical. Determine whether or not you really need that

additional space. If you decide you do, consider whether there is some other way of creating it without having to construct an addition—for example, by developing your basement or attic space. If this isn't feasible, then take a look at one of the easiest and most effective additions: a greenhouse. There are certainly enough styles and prices to accommodate almost everyone's needs and budget, and the needed space will have been created in an appealing and unique way.

Another way to add space is to expand into the garage. There are companies that specialize in this type of work, but they are expensive, and the resulting loss of a garage for cars would negatively affect the resale value of your house. Instead, you could build up the garage roof to allow for a second story. Many people do this to make small apartments or studios out of them. This type of addition can be worth the investment, since the prospective buyer would regard it as useful space or even as an income-producing rental apartment.

We all tend to look at the house we own as the permanent place for our family. Every time we move into a new place, we vow that it is the last move and that we'll stay there forever. Normally, we follow this up with major investments in the house and its surroundings. Unless carefully chosen, these improvements could be very costly because we *will* move again, and in the near future. The improvements made must pay off when we leave. The key is to keep thinking about that next move and continually prepare ourselves, our families, and our homes for that future inevitability.

NOTES

1. As the chart in this chapter indicates, U-Haul presently has the largest available van, a 24-footer with a capacity of 1,128 cubic feet according to their current moving guide. The largest Ryder van is a 22-footer which, according to their moving guide, has a larger capacity (1,200 cubic feet) than the 24-foot U-Haul. It is hard to say whether these figures are just estimates or whether the vans differ greatly in design, bed size, or height, which might account for the apparent discrepancy in the capacities. You should be the ultimate judge by visiting each of these outlets to look at the vans offered and by measuring them yourself.

2. A 1977 article in *The New York Times* talked about the containerized method of moving that is available from Smyth, a division of the Golden Circle Corporation, Colorado Springs. It also states that Allied Van Lines and Imperial Van Lines have container service but on a very limited basis. Other companies like Global Van Lines and Mayflower provide containers for their overseas customers and may do the same for cross-country moves. My general impression is that it doesn't pay the companies enough to adapt to this method because the consumer is not demanding it; and the consumer isn't interested because of the additional expense. A vicious circle. It appears to present a great opportunity for a new, specialized cross-country moving company that deals exclusively with containerized shipments.

3. In their latest guide, U-Haul mentions savings of up to 50 percent when you rent a truck and do it yourself. They additionally claim up to a 75 percent savings if the move is with a trailer. It seems, then, that a trailer can be 25 percent cheaper than a van for do-it-yourself movers and that quite a savings can be had by dropping down to a load small enough to be trailerable.

4. Currently, Ryder is charging 95¢ each for book cartons and $1.25 each for utility cartons. W. W. Grainger, an industrial wholesaler based in Chicago, is charging $10.75 for a bundle of twenty-five comparably sized boxes, which comes to about 43¢ each. A surplus-carton or used-box dealer should be able to halve that amount. What about the company you work for?

5. To give you an idea of prices, the local swap sheet lists seven possible used trucks, ranging from a 1966 Ford 500 for $500 to a relatively new 1973 International 12-foot Box for $1,850. The best buy appears to be a 1970 International 16-foot Box in good condition and with good tires, selling for $900. So much for upper New York State.

6. In my local phone book there are three major companies listed in this column that do cross-country transporting: AACON Auto Transport, Inc.; Auto Delivery Division of Drivers Exchange, Inc.; and the Auto Driveaway Company.

7. You may be thinking such places just don't exist but not so! Many people who move to a temporary job for a year or two leave their homes entirely furnished and rent them to reliable people. When I first came to Rochester, such an opportunity was presented to me. The owner was a Japanese businessman who represented his company in the United States. He was called back to Japan for two years and was desperate to find someone to whom he could lease his entirely furnished home.

The well-known designer and educator Vic Papanek told me of a similar situation he took advantage of in Denmark, where he was a visiting lecturer at the Royal Danish Academy. The apartment he lived in was owned by a banking firm and was used for visiting businessmen and educators on a yearly basis. It, too, was entirely furnished.

Your local realtors who specialize in renting and leasing would be able to steer you to this kind of option.

8. See the discussion of the Telescope director's chair in James Hennessey and Victor Papanek *Nomadic Furniture 1* (New York: Pantheon Books, 1973), along with other portable furniture ideas. Be aware that Telescope has a cheaper chair of lesser quality on the market, which you should avoid. Buy only the one with the smooth arms (not sharp right angles), six screws per hinge (not four), and nylon pads or glides.

9. In addition to your local Scandinavian import house, I would suggest the services of SCAN, a cooperative that has terrific buys on imported furniture and furnishings of quality. Write to them at: SCAN, Corridor 1, Corridor Industrial Park, 8406 Greenwood Place, Savage, Maryland 20863. Their worthwhile catalog costs $1.00.

10. One of the nicest selections of well-designed and well-made play structures I've seen lately comes from Child Life, Play Specialties, Inc. They have structures at affordable prices that can be added to as your budget allows. You can obtain their catalog of fine wooden playground equipment for free by writing to: Child Life, Play Specialties, Inc., 55 Whitney Street, Holliston, Massachusetts 01746.

11. Lindahl sent along a reprint from an article that appeared in *Vacation Homes and Leisure Living* (Spring/ Summer 1974). It is pretty honest about building a home without prior experience, and it outlines some of the problems one could encounter.

12. The viability of such a design was taken from the work of Swedish architect Bengt Warne in collaboration with bio-engineer Carl Lindström. The results of their combined efforts appeared in the article "Bio-conversion," *Sweden Now*, March 1977, p. 34.

13. It is amazing how many different companies are now producing products for wind and water generation. At one time the only major resource for manufacturers was the *Whole Earth Catalog*. While it is still a good reference, since its publication quite a few more companies have entered the marketplace. I have seen all kinds of ads in how-to magazines and science publications like *Popular Science, Popular Mechanics*, and *Mechanics Illustrated*; and these would tend to outline the more current companies. As some of these could be "rip-off" companies, be extremely selective.

My favorite source is the catalog from Cumberland General Store. They have very clear illustrations and explanations, and they offer well-made farm-tested products, such as Hoppes hydroelectric turbines, Windcharger wind-driven generators, and Baker windmills with towers up to 60 feet high. Their catalog costs $3.00, but its price can be deducted from your first order. It is well worth the money because of all the tremendous products they offer for people who are living on and working their own land. Write to: Cumberland General Store, Route 3, Crossville, Tennessee 38555.

14. *Nomadic Furniture 1*, p. 98; and James Hennessey and Victor Papanek, *Nomadic Furniture 2* (New York: Pantheon Books, 1974), p. 69.

15. *Nomadic Furniture 2*, pp. 81, 82.

16. For people who are restoring an old house and want to maintain things as they originally were, there is *The Old House Journal*, a periodical specifically oriented to restoration. In addition to articles about Victorian or colonial fads and fashions, this simple publication offers a great deal of how-to information, as well as a list of current suppliers of reproduction hardware and fixtures. A one-year subscription is $12, and they also offer a buyer's guide for $5.50 ($3.50 for subscribers). Write to: The Old House Journal, 199 Berkeley Place, Brooklyn, New York 11217.

BIBLIOGRAPHY

AIA Research Corp. *A Survey of Passive Solar Buildings.* Washington, D.C.: U.S. Government Printing Office, 1977.

Anderson, Bruce, and Riordan, Michael. *The Solar Home Book.* Harrisville, N.H.: Cheshire Books, 1976.

Arthur, Eric. *The Barn.* Greenwich, Conn.: New York Graphic Society, 1972.

ASE. *Alternative Sources of Energy.* Minong, Wisc.: ASE, bimonthly periodical.

Clough, Rodney. "Is There Hope for the Mobile Home?" *Industrial Design,* September/October, 1978.

der Ryn, Sim Van. *The Toilet Papers: Designs to Recycle Human Waste and Water.* Santa Barbara, Cal.: Capra Press, 1978.

Fracchia, Charles A., and Bragstad, Jeremiah O. *Converted into Houses.* New York: Penguin Books, 1977.

Hennessey, James, and Papanek, Victor. *How Things Don't Work.* New York: Pantheon Books, 1977.

———. *Nomadic Furniture 1.* New York: Pantheon Books, 1973.

———. *Nomadic Furniture 2.* New York: Pantheon Books, 1974.

Hix, John. *The Glass House.* Cambridge, Mass.: MIT Press, 1074.

Interstate Commerce Commission. *Summary of Information for Shippers of Household Goods.* rev. ed. Washington, D.C.: U.S. Government Printing Office, 1974.

Isaacs, Ken. *How to Build Your Own Living Structures.* New York: Crown Publishers, 1974.

Jacopetti, Roland, Van Meter, Ben, and McCall, Wayne. *Rescued Buildings.* Santa Barbara, Cal.: Capra Press, 1977.

Johannson, Francia Faust, ed. *Home Buying II: A Piece of the Block.* Owings Mills, Md.: Maryland Center for Public Broadcasting, 1976. A Consumer Survival Kit.

————. *Moving: Let's Get Loaded*. Owings Mills, Md.: Maryland Center for Public Broadcasting, 1977. A Consumer Survival Kit.

————. *My House Has a Flat: Mobile Homes*. Owings Mills, Md.: Maryland Center for Public Broadcasting, 1976. A Consumer Survival Kit.

Kahn, Lloyd. *Domebook Two*. Menlo Park, Cal.: Pacific Domes, 1971.

————, ed. *Shelter*. New York: Random House, 1973.

————, ed. *Shelter II*. New York: Random House, 1978.

Kern, Ken. *The Owner Built Home*. Oakhurst, Cal.: Ken Kern Drafting, 1961.

Kira, Alexander. *The Bathdoom*. rev. ed. New York: Viking Press, 1976.

Lindström, Carl. "Bio-conversion." *Sweden Now*, March 1977, p. 34.

Loftness, Vivian, and Reeder, Belinda. "Recent Work in Passive Solar Design: The Use of Architecture Itself as the Primary Energy Device." *AIA Journal*, April 1978, pp. 52–81.

Los Alamos Scientific Laboratory. *Passive Solar Heating and Cooling*. Springfield, Md.: U.S. Department of Commerce, 1976.

Qvist, Leif. "Bio-living." *Sweden Now*, March 1977, p. 32.

Reynolds, John. *Windmills and Watermills*. New York: Praeger Publishers, 1970.

Roland, Conrad. *Frei Otto: Tension Structures*. New York: Praeger Publishers, 1970.

Rosefsky, Robert S. *The Ins and Outs of Moving*. Chicago: Follett Publishing Co., 1972.

U.S. Department of Housing and Urban Development. *Intermediate Minimum Property Standards for Solar Heating and Domestic Hot Water*. Washington, D.C.: U.S. Government Printing Office, 1977.

Wells, Malcom. *Underground Designs*. Brewster, Md.: Malcom Wells, 1976.

Wilson, Jim. *The Loft Book*. Philadelphia, Pa.: Running Press, 1975.

Wren, Jack. *Home Buyer's Guide*. New York: Barnes and Noble Books, 1970.

Wright, David. *Natural Solar Architecture: A Passive Primer*. New York: Van Nostrand Reinhold, 1977.

Zimiles, Murray, and Zimiles, Martha. *Early American Mills*. New York: Clarkson N. Potter, 1973.

Index

Shelter Kit, Inc., 206–10
Shopping News, 114
silos and towers, 268–71
single-room living, 281–301; box-
inside-a-room, 289–90; furnishings and accessories, 292–
5; illusion of space, 295–301;
kitchen-dining areas, 281–5;
lighting, 297–300; mirrors,
295–7; room-in-a-box, 290–4;
space simplification, 281–2,
289–95; storage, 281–9; wall
coverings, 300–1. *See also*
apartment living
site-built houses, 161, 195–209;
financing, 196; waste-disposal
systems, 223. *See also* experimental and kit homes
Small Business Administration,
265
solar heating, 236–41, 274–7; log
home kits with, 191–3; passive, 176, 239–41; water-run,
236–9
solar ovens, 176
Solartran Corporation, 191–3
sound insulation, 312
space, *see* single-room living;
storage
stereo components, 96
storage, 25, 281–9, 292; bed,
285–9; wall, 331
store-it-yourself companies, 25
storefronts, 263–5
suitcases, 129, 132
swap meets, 77, 119–20
swap sheets, 114, 186–7, 338
Sweden Now, 339
swimming pools, 219, 220

tables, 86, 90, 94, 96
TAG Modular Travel System,
133–4
tax deductions, 61, 119, 154
telephone company, 140
television sets, 46, 98
tension-compression structures,
159, 161–3

tents and tent campers, 162–3,
166
theft insurance, 34–35
tires, 36–37
Toa-Throne, 226–9
tools and tool box, 46, 91, 98
tote bags, 131–4
tract developments, 195–6
trailers, 76, 166
Triad, 159, 160–1
trickle tank, 230
trucks: borrowing, 75–77; buying, 73–75, 338; living in, 80;
packing, 107–8; size, 39–43,
337. *See also* do-it-yourself
move; rental companies
Turner Greenhouses, 181–2
typewriters, 46

U-Haul, 25, 31, 32, 37, 43, 57,
207, 337; optional insurance
policies, 34–36
Uncommon Market, 131, 132,
133–4, 292–3
underground housing, 159–61,
173–6
United Farm Agency, 214
unpacking, 25, 27–28
urban-renewal projects, 148–9
U.S. Department of Housing and
Urban Development (HUD),
see HUD
utilities, 125, 129, 231. *See also*
heating; power and energy

vacation homes: geodesics, 171;
greenhouses, 176, 181–4; in-
flatable, 166; trailer, 76
*Vacation Homes and Leisure
Living*, 339
Veterans-insured loans, 196

wagon, 99
walls and wall coverings, 300–1;
apartment, 309–10; improving, 317–18; kitchen, 325
Ward Cabin Company, 189–91
wardrobe cartons, 42, 84, 126
wardrobe closet (armoire), 99